EU DEVELOPMENT POLICY IN A CHANGING WORLD

EU Development Policy in a Changing World

Challenges for the 21st Century

Edited by
Andrew Mold

Amsterdam University Press

The publication of this book is made possible by a grant from the European Association of Development and Research Training Institutes (EADI).

Cover design: Mesika Design, Hilversum
Lay-out: v3-Services, Baarn

ISBN 978 90 5356 976 4
NUR 754 / 759

Table of Contents

Foreword and Acknowledgements

The editor of this collection would like to thank the following people for their constant encouragement and support in ensuring that this project finally saw the light of day: Thomas Lawo and Susanne von Itter, Maja Bucar, Isa Baud, Jean Luc-Maurer and the team at Amsterdam University Press. Also a special mention goes to Louk de la Rive Box during his time as President of the European Association of Development and Research Training Institutes (EADI) for his unflagging support to both this project and the European Journal of Development Research. The contributors to this volume themselves deserve my thanks too for their patience in what turned out to be a long and drawn out process.

Special thanks to Beatriz Suso who provided the cover photos, taken while she was working in Darfur over 18 months between 2005-6. The front photo shows a typical well in the North of Darfur in an area called Malha, the photo being taken in February 2006.

Several people around me have been enormously supportive during the writing the editing of this book – Zahra Kamil in particular, and friends and colleagues in Addis Ababa. A special mention in this context goes to Dagma, Edu and Schumene – here's hoping that development one day will work for you too.

Finally, for an edited collection like the present book this is not common practice, but with the indulgence of my co-authors I would like to dedicate this book to my father, Norman Brede Mold, who passed away while the book was in the final stages of preparation. He was a loving supportive father who will be sorely missed by my sister, mother and myself.

I The Evolution of EU Development Policy – Enlargement and a Changing World

Andrew Mold and Sheila Page[1]

1. Introduction

Half a century after its foundation with the signing of the Treaty of Rome in 1957, the European Union (EU) is moving slowly but surely towards a different stage in its development. It originally consisted of a group of six relatively homogenous member states but now comprises of a much more diversified heterogeneous grouping of 27 member states. Needless to say, the ongoing process of enlargement implies not only a quantitative, but also qualitative transformation in the outlook of the EU. Moreover, the most recent enlargements in 2004 and 2007, from 15 to 27 members, have been different from previous ones, in the sense that whereas previous enlargements had been generally welcomed, and even celebrated, by existing members, this time enlargement was looked upon with much trepidation. Public opinion polls consistently showed that there was little support for enlargement. On the contrary, many citizens showed an open hostility to the process and fears were frequently voiced about the dangers of an influx of illegal immigrants, of the threat to jobs from competition from low-wage workers in Eastern Europe, and the perceived impossibilities of meeting the budgetary pressures which the enlargement supposed. If these reactions sound familiar, it is because they are – they reflect the standard conservative response to the problems posed by interaction with developing countries, including the fear of immigration, complaints about the costs of 'wasted' aid, and concerns over 'unfair' low-wage competition.

This book deals fundamentally with the evolution of EU development policy, both in the context of the changes in the global political environment and within the EU itself. As the subtitle of the book ('Challenges for the 21st Century') suggests, the broad focus is on long-term strategic questions. The questions that will be asked are: How has the EU's expansion to the east been affecting political and economic relations with the developing world? In the post-9/11 world, security concerns have come to play an increasingly dominant role. How will the EU make its security policy compatible with its development policy? Can the EU design a coherent approach to developing countries or will its other interests, such as protectionism in agriculture or its neighbourhood policy, constrain its development policy? What would a 'development-friendly' trade policy look like?

EU development policy and the influence of the EU on the developing world are of course multi-dimensional, and thus in trying to answer questions like these it is not sufficient to simply look at the activities of the Directorate General of Development of the European Commission. Indeed, the interaction between the different dimensions of EU policy with the developing world (as well as with other industrialised countries or groups of countries) is becoming increasingly complex. A helpful typology for understanding these different dimensions to EU development policy is provided by Maxwell et al. (2006), who consider three clusters of challenges. Cluster one involves the post 9/11 'development and security agenda, which focuses on weak societies (like Afghanistan) and 'difficult/fragile states' (like Sudan, Iran, North Korea, or Syria). Development policies in the areas of conflict prevention, conflict management, political stabilisation, nation building and democratisation are consequently gaining in importance. The second cluster concerns growing problems related to the provision of global public goods and global governance which cross national frontiers and which require coordinated responses from both rich and poor countries. Climate change is a prime example of this. Other such problems include environmental degradation, disease threats, migration, and nuclear proliferation. Finally, there are the challenges to the established development agenda produced by other fundamental shifts in the global political and economic environment. These include the tensions between Europe ('the Western world') and the Islamic countries, the rise of China and India, demographic shifts, the rapid pace of technological change, and a deepening of the process of economic globalisation.

Confronted by such a complex panorama, EU development policy is currently at a critical juncture on a number of fronts. The apparent impasse in the Doha Round of multilateral trade negotiations has lent a new impetus to bilateral trade agreements. The EU is currently negotiating an extremely ambitious set of agreements (the Economic Partnership Agreements) with the African, Caribbean, and Pacific (ACP) group of countries. Its foreign policy stance (and, by extension, its developmental policy) towards its near neighbours in North Africa and the Middle East has been eclipsed by the aggressive (and arguably fundamentally flawed) policy of the United States towards the region. Relations with Latin America are floundering. Clearly, it is an opportune moment for critical reflection on the current state of EU development policy and to consider options for the future. This short introductory chapter focuses on the way in which enlargement itself may be affecting EU – developing country relations.

2. Are there Lessons to be Learned for Developing Countries from Recent European History?

Most of the contributions to this edited collection try to illuminate the development challenges facing Southern countries, with a view to providing some pointers for EU development policy. But lessons can of course be learned both ways. The experience of developing countries with economic reform, social change, and political upheavals is often directly relevant to Europe itself. In the past, many members of the European Association of Development Research and Training Institutes (EADI), the leading pan-European network of research centres on developing countries, have promoted this viewpoint. Dudley Seers, the first elected president of EADI, was a pioneer in applying the lessons from developmental research to the problems of peripheral Europe. His edited volume, *Underdeveloped Europe: Studies in Core-Periphery Relations* (1979)) was a classic study in how to apply structuralist concepts to the analysis of underdevelopment in Southern and Eastern Europe. The theme has been a recurring one for EADI. In 1994, for instance, the *European Journal of Development Research* published papers from the 1993 EADI conference 'Transformation and Development: Eastern Europe and the South'. In that volume, Tony Killick traces the economic crises of the 1980s in Africa and Eastern Europe to a common cause:

> The 1980s economic crisis of Eastern Europe can rather obviously be attributed to the failings of the political systems then in place there. A persuasive case can similarly be made in tracing the relative economic decline of Africa to generally dysfunctional political systems, marked by personal rule and a consequential distortion of incentives and structures. (1994: 8)

In fact, the parallels between the experiences of Africa and Eastern Europe may be deeper than simple transitory coincidences such as failed political systems at a particular point in time. Basil Davidson, one of the doyens of historians of Africa, once pointed out that Central and Eastern Europe saw their autonomy and political independence trampled on in a similar way, and for a similar duration, to the African countries under European colonialism (Davidson, 1992: chap. 9). Their freedom disappeared under Hapsburg domination and, after a short respite in the years after World War I, they fell under the yoke of Nazi Germany and finally under Soviet 'neocolonialism.'[2] Although the effect is somewhat intangible and difficult to quantify, most development researchers would agree that subjugation of this kind leaves an indelible mark on a nation's collective psyche, and makes development a far more difficult task than it would have been otherwise.[3]

Regarding the economic effects of the transition to a market economy, although great progress has been made in a number of countries, the process has been far more difficult than most observers anticipated. In a story again familiar to scholars and students of international development, bad policy advice (sometimes *disastrous* policy advice) from big-league international consultants contributed to great economic and social suffering in the initial stages of the transition.[4] The road to recovery proved to be much longer than expected. In the first years of reform, countries like Poland, Romania, and Bulgaria suffered serious falls in output (exceeding 20 percent) and triple-digit inflation. Some of the structural problems which arose in that period, like the elevated levels of unemployment (currently at around 15 percent on average, reaching 20 percent in the case of Poland), have yet to be resolved.

Indeed, although their point of departure is so different, in some senses the economic outcome in Eastern Europe in the first decade after the collapse of communism closely mirrors how globalisation has affected developing countries. For instance, Ellman's (2003: 178) description of the economic hardships endured by Eastern Europeans is easily transferable to many of the developing countries which underwent structural adjustment in the 1980s and 1990s:

> The transformation in Eastern Europe has been marked by a sharp polarization, both between and within countries. Not all the countries have made great progress with transformation. Even in relatively successful countries, not all the population has enjoyed the fruits of this success... the winners are the new business elite (owners of profitable firms, specialists in business services such as law, marketing, advertising, financial services) and those members of the political and criminal elites who have been able to enrich themselves. The losers have tended to include older (former) employees, those working in agriculture, manufacturing, coal mining, and the state sector, the newly unemployed, ethnic minorities...children, large families and the less educated.

Of course, because of the sheer novelty of the situation, the transition was always going to prove difficult – when Eastern European communism was (forcibly) established in the aftermath of World War II, the existing capitalist economies were dismantled and a socialist mode of production installed in place of the market. But the converse case, of an economy having to shift from a collective mindset to one embodying capitalist ideals and institutions, had never occurred in the whole history of development.

Under such circumstances, it is understandable that mistakes were going to be made. And from a purely economic perspective, there is nothing wrong with high rewards going to those who move into new activities first. The problem was that the whole process was conducted in a way that was deeply divisive. The architects of the transition showed scant consideration regarding how to foster the development of a new capitalist class. Instead, following perhaps Milton Friedman's view that it does not matter so much *what* the system of property rights is, the important thing is that it is established and subsequently enforced, Eastern European countries rushed headlong into a 'fire sale' privatisation programme (Nolan, 1995). The resulting inequities in the scramble for assets were thus hardly surprising. Underlying all this is the question of how property rights are determined – perhaps one of the central issues in development economics. It is a controversy that refuses to go away. In Latin America, land reform continues to be the source of much controversy. In the face of communal systems of land tenure, in Africa there is still much uncertainty as to how to ascribe property rights at all.[5]

Another curious lesson from Eastern European economic history for the development community is the way that different economic systems have failed to make much of an impact on relative wealth in Eastern Europe. John Kenneth Galbraith (1980) once observed that if around 1880 someone embarked on a train journey around Eastern Europe, the highest and best-distributed standard of living would have been found in what was by 1980 the German Democratic Republic. The next highest would have been in Bohemia (then Czechoslovakia), followed by Slovenia and Croatia. Hungary and the German parts of Poland, Romania, and Bulgaria would have been yet poorer, and poorer still were Macedonia, Montenegro, and parts of Serbia. A hundred years later, and after more than 30 years of communist rule, the same journey would have showed virtually the same *relative* states of prosperity and poverty. Seen in this light, economic planning and scientific socialism achieved little. One might add that the post-communist revolution and dramatic return to a market system in the 1990s has similarly failed to alter this hierarchical pyramid of relative prosperity – if anything, it has compounded it.

Such observations are disturbing for development economists because it would seem to suggest that an imperceptible but powerful ironclad law might exist that condemns countries to permanent relative states of poverty or prosperity according to their geography, a law from which moreover it is very difficult to escape. Such a conclusion would, however, be misleading. The dramatic change in the situation in a country such as South Korea, which has been transformed from one of the poorest developing countries in the world to having a higher income per capita than Portugal in a period of just 40 years, shows that it *is* possible to escape from the rigid straight-jacket of economic geography. There are, to use Stephen Haggard's words, *pathways from the periphery* (1991). Nonetheless, the observation that relative wealth within Central and Eastern Europe has been fairly static does provide food for thought as to how ingrained structural and societal impediments to convergence and development may be.

At a time when there are many propositions in favour of a 'big push' on development aid, especially for the African continent (see, *inter alia*, UNCTAD, 2006 and Sachs, 2005), another major lesson that can be derived from the Central and Eastern European experience is the limited transformative power of financial resources alone. Since the end of communism the massive fiscal transfers dedicated to German reunion have not proved enough to overcome underlying economic and social problems and disparities between East and West. By the end of 2003, net transfers from West to East Germany to fund unification had reached about €800 billion (*The Economist*, 2003). That makes it the most generous aid programme ever, far outstripping the total cost of the post-war Marshall Plan. Yet despite these enormous transfers, progress has been slow: from the end of the 1995 construction-driven boom until 2003, the east-German economy had grown at about half the (already slow) pace of Germany's western states; unemployment stood at around 20 percent; and average wages were only 77 percent the level of west German levels (and barely 60 percent if Berlin was excluded from the figures).

This disappointing outcome should, at the very least, cause the development community to reflect upon the potential of aid to significantly change the growth and development perspectives of poor countries – if aid on such a scale, and in the context of such a strong social and cultural affinity between donor and recipient, is incapable of making a dramatic impact, then what are the chances of aid-led development in the context of the poorest developing countries? Read between the lines and this conclusion is what multi-disciplinary researchers into development have been saying all along – that the key to successful development is not simply a technical question to be resolved by, say, more aid or higher rates of investment: there is a qualitative, social dimension related to cultural attitudes, institution building, etc., which economists in particular are poorly equipped to explain, let alone offer advice upon.[6] Consequently, recent ambitious proposals, like those emanating from the United Nations (UN)-led Millennium Project, or the UK government's Commission for Africa, for a massive increase in aid are at best only part of the solution to much deeper problems.[7]

High aid dependency also creates other difficulties, which we see in the relations of the EU with both Eastern Europe and developing countries. As aid recipients, developing countries are looked upon as disadvantaged objects for assistance, dependent on the decisions of donors. But they are also partners and rivals in trade: they have market access to offer and demand; they attract and work with foreign investors, and demand the right to participate fully in international decisions and governance. This simultaneous existence of reciprocal and client-type relationships requires sensitivity and a consistent approach. The EU has faced difficulties in reconciling its dictatorial approach as donor with the need to negotiate with increasingly strong developing country interests in the World Trade Organization (WTO). It has shifted uneasily between offering preferences and proposing reciprocal liberalisation. The difficulty of this dual relationship both for the acceding countries and for developing countries is an underlying theme of this book.

3. Effects of Enlargement

What of the influence of the process of consecutive enlargements on developing countries? As chapter 2 of this volume, by Mirjam van Reisen, makes plain, the influence contains at least two different elements. One is the differing attitudes of the new members towards developing countries. In the early years of European integration, France, followed by the UK, then Spain, and Portugal maintained (and continue to maintain) traditional ties and economic relationships with countries outside of Europe. Subsequently, Germany, whose power and willingness to make its influence felt have been increasing, has jealously guarded its links with Eastern European countries, while these in turn are for the moment more concerned with their own transformations than with helping other countries to develop.

The second influence that enlargement is exerting on the developing world is economic. It should be remembered that previous enlargements have often prejudiced the economic interests of developing countries. For instance, Northern African countries like Tunisia and Morocco were very much disadvantaged by the expansion of the EU to include Greece, Portugal, and Spain (White, 2001). Prior to the second enlargement of the EU in the 1980s, the European Union was not self-sufficient in many Mediterranean agricultural products and was dependent on imports from North Africa. The admission of the southern European countries into the EC significantly cut their access to the EC market for a number of their key export products, such as olive oil and oranges.

Arguably, one of the major ways in which European integration has harmed developing country interest has been through the workings of the Common Agricultural Policy (CAP). It is commonly pointed out that the subsidisation of European farmers (who moreover only constitute around 1-2 percent of the active population) costs far more than the total aid budget dedicated to developing countries. In recent years, there has been an enormous groundswell of criticism that the CAP has not only closed off one of the potentially most lucrative agricultural export markets for developing countries, it has also undermined agricultural prices on world markets and exacerbated food insecurity in the poorest developing countries.[8] Although it is true that the African, Caribbean, and Pacific countries (ACP) have enjoyed since 1975 the benefits of preferential market access to the European market, most observers agree that it has proved totally inadequate for offsetting the distortions of world agricultural trade brought about by the CAP (see, for instance, Grant, 1997). It has been particularly damaging to the large, poor countries in Asia and Latin America where most of the world's poor live, and which do not even enjoy the limited benefits of the ACP. One particularly beneficial impact of European enlargement may be the way in which it makes the existing system of agricultural subsidisation unsustainable, as new entrants claim the same entitlements as those given to existing members to protect their agricultural sectors.[9]

Some observers argue that European enlargement distracts attention from the problems of the Third World – Europe still provides around 50 percent of total aid flows and, so the argument goes, enlargement may simply divert financial and human resources away from the more pressing problems of the developing world. While it may be true that the European Commission is overstretched, and the budgetary implications of enlargement mean that there will be less money to go round, we should not overplay the extent to which the developing countries can potentially lose from the enlargement. Over a decade ago, Mkandawire (1994: 86) made some pertinent comments on this issue, words that still ring true:

> It is symptomatic of what is wrong with Africa's position in the world that democratisation and economic recovery in Eastern Europe should be considered threats to Africa's well-being. To the extent that changes in Eastern Europe signal the end of imperial domination and the beginning of a new society based on respect for human rights, Africa can only benefit from such a change.

4. The EU's Other Foreign Policy Interests

Within the whole panoply of the EU's foreign policy interests, there is no hiding the fact that developing countries and development objectives take a relatively secondary place. That is why relations with the poorer developing countries are more often delegated to the European level than are relations with the US or other major countries. Particularly for countries without strong traditional interests in particular developing regions (such as Italy and Greece), the importance of what is called the 'near abroad' and security questions will ultimately determine which countries are the focus of interest and what types of assistance are offered.

Nevertheless, as some Asian and Latin American countries become economically or politically important, they attract increasing attention. This is also true of course of the more developed African countries, such as South Africa or Egypt. Here, the EU's approach to them will undoubtedly differ from a traditional development relationship. In all developing countries the EU's policy will reflect a combination of motives, with economic or political development only part of the picture. In examining how EU development policy is evolving, these other components of foreign relations must not be neglected.

Finally, despite all the problems and tensions, the EU continues to exert a strong political and social appeal (what Joseph Nye once termed 'soft power') upon many developing regions, in the sense that it offers an apparent alternative to what is seen as the unbridled capitalism of the United States model. Social justice has been intrinsically a part of the European project, with a central role given to welfare policies. The economic model has been different, too, with a greater stress on regulation and socially-inclusive corporatism. Thus whereas the United States' regional integration with Mexico, under the North American Free Trade Association (NAFTA), has come to be viewed as singularly one-sided, with the lion share of the benefits accruing to US-based corporations and relatively few tangible benefits for the poorer partner Mexico,[10] with its Structural Funds and other compensatory schemes for poorer regions the EU model of regional integration holds out the possibility of a more progressive approach. One concern raised in this book is precisely that in its dealings with developing countries the EU may be moving towards a limited, business-like and mercantalistic approach, more akin to the US model.

To sum up, therefore, the picture is an extremely complex one. It is not immediately evident as to how the deepening of the process of European integration will affect developing countries. However, EU enlargement clearly represents an important catalyst for change. It is also worth stressing the difficulties of articulating a coherent development policy in a world in which classical regional and development classifications are in a state of flux. Old boundaries, such as those between 'least developed' and those which are simply 'developing', are breaking down. It is now clear that there is no monotonic scale. Different definitions of development give different rankings: not just by income, but by human development or by capital, both economic and political, or by history and experience. It is not only in Europe that regions have changed. In the Western Hemisphere, Africa, and Asia, there are increasing groupings and alliances that cut across traditional areas, such as the Cairns Group of agricultural exporters, or the G-20, or indeed, the countervailing axis to US power and influence currently being driven by Venezuela, Iran, and North Korea (all alliances spanning no fewer than three continents). But the shift is more fundamental than these intra-classification changes suggest. While traditional and new regional loyalties or income and development classifications continue to provide common interests and the basis for international action, other interest groups have emerged: in trade, those who produce or import certain kinds of goods are an obvious example (African cotton, for instance), but there are also those with different approaches to free trade or to national economic intervention. Similar divisions can be derived from other international interactions on issues such as climate change or security. This does not mean that the concepts of 'Europe' and 'developing countries' are no longer meaningful, but they must be seen, as they are here, against a complex backdrop. It is in this context that this volume is intended as a modest but forthright contribution to the analysis of evolving policies and strategies of the enlarged EU towards the developing countries.

5. Contents of the Book

Each chapter in this book deals with a different thematic issue. In chapter 2, Mirjam van Reisen speculates on the future of Europe's relations with the South in an enlarged EU by looking at the historical record of its dealings with developing countries and, in particular, the impact of previous processes of enlargement. Van Reisen warns that, in the post-enlargement, post 9/11 world, EU development co-operation may become increasingly subordinated to other policy objectives, such as the common foreign and security policy. Nonetheless, because of the symbiotic nature of the relationship, the EU will continue to need the South for its energy products, raw materials, labour force, export markets, and as a destination for foreign direct investment. Beyond straightforward material interest, van Reisen argues that in its relations with the developing world the EU needs to actively promote the values upon which it was founded: the European values of social democracy, the promotion of human rights, and accountable and transparent governance. If the EU is to succeed in its objective of rejecting the notion of a unipolar world dominated by the United States it will inevitably need alliances with the South more than ever.

Chapter 3, by Marjorie Lister, addresses the question of how globalisation has affected the international development agenda. For the EU, the advent of the single currency, the consolidation of the European single market and the EU's ability to act cohesively in international fora such as the WTO potentially offer it great power. At the same time, in consonance with what we have argued above, Lister argues that the Third World as a political and geographical entity is becoming increasingly fragmented. This fragmentation necessarily implies division and weakness vis-à-vis the EU. Despite initiatives like the Cotonou Agreement, which stress that the ownership (i.e., responsibility) for development programmes lies mainly with the developing countries themselves, Lister argues that the EU's relations with these countries are impossible to understand without reference to the historical experience of colonialisation and subordination.

In a controversial reflection on the current state of Euro-Mediterranean relations, in chapter 4 Roderick Pace discusses the relevance of Samuel Huntington's theory on the 'clash of civilisations'. Significantly, the EU has attached much importance to the *'dialogue of civilisations'* and the need for the development of more links between the civil societies on both sides of the Mediterranean (indeed, this was supposed to be one of the great innovations of the Barcelona Process which was initiated in 1995). Attempts to intensify the 'dialogue of civilisations' were also made in the aftermath of the terrorist attacks of September 11th and the subsequent attacks carried out in Turkey, Morocco, and Madrid. Yet the EU's own actions suggest a tacit acceptance of the 'clash of civilisations' hypothesis that differences of culture and civilisation exercise a strong influence on relations in the Mediterranean region. Pace dissents from this view, and argues that the 'clash of civilisations' hypothesis is essentially flawed: the differences are exaggerated and traditional sources of conflicts ignored. On the political front, for example, Pace suggests that there is no essential incompatibility between Islam and democracy – with leaders like Ben Ali in Tunisia and Mubarak in Egypt trying to conserve their power base, the resistance to political and democratic reform owes more to internal political considerations than to a clash of cultural or civilisational values.

Similarly, Pace argues that the achievements of North African countries like Egypt in the 1960s and 1970s, and Tunisia in the 1990s, in attaining a fast growing economy shows that there is no intrinsic incompatibility between Islam and economic growth – just as the idea that India could never escape from the sluggish 'Hindu rate of growth' was shown to be false in the 1990s, so too it would seem to be an absurdity to allege that Islamic countries are incapable of achieving a dynamic economic performance or an acceptable degree of development. The economic values of Islamic movements – such as respect for private property, promotion of fiscal good management and discouragement of corruption are clearly compatible with economic development. For the true source of the Mediterranean region's conflicts, Pace concludes that we need to look to the underlying causes, those normally associated with human conflicts, namely, clashes of 'interests' not clashes of 'civilisations'.

Chapter 5, by Andrew Mold, analyses the economic and social implications of the European-Mediterranean agreements (EMAs). At a time when the EU is aggressively pursuing similar deals with the ACP countries (the Economic Partnership Agreements), it is important to take stock of progress regarding the EMAs, the first of which were signed over 10 years ago. In this context, Mold reviews existing studies and carries out a computable general equilibrium analysis for the different scenarios for liberalisation for three North African economies – Egypt, Morocco, and Tunisia. Using a realistic closure for the model, which takes into account both the high levels of unemployment in the region and the probable replacement of tariff revenue with other kinds of fiscal pressure, Mold explores the different responses of the North African economies to the EMAs. Two of the key issues here are the questions of reciprocity and the inclusion of agriculture within the agreements. Regarding the latter, despite some scope for expanding agricultural exports from the North African economies, it is argued that these countries as net food importers stand to gain little from liberalisation of agricultural trade.[11] On the second issue of reciprocity, Mold finds that this is indeed one of the fundamental problems with the agreements – North African industry is simply not sufficiently competitive to sustain head-on competition with the EU. Yet as in the case of the ongoing Economic Partnership Agreements (EPAs) negotiations with the ACP countries, reciprocity is one of the key premises on which these agreements are built. In their present form, it is thus argued that the EMAs are potentially damaging to the North African economies, and will do little or nothing to alleviate the difficult economic and social situation in these countries. In the conclusions, a number of particularly problematic elements in the agreements are discussed and some suggestions are made as to how to make the EMAs more pro-developmental.

In chapter 6, Christian Freres documents the evolving political and economic relations between the EU and Latin America. As a result of the incorporation of Spain and Portugal into the EU in 1986, Latin America attracted greater interest from the European authorities. With the subsequent enlargements, however, that interest has waned. Freres asks several important questions regarding the kind of partnership that might be possible over the medium- and long-term. He argues that in principle it should be possible to have a network of Association Agreements covering all the countries in the region. The December 2005 Communication of the European Commission appears to show Europe's political will to achieve this objective. Nevertheless, Freres argues that in the future these agreements should be more ambitious. In the case of Mexico, the agreement signed barely goes beyond a simple free trade agreement. The association agreements hold much more potential than just expanding trade or investments or even aid. A partnership implies opening up new fields of co-operation, which in turn provides possibilities for new stakeholders on both sides to get involved. Future association agreements should base themselves on this principle, Freres argues.

In chapter 7, Gordon Crawford contrasts EU democracy promotion policy in Africa with the reality of its implementation in Ghana. He finds that the EU's policy in Ghana is high on rhetoric but remains low on delivery. He argues that if policy performance is poor in Ghana (by most standards in Africa, a relatively favourable political environment), then it is unlikely to be better elsewhere. Crawford outlines three possible explanations of the rhetoric-reality gap – one bureaucratic, one political, and one economic. These explanations are then applied to the Ghanaian case. The conclusions are two-fold. First, the EU's political activities in Africa are driven more by its self-interests than by the norms and principles of democratic governance. Secondly, consistent with hegemonic neo-liberalism, Crawford argues that democracy is narrowly conceived by the EU and is more concerned with limiting state power than extending popular control.

In chapter 8 Oliver Morrissey, Chris Milner, and Andrew McKay discuss an issue which is generating much controversy among the African, Caribbean, and Pacific (ACP) countries – the proposed Economic Partnership Agreements (EPAs). ACP countries entering such arrangements would preserve preferential access to the EU market but, as in the case of the Euro-Mediterranean agreements (chapter 5), must offer reciprocal access in return; potentially they will attract more aid and investment from the EU. Morrissey et al. present a method for measuring the likely welfare consequences of such an arrangement for ACP countries, using the example of the East African Community (EAC, comprising Kenya, Tanzania, and Uganda). If under the EPAs the EAC countries are required to liberalise substantially and quickly they conclude that this will have an adverse welfare impact and cause a significant loss of government revenue from the elimination of tariffs on imports from the EU. Morrissey et al. conclude that the ACP countries have little to gain from a reciprocal agreement with the EU.

In chapter 9, Chris Stevens asks a simple but important question – how can EU trade policy be made more 'development-friendly'? He outlines the major characteristics of EU trade policy and makes several suggestions for how to mitigate the negative effects and enhance the positive ones. In this context, he extensively explores the recent reforms to the 'backbone' of the EU preference system, the Generalised System of Preferences (GSP), and suggests ways in which the EU could revise and strengthen the GSP+ regime. Stevens stresses that simply extending the product coverage of GSP+ (i.e., increasing the number of products for which tariffs are reduced or eliminated) is no longer sufficient. From the point of view of achieving a development-friendly trade policy, any acceptable reform to the GSP would need to introduce greater certainty and dispute settlement mechanisms.

Finally, in chapter 10, Andrew Mold draws some conclusions regarding both EU economic and also political ties with the developing world. In the first place, the fact that development policy rhetoric so often outstrips performance implies that expectations need to be toned down. Secondly, the weaknesses observed and the lack of overall coherence in EU development policy might actually be more deeply rooted rather than a simple reflection of a lack of resolve on the part of the European Commission and the EU member states – they have deeper structural causes. Part of the problem stems from institutional limitations, but it is also suggested that one of the underlying causes of what might be described as the 'malaise of development economics' – that is, the apparent inability of the economics profession to provide answers to the key problems confronting developing countries – unemployment, poverty, and relatively poor growth performance. In order to compensate for the excessive influence of the international financial institutions (IFIs) and their neoliberal conceptions of development, part of the solution resides in greater efforts by the EU to articulate a differentiated approach – one that builds on the historical experience of European countries themselves. But it also relies on allowing developing countries greater 'policy space' – the ability to experiment and eventually find their own 'paths from the periphery'.

Notes

1 The views expressed herein are those of the authors and do not necessarily reflect the views of the United Nations. The authors would like to thank Gordon Crawford and Andrew Allimadi for comments on an earlier draft of this chapter. The authors are of course responsible for any remaining errors.

2 Lest the phrase Soviet 'neo-colonialism' appears excessive, Davidson (1992: 271) claims that 'this Soviet "neo-colonial" control was extremely close, closer even than anything of its kind that appeared in Africa. There was even an oil refinery in Bulgaria, it appears, which was incapable of refining any oil except Soviet-produced oil. One may compare this with the American-financed bauxite smelter built in Ghana that was unable, in practice, to smelt Ghanaian-produced Bauxite.'

3 See, for instance, Easterly (2006).

4 See, for instance, 'Selling the Capitalist Miracle' (*The Guardian*, 2 March, 1992, page 21). Ellman (2003: 192) tells the sad story of the policy advice given on privatisation to the Russian government by the Harvard Institute for International Development (HIID), financed by USAID, and the corruption associated with it. After official US investigations, HIID was eventually closed down.

5 See, for example, De Soto's (2001) provocative (and highly ideological) book on how the poor have allegedly been 'disempowered' by the lack of recognition of their property rights. On the problems of defining land rights in Africa, see the special issue of the *European Journal of Development Research* edited by Benjaminsen and Lund (2002).

6 This, in essence, is the message that William Easterly (2006) tries to convey in his controversial, but highly engaging, recent book *The White Man's Burden – Why the West's Efforts to Aid the Rest have Done so Much Ill and So Little Good.*

7 For a critical evaluation of these two proposals, see Mold (2005).

8 See, for instance, Oxfam (2002).

9 At the same time there is much controversy as to whether the poorest developing countries would now benefit much from the elimination of the CAP. Empirical studies tend to show that the major benefits would accrue to the Cairn Group of countries – large agricultural exporters like Argentina, Canada, Brazil, etc. Being net food importers, some of the poorest developing countries may actually lose out, at least over the short run, because food imports would become more expensive (Piermartini and Teh, 2005). Nevertheless, this story misses the dynamics of the process. Up until the late 1970s, for instance, Africa was a net exporter of food and agricultural products. The deficits opened up in the 1980s and 1990s after African governments liberalised their trade regimes, under considerable pressure from the Bretton Woods institutions. They pursued this policy despite the threat of competition from massively subsidised farm exports (both from the EU and other developed countries like the United States which pursue similar policies). Far from saving African countries, then, the policy of the EU and other industrialised countries has contributed to undermining the African continent's agricultural production in a very damaging way. To say then that 'agricultural subsidies in the OECD help poor developing countries is akin to saying heroin helps a drug addict' (Mold, 2005b).

10 See, for example, Mold and Rozo (2006), which analyses the disappointing impact of NAFTA on its southern partner, Mexico.

11 Moreover, it has to be borne in mind that there is no 'level-playing field' – the massive subsidisation of EU agriculture makes it very difficult for North African economies to compete in agricultural production, even in crops where they have a natural comparative advantage.

References

Audley, John, Sandra Polaski, Demetrios G. Papademetriou, and Scott Vaughan (2003),'NAFTA's Promise and Reality: Lessons from Mexico for the Hemisphere', Washington: Carnegie Endowment for International Peace, available at http://www.ceip.org/files/publications/NAFTA_Report_full.asp

Benjaminsen, Tor and Christian Lund (eds.) (2002), 'Securing Land Rights in Africa', *The European Journal of Development Research*, vol.14, no.2, December.

Davidson, Basil (1992), 'The Black Man's Burden – Africa and the Curse of the Nation-State', Nairobi: E.A.E.P.

Easterly, William (2006), 'The White Man's Burden – How the West's Efforts to Aid the Rest have done so much Ill and so little Good', New York, The Penguin Press.

Economist, The (2003), 'When East Meets West – A Survey of EU Enlargement', Nov. 22.

Ellman, Michael (2003), 'Transition Economies', in H-J. Chang (ed.) *Rethinking Development Economics*, London: Anthem Press, pp. 179-198.

Grant, Wyn (1997), *The Common Agricultural Policy*, Basingstoke: MacMillan Press Ltd.

Mkandawire, Thandika (1994), 'Africa and the Changes in Eastern Europe', *The European Journal of Development Research*, vol 6, no.1, June, pp.77-88.

Maxwell, Simon, Dirk Messner, Francoise Moreau, and Laurence Tubiana (2006), 'European Development Report – A Prospectus', mimeo produced for DG Development, European Commission.

Mold, Andrew (2005), 'Africa's Last "Last Chance"? Reflections on the Commission for Africa and Millennium Project Reports', Real Instituto Elcano de Estudios Internacionales y Estrategicos, Working Paper 42/2005, September.

Mold, Andrew (2005b), 'Down on the Farm', *The Economist*, April 16[t], page 16 (letters).

Mold, Andrew and Carlos Rozo (2006), 'Liberalisation, growth and welfare: the "maquiliacion" of the Mexican economy', in Kishor Sharma and Oliver Morrissey (eds), *Trade, Growth and Inequality in the Era of Globlization*, Abingdon: Routledge.

Nolan, Peter (1995), *China's Rise, Russia's Fall – Politics, Economics and Planning in the Transition from Stalinism*, London: Macmillan Press.

Oxfam (2002), 'Rigged Rules and Double Standards – trade, globalisation, and the fight against poverty', available at www.maketradefair.com.

Peters, Enrique Dussel (2000), 'El Tratado de Libre Comercio de Norteamérica y el Desempeño de la Economía en México', Mexico DF: Economic Commission for Latin America and the Caribbean (ECLAC).

Piermartini, Roberta and Robert Teh (2005), 'Demystifying Modelling Methods for Trade Policy', WTO Discussion Papers, no. 10.
Sachs, Jeffrey (2005), *The End of Poverty – How We Can Make it Happen in our Lifetime*, London: Penguin.
Seers, Dudley (1979), *Underdeveloped Europe: Studies in Core-Periphery Relations*, Brighton: Institute of Development Studies.
de Soto, Hernando (2001), *The Mystery of Capital – Why Capitalism Triumphs in the West and Fails Everywhere Else*, London: Black Swan.
UNCTAD (2006), 'Doubling Aid: Making the "Big Push" Work', Geneva: UNCTAD.
White, Gordon (2001), *A Comparative Political Economy of Tunisia and Morocco – On the Outside of Europe Looking In*, New York, State University of New York Press.

2 The Enlarged European Union and the Developing World: What Future?

Mirjam van Reisen[1]

The past is not dead – it is not even past.
William Faulkner

A necessary stage on humanity's path toward a new state of being must be, and cannot help but be, a renewal of its thinking.
Mikhail Gorbachev

1. Introduction

The restructuring of Europe's relations with its colonies and former colonies was a substantive and essential part of the establishment of the (then) European Community (EC). The creation of the European Union (EU) was a clear product of the new world order following World War II, in which the division of Europe between East and West was a defining factor. The creation of Europe was rooted in the East-West divide on the one hand and the decolonisation process on the other hand. These three historical processes – the creation of a European Community, the East-West conflict, and the decolonisation – are intrinsically linked since they were distinct but parallel responses to a new global division of power.

Today the EU is a global actor in development and its activities have continuously expanded. In 2004 the EU's Official Development Assistance (ODA), which is managed by the European Commission, made up 11 percent of total Development Co-operation Directorate of the OECD (DAC) ODA disbursements, amounting to US$ 8.7 billion for ODA and an additional US$ 4.2 billion worth of aid for the countries of Eastern Europe (OA). If bilateral aid from member states is included as well, the total EU ODA amounts to 54 percent of the total DAC

ODA, equivalent to US$ 42.9 billion in 2004. With the fundamental change in East-West relations at least one of the components of the world order was removed. The end of the East-West divide was marked by the accession of ten new member states from the former Eastern Bloc into the EU in 2004. This begs the question as to how this fundamental change will impact on the future relations of the EU with the South. This chapter will consider the future of these relations, beginning with an examination of the impact of previous processes of enlargement on development policy.

The first part will consider the history of the EU's relations with developing countries, including the origin of EU North-South relations in Europe's colonial past and the impact of the Cold War on Europe's relations with the Third World. The creation of the EU itself, together with the contribution of subsequent enlargement processes, will be stressed as a factor of change in traditional North-South relations. In the following section the impact of the end of the Cold War on Europe's development policy will be highlighted. This will include (i) an examination of current changes of the legal definition of the EU competence in development policy, (ii) changes resulting from the 2004 eastward enlargement, (iii) a review of the accompanying institutional reforms, and (iv) an examination of the contradictory trends in EU policy with regards to development co-operation in the period after the fall of the Berlin Wall. Based on an assessment of recent trends, the chapter will conclude with some observations regarding the future prospects of development co-operation in the enlarged European Union.

2. Europe and Its Colonial Past

Europe's colonial past is still seen by many scholars as an important influence on European aid. Emphasizing the impact of French colonial history on the creation of EC aid Bretherton and Vogler conclude:

> In a very real sense the EC was to be associated with French policy towards Africa; to share with France some of the potential trade benefits, but also the financial burden, of French colonialism – and subsequently of the decolonization process and its aftermath. Consequently it is appropriate, in the early years, to regard the EC role in North/South relations as an adjunct to French policy rather than a distinctive Community approach to development (1999: 113).

There is extensive historical evidence that substantiates this position. It can be shown that Europe's relations with developing countries were built and expanded upon the basis of previous colonial connections. It can also be demonstrated that the developing countries were seen as an all-important source of energy and raw materials, necessary for the economic development of Europe. Europe's weakness in its limited access to raw materials and energy was well understood by the founders of the EU. Indeed, the instrument of Marshall aid was created explicitly on the understanding that Europe would need access to the Third World to support its recovery, which in turn was seen as necessary for the economic expansion of the post-war American economy.

The objective of US foreign policy in the early post-World War II period was to construct a 'Grand Area', which specifically included the Western Hemisphere, Western Europe, the Far East, the former British Empire – which was to be further 'dismantled' – and the Middle East. Different functions were assigned to the various regions, such as industrial production, the supply of raw materials, and the provision of energy resources.[2] Chomsky quotes a memo from the US State Department in 1949, which stated that the Third World was to:

> ... fulfil its major function as a source of raw materials and a market' for the industrial capitalist societies. (...) It was to be exploited for the reconstruction of Europe and Japan (1992: 12).

The Treaty of Rome (1957) arranged the 'association' of the former French and Belgium colonies with the EC. It involved two important elements for a viable common economic market: the supply of raw materials and the expansion of export markets. This would ensure free access to the common market for colonial exports and would extend France's preferential access to the markets of its former colonies to other EC members. The fact that General De Gaulle threatened to break off negotiations on the Treaty of Rome if the other parties to the negotiations did not agree to the association of the French Overseas Countries and Territories appears to give strength to the idea that Europe's relations with the South were originally intended to protect French interests. Moreover, in the second half of the 1950s, with a recession looming in Europe, France's economic interests in its colonies regained importance.[3]

Eventually France, with the support of Belgium and Luxembourg, secured the principle of 'association' for the Overseas Countries and Territories in the Treaty of Rome, in exchange for a number of concessions to Germany and the Netherlands, who were strongly opposed to the initial proposals for 'association'. France conceded that enterprises from all member states were free to establish subsidiaries in the associated countries on equal terms and that special preferential tariffs and trade arrangements should also apply to all EC states. Associated countries and territories would gradually and progressively receive free access for their products to the markets of the member states. Based on a specific arrangement West Germany would continue to import bananas from Latin America.

While it is evident that colonial relations, as they existed at the time, were the primary basis for the EC's policy towards developing countries, it is worth stressing some additional elements. Firstly, it is interesting to note that the French introduced the subject of 'association' and its future relations with its colonies as late as 1956 in the negotiation with their European partners. Long before leaders of the African countries had expressed their apprehension about their future role in the project of European integration – following the obvious success of the European Coal and Steel Community (ECSC) – and were pushing the French government to take action with regard to their inclusion in a European arrangement. In 1953 an ad hoc assembly was set up to identify the future shape of relations between African colonies and European countries. The representative of Sénégal in the French government, Léopold Sédar Senghor, who had served in the French army during World War II, made the constitutional argument that the Overseas Countries and Territories should be fully entitled to be part of the European Community.[4] He proceeded with a political warning about the risk that the Treaty might not be ratified due to opposition from the delegates of the Overseas Countries and Territories, who had seats in the French Parliament under the constitution of the Fourth Republic. Senghor's idea of a federation in the framework of a French-African Community was consistent with the French approach of viewing colonisation as assimilation. The French did indeed, at one point, introduce a proposal that the colonies should be fully included in the European Economic Community (EEC). In France different levels of association and assimilation were maintained, with Algeria, Martinique and Vietnam in particular being seen as an integral part of France.

Yet on the other side of the political spectrum of nationalist politics the pressure for a change in colonial policy became intense between 1953 and 1956. African leaders, such as Nkrumah from Ghana and Sekou Touré from Guinea, promoted African unity with the objective of achieving complete independence and full sovereignty. Between 1953 and 1956 the French defeat in Diên Biên Phu and the subsequent end of French rule in Indochina, as well as the outbreak of the Algerian war in 1954, and tensions arising in Tunisia and Morocco, forced the leadership of the Fourth Republic to review the premises of relations with the colonies. At the same time, under mounting pressure in the Congo, the Belgian government was forced to present a plan in 1955 accepting that independence of its colony would be inevitable.

Within this political climate, and given the important role played by African troops during World War II, there was serious pressure on France to reshape its colonial relations. The introduction of a policy of 'association' should be understood as an alternative to traditional French colonial policies of 'assimilation' and 'integration'. Today the notion of 'association' appears to be derived from old colonial policies – and it was obviously grafted on these. However, it introduced a new style of colonialism, based on the recognition that influence in the colonies could only be maintained if various degrees of autonomy were allowed.

In 1958 De Gaulle tried to guarantee French influence in West Africa by creating the French Community. Pan-Africanists such as Sekou Touré in Guinea rejected this proposal, whereas moderate Francophone and Anglophone African leaders were looking for ways to continue close collaboration with Europe. The great dependency of the (former) colonies in terms of trade with European markets, as well as aid received (in particular from France), was one of the decisive elements in the Euro-African perspective. Hence European integration facilitated a fundamental change in policy towards the colonies. The Treaty of Rome was based on the principles of 'association', as opposed to 'assimilation', and on principles of non-discriminatory trade access by other European member states. These principles ushered in a new period of relations between the European countries and their colonies. These colonial relations were set on a new footing through the Treaty of Rome (Art. 131-136), which unilaterally established an association between the Community and the Overseas Countries and Territories, 'Europeanising' the former exclusive relations between colonisers and colonised. The association basically created a free trade area between the EC and the colonies, giving the right of establishment to firms and nationals from all parties.

The Treaty of Rome also created an instrument to collectively share the burden of financial assistance to the colonies, in the form of the European Development Fund (EDF). These contributions of member states to the association countries were arranged separately, outside the Community budget, but were administered by the Community. Germany and the Netherlands made a substantial contribution, which was all the more remarkable given their original opposition to the regional focus of the fund, especially in view of the fact that none of the Dutch dependencies or former German ones were included. Germany's contribution matched that of France with 34 percent of the total and the Netherlands contributed 12 percent of the fund's resources.

Twenty-three countries of sub-Saharan Africa gained independence between 1956 and 1960. This unexpected change triggered new negotiations for a pioneering association agreement with the newly independent countries. An agreement arranging preferential trade and aid provisions, along the lines of the provisions for Overseas Countries and Territories in the Treaty of Rome, was signed between the Community and 17 African states and Madagascar in Yaoundé, Cameroon in 1963, valid for a period of five years. The group was composed of former French and Belgian colonies, organised in the Associated African and Malagasy States (AAMS).

3. Europe's Early Unification: From Colonialism to Multilateralism

In the aftermath of the Second World War, the decline of French and British power in the developing world was very much accelerated to the benefit of the United States. While Europe suffered enormous economic losses, US productive capacity expanded dramatically. US capital began to move into Africa, Asia, and Europe. Although Latin America remained the largest source of mineral imports for the US, the US also invested heavily in the Congo/Zaire, Gabon, Ghana, Libya, Liberia, and South Africa. The expansion of US investments in African mining was mainly provoked by a worldwide shortage of minerals. The American armament industry utilised virtually all available supplies during the Second World War and the Korean War. American experts explored every corner of Africa for mineral wealth, and aid through the Marshall Plan went to support these initiatives. The International Bank for Reconstruction and Development (IBRD or World Bank), set up to manage the Marshall Plan, administered these activities.

Rebalancing the power between Europe and the US was a principal element underpinning the new co-operation efforts with the developing world at this stage. The increased influence of the US in the (ex-) colonies went hand in hand with the introduction of a new lexicon – notably through the appearance of terms such as 'development', 'co-operation' and 'partnership' – in order to set US intentions apart from the despised colonial project. This new lexicon was reflected in official European overseas policies, which was increasingly aligned to American policy. In 1962 the objective of French overseas policy was re-formulated in the following fashion:

> It is a matter of helping the people who need our support for their modern development and, above all, a matter of our co-operation with those countries from Africa, Asia and Latin America who wish to accept France's co-operation (cited in Uribe 1984: 244-245).

The change in policy was particularly notable in that 'co-operation' was no longer explicitly linked to the colonies. The driving force of France's policy in the developing world was the desire of its leaders for the country to be a global power. What had changed was that this objective was now seen in the context of European integration.

Yet the creation of the European co-operation programme with the African, Caribbean, and Pacific countries represented both a continuation of colonial policies and practices, as well as a fundamental change. As Lanning and Mueller (1979: 105) commented:

> Recent efforts to persuade African states to affiliate and associate themselves with the EEC may be seen partly as a continuation and reinforcement of the colonial pattern of trade and dependency, and partly as a defensive move against the incursions of the US into what had hitherto been regarded as the exclusive preserves of France and Britain.

This strategy opened new avenues for France to pursue a broader global presence and increase its political power. Co-operation was, therefore, not limited exclusively to the (ex)-colonies, but to the 'Third World' in its entirety, now called more optimistically 'developing countries'.

One of the first political expressions of this new concept of co-operation with countries outside the French sphere of influence – and the desire to move the centre of gravity of French foreign policy to include new horizons in Africa, Asia, and Latin America, was De Gaulle's visit in 1964 to Mexico. De Gaulle himself heralded the 'beginning of a new orientation':

> A policy has been laid out (...) for the whole world to see. Yes! For the whole world to see! Although this policy is French-Mexican, it is at the same time worldwide. The fact that special links should be established between your country, the living heart of Latin America, and my country, essential to Europe but also with a deep influence and activity in Africa and Asia, this is a fact from which happy consequences could follow, which go well beyond our own countries (cited in Uribe 1984: 248).

De Gaulle insisted on policies that would ensure France's independence from the United States, and would be able to act as an independent player in the international arena – using European integration to achieve this objective. In his view the visit to Mexico was successful in making this point to the United States:

> I have concluded, and everybody has reached the same conclusion, that the international situation of our country is more brilliant, more secure than ever before. We are a great nation (cited in Uribe 1984: 248).

Particularly in the context of the negotiation of Britain's entry in the community, Europe provided another route for the expansion of French relations overseas. The collapse of negotiations with Great Britain following De Gaulle's veto of British membership in the Community in 1962 did not close the door for the members of the British Commonwealth. In 1963, several months after the first collapse of negotiations on British entry, the six adopted a declaration that confirmed that the EC was open to all requests by third countries which had an economic structure comparable to that of the AAMS and who wished to join the Yaoundé Convention or to form a different kind of association. According to Harry Dyett (1998: 11) "this offer, the Community Declaration of Intent, was at the same time a lever to prod Britain to become a part of Europe" and to come to terms with the new international realities. This included both decolonisation, leading to a diminishing influence of Britain over its former colonies, and a greater international role for an integrated European Community. Dyett concludes that this "was an indication that the Community was ready to widen the scope of its association with developing countries and give teeth to its development policies with or without Britain." The Community Declaration of Intent made clear that Europe did not wish, and saw no justification, for its policy to be based on the ex-colonies of its member states.

The EEC's increased power and emphasis on Africa was a direct challenge to Britain, which was heavily dependent economically on cheap imports from its (former) colonies. Under pressure, the British government announced in November 1966 that it would again explore the possibilities for British entry into the Community. In 1969 an association agreement was signed between the Community and three former British African colonies – Kenya, Tanzania, and Uganda – called the Arusha Agreement. This was seen as a substantial improvement on the Yaoundé Convention. Hence the relationship with the (ex-) colonies became a key aspect of the process of European integration.

4. Expanding the Focus of the EC towards the Mediterranean

In the early 1970s the Commission published the first policy documents on EC aid justifying its exclusive regional focus on Africa while, at the same time, emphasizing the strength of the Community institutions as having no association with the colonial era, and, therefore, being particularly suited to foster a globalisation of European aid relations. This apparent contradiction between exclusive regionalism and globalism was built intrinsically into the Treaty of Rome, which allowed for these parallel objectives by ensuring that the right to association was not exclusive to former dependencies. The Treaty of Rome (Art. 238) established the possibility of concluding an association agreement with a third country, union of states, or an international organisation 'embodying reciprocal rights and obligations, joint actions and special procedures' (Art. 238). This would allow former colonies that had gained independence to maintain a close relationship with the EC, and allowed the conclusion of special arrangements with third countries in general. In the Treaty's Declaration of Intent, emphasis was given to the wish to achieve association with the Mediterranean countries. Initially this focussed on the former French colonies of Morocco and Tunisia. The first Mediterranean policy included all countries north and south of the Mediterranean, with the exception of Libya.

Article 238 could also be invoked for a range of future potential situations, including accession of future members – limited to the not specifically defined term 'European countries'. This article was agreed with the aim of accommodating possible future enlargements, particularly with regard to Northern Mediterranean countries, such as Greece, Spain, and Portugal, and the countries of Eastern Europe. Negotiations for the association of Greece started as early as 1959 and came into force in 1962. Turkey signed an association agreement with the EC in 1963. Morocco and Tunisia also approached the Community for an agreement in 1963 but nothing was signed until 1969. In 1970 controversial preferential trade agreements were signed with the dictatorial Spanish regime as well as with Israel, despite growing tension in the Middle East.

The policy towards the Mediterranean (including the Middle East) was strongly reinforced by the outbreak of the oil crisis in 1973. In his 1975 annual address to the European Parliament, the President of the Commission François-Xavier Ortoli warned that

> We are losing our independence ... For thirty years or so Europe was happily able to ignore the unpleasant fact that its energy and raw material re-

> sources were limited. There is no avoiding the truth today. ... The United States has energy and raw material resources on a continental scale. It is natural that it should want to exert all the influence of its increased dominance in a difficult and unstable situation (Ortoli,1975: x).

Indeed, there is evidence that one of the factors in the increase in oil prices in the early 1970s was an arrangement between some OPEC countries – Saudi Arabia in particular – and US oil-related multinationals with the joint objectives of keeping US control over oil reserves in the Middle East and ensuring that exploration investments could be made profitable and reinvested in the US to avoid further devaluation and erosion of the dollar.[5] No matter what the exact details and motives were, the increase in oil prices resulting from the oil embargo on the countries that supported Israel in the 1973 Arab-Israeli war had particularly negative effects for the European Community.

As a result the access to affordable fuel resources became an increasingly important issue for the EC. One of the few options the EC had to secure energy imports was to urgently intensify its relations with the southern Mediterranean and Arab countries, with Algeria and Libya and to a lesser extent Egypt and Syria being the most significant suppliers of petroleum and gas in the region. The increased interest in the Middle East and Mediterranean gave rise to an expansion of negotiations with the countries of the Mediterranean Basin and the Middle East.

In July 1974 a Euro-Arab dialogue was initiated in order to intensify the degree of co-operation between Europe and the Arab world. The success of this process was limited as the European side was unable or unwilling to politically deal with issues that would go overtly against the position of the United States (and Israel), while the Arab side was not ready to give 'specific assurances' with regards to the supply of oil to European countries. In the December 1974 Paris Summit the EC's leaders agreed that the Mediterranean agreements were of vital importance. At the same time the Commission initiated a reorganisation of the various bilateral relations with countries of the Mediterranean into an overall 'Global Mediterranean Policy'. This increased activity resulted in the conclusion of agreements and protocols on financial and technical co-operation with 17 Mediterranean and Middle Eastern States, including loans and grants. The protocols related to the association agreements with these countries were financed by resources from the EC budget. In this way a first distinction was made between the sourcing of Community assistance to developing countries through the EDF and through the budget.

5. The First Enlargement and the Increased Scope for Development Aid

The enlargement of the European Community to include the United Kingdom, Ireland, and Denmark represented a turning point for EC development policy. How the areas of enlargement and development aid became intertwined is noticeable from the division of portfolios within the Commission. While the first two commissions included a Commissioner for Overseas Countries and Territories, and the next one, for development aid, the fourth Commission (1970-1973) incorporated Commissioner Jean-François Deniau to take charge of the combined portfolio for 'enlargement and development aid'. It was not coincidental that the four first Commissioners all had French nationality.

When the negotiations started on how the relationships between the colonies and former colonies would be arranged in an enlarged community, Britain's relations with these countries had already evolved substantially, and many were already independent, such as Iraq, Egypt, India, Ghana, and Tanzania. The British Commonwealth was established in 1931 in order to include the 'white' dominions of the British Empire into an arrangement that granted them more independence. In 1949 the criteria for membership in the Commonwealth were changed so as to allow 'non-white' developing countries – at that stage particularly India – to join the Commonwealth. By the time Britain prepared its accession to the EEC, and the discussions started on the association of the members of the Association of Commonwealth States (ACWS) in 1971, the basis for negotiations was entirely different from that of the provisions for association in the Treaty of Rome. The period in which the negotiations on enlargement went hand in hand with the increase in scope of European development aid is sometimes portrayed as the first 'breakthrough' by those advocating a 'globalised aid approach'. Based on the reality of special interests and ties with former colonies the Community was multilateralising these previously exclusive contacts – and so fundamentally changing the basis of relations with the former colonies.[6]

The three options put on the table for the members of the ACWS – accession to a successor agreement of the Yaoundé Convention, association through the right of association under the Treaty of Rome, and a trade agreement under the EC's common commercial policy – were all based on the concept of 'association' with the EC, which to some had the connotation of a senior/junior relationship. A number of the developing countries in Africa, the Caribbean, and Pacific who were members of the British Commonwealth (the so-called 'Commonwealth associables') saw in the three offers a 'political arrangement, which would institutionalise second-class membership' based on an unequal relationship between Europe and the South.[7] Nigeria reacted strongly against the political implications of Britain's application for membership and its relations with the UK soured. The Commonwealth associables were acutely aware that the association arrangements under the Yaoundé Conventions were first and foremost political and intended to maintain 'privileged relationships'. The main problem identified by the Commonwealth associables was the limitation in establishing an independent trade policy under the Yaoundé Convention, and this gave rise to 'the accusation in many quarters of political subservience on the part of the States in the Yaoundé Convention, and more particularly the Francophone associated countries' (Dyett 1998: 37). The Commonwealth independent states thought of this as offensive and made repeated accusations of these being neo-colonialist policies by the European Community.

The original group joined with the Commonwealth associables and managed to negotiate on the basis of commonly agreed principles, of which the element of non-reciprocity was the most important aspect. Non-reciprocity was considered essential for developing countries to build and protect their nascent economic potential without being subject to rivalry from strong competitors. Despite French opposition, the inclusion of the principle was achieved with the support of Britain, Germany, and the Netherlands. This construed an important, and perhaps even remarkable, advance, particularly since the Treaty of Rome was entirely based on the concept of reciprocity. Nevertheless in some areas of agricultural products, Commonwealth associables had to accept a decrease of access to the EC market compared to the free market access they had previously enjoyed to the British market.

Another major achievement was the introduction of a scheme for export stabilization, STABEX. Although endowed with limited resources, this was recognition of the need for instruments to compensate for demand and price fluctuations, in order to create more economic stability in countries heavily dependent upon exports of basic commodities. Moreover, the inclusion of iron ore in STABEX was seen as a major victory for the ACP countries. Finally, through specific protocols, such as on sugar, rum, and bananas, the access that former British colonies had to the UK was extended to the EC as a whole.

The timing of the negotiations, which paralleled the negotiations in the UN General Assembly on a New International Economic Order (NIEO), coincided with the quadrupling of oil prices by OPEC in 1973 and was advantageous to the outcome of the Lomé I negotiations. The need for smoother co-operation with the developing countries in other sensitive areas benefited the agreement with the ACP countries which was agreed at a higher price than perhaps originally anticipated.[8] In 1975 the first Lomé Convention was signed with 46 countries; 19 countries from Yaoundé II, 21 Commonwealth associables and eight other African countries.

6. The European Development Fund and the Budget

The European Development Fund (EDF) agreed for the Lomé I Convention was considerably more generous than its predecessors under Yaoundé.[9] However if inflation is taken into account the increase is a great deal less. The per capita allocation increased between Yaoundé II and Lomé I and has continued to increase in subsequent EDFs (table 1).[10]

Table 1 **Value of EDF Financial Aid Allocation to Associated Countries, in Million ECUs/Euros[11]**

	Rome Treaty 1957	Yaoundé I 1963-9	Yaoundé II 1969-75	Lomé I 1975	Lomé II 1979	Lomé III 1984	Lomé IV 1990-1995	Lomé IVbis 1995-2000	Cotonou 2000-2020
	EDF1	EDF2	EDF3	EDF4	EDF5	EDF6	EDF7	EDF8	EDF9
Year	1957	1963	1969	1975	1980	1985	1990	1995	2000
EDF	569	730	887	3,053	4,207	7,882	11,583	13,151	14,300
% ACP countries	-	18	18	46	58	65	68	70	77
% EU countries	-	6	6	9	9	10	12	15	15
EDF/per capita current prices	10.5	9.7	10.5	12.3	13.5	17.9	21.9	21.3	20.7

In 1979 the European Parliament reinforced efforts to strengthen a global approach towards Community aid when it again requested that the European Development Fund be integrated into the Community Budget. This coincided with the signing of the second Lomé Convention between the Community and 56 ACP states. The Commission supported the Parliament in this effort but the Council did not approve it and therefore the distinction between co-operation through the EDF and the budget remained.

The first enlargement with the UK, Ireland, and Denmark initiated a period not only of increased co-operation with associated countries but also with non-associated countries. For the EC several former British colonies (in particular those in Asia) were unsuited to join the successor of the Yaoundé Convention as fears were raised that they would seriously compete with domestic agricultural and industrial European sectors, as well as in textile and clothing. Hence it became clear that, in order to adopt a foreign policy that was more global in scope, additional instruments were necessary, primarily focused on trade and agriculture, the two principal domains of Community policy. Even though a small budget line for development co-operation was created in 1974, the non-associated countries in Asia and Latin America did not yet have a specific place in European development policy. In April and July 1974 the Development Council adopted two resolutions on technical and financial aid with non-associated countries following Commission proposals. Moreover, in 1974 trade co-operation agreements with India, Uruguay, and Brazil were concluded. In 1976 a budget line for extending financial aid to the non-associated countries from Asia and Latin America (ALA) was included in the budget. But the resources of this budget line remained limited in scope.

Previously some arrangements had been made through the budget for development aid. This was in the area of food aid, which was directly funded from the European Agricultural Guidance and Guarantee Fund (EAGGF). The food aid programme was initially established as an instrument to dispose of the massive overproduction resulting from the progress in agricultural production technology and the unrestricted guarantee of prices under the Common Agricultural Policy (CAP), which were set higher than world market prices as a subsidy to the farmers. The food aid programme was not restricted to particular countries, although there was no food aid to Eastern Europe. The largest recipients of food aid (in cereals) were Bangladesh followed by Pakistan. The food aid programme also included emergency food aid. Alongside these programmes the EC initiated a Generalised System of Preferences (GSP) in 1971. This was an instrument that provided a global application of preferential market access for imports from the associated countries. While the measure was intended to move forward from a restrictive regional Euro-African development approach, the proliferation of instruments granting preferential treatment quickly eroded their value to the partner countries.

7. Towards a New Relationship with the Third World

The oil crisis forced the EC to look again at its relationship with the developing countries. The Commission now recognised that the EC's ability to achieve a dynamic economic performance depended at least in part upon the Community's ability to establish a new relationship with the developing world:

> Europe, for its part, must, even more than other industrial areas, remain in a position to import energy and raw materials in order to keep up its expansion. It therefore needs to export more than in the past, with a different market pattern giving more prominence to new emerging markets (Ortoli, 1975: xx).

Ortoli stressed the 'real interdependence between them and the countries of the Third World', and acknowledged the fact that EC member states, more than other industrialised countries, were dependent for 'both their supplies and markets upon the existence of a favourable climate in international economic relations.' In this context, the 1970s marked 'a breakthrough from the development aid era to that of co-operation in the true sense of the term' (Ortoli, 1975: xxi). In a series of policy papers the Commission addressed this question, aiming to establish a three-sided arrangement between the developing countries, which would supply energy, raw materials, and newly emerging markets for Europe's exports. The Community's ability to achieve such a trilateral relationship would determine its capacity to act as an independent player in the international arena.

During the 1970s European development policy took on an increasingly global perspective. As observed above, in the aftermath of the oil crisis it was recognized more than ever that relations with developing countries would be an essential part of any future European economic strategy. Among the ACP countries, Nigeria became an important exporter of crude oil to Europe. At the same time, the historic element of Europe's relations with Asia, Africa, and America was accepted as an essential part of its policy. Finally, solidarity with the world's impoverished people was now introduced as an objective in itself, bearing in mind the concept that the Community 'stands for democracy, inspired by principles of fairness and brotherhood' (Ortoli, 1975: xxi).

The dividing line between the contrasting views on European co-operation from either a regional Euro-African or global perspective, was blurred during these years. Europe's role as a global player was increasingly defined on the basis of its ability to assert a strong regional partnership with Africa, and its capacity to be partner and player outside the regional arena. The signing of the agreements with the Mediterranean countries and the successful negotiations on Lomé I now ensured that the whole of the African continent was embraced. These achievements were used to send a message to the international community, in particular to the US. According to the then Commissioner Cheysson, the Lomé Convention proved at once the strength and quality of European-African relations, 'surpassing the US-Latin American connection', as another way of saying that the European Community had not lost its ambition, or its potential, to be a global player alongside the United States and the Soviet Union.

At the same time, there was an increasing awareness that some commonality and definition was required between the efforts of the Community member states and the Commission's activities in development co-operation. In 1973 the Council adopted various conclusions and resolutions on the harmonisation of national and community policies. In general terms the approach consisted of putting into practice close coordination between member states and the Community. At the same time, member states jointly set themselves the objective of increasing official development assistance and insulating their aid flows as far as possible from any budgetary and balance of payments difficulties. For the first time members confirmed or expressed their desire to attain as soon as possible the objective of an annual ODA flow corresponding with 0.7 percent of GNP, an objective set by the UN for the second development decade. Member states also agreed to exchange information between themselves and the Community on the geographic distribution of aid.

8. Second Enlargement: Further Expansion of Community Aid

In 1979 oil prices reached a new peak. The precarious economic situation in certain countries and the tight budgetary situation virtually ruled out any new policies funded from the general budget. To put the brake on inflation and reduce their budget deficits governments pursued restrictive financial policies at home, which had a noticeable effect on the Community, which was 'fast approaching the financial limit of its activity' (European Commission 1981: 21). As a result of the war between Iran and Iraq, which followed in 1980, oil supplies dried up even further. Moreover, the Strait of Hormuz, the artery through which 48 percent of EU oil flowed, was being threatened. These developments gave new impetus to the Communities' relations with Turkey and relations with the countries of the Mediterranean and the Middle East. Moreover, European member states also began to explore the unused potential of energy reserves in the Soviet Union.

At this stage, Greece, Portugal, and Spain were all recipients of the Community development programme after the military regimes had given way to democratic governments in 1974 and 1975. In 1979 a treaty was signed regarding the accession of Greece to the EEC. Negotiations restarted with Spain on its accession in the same year and the Council speeded up the implementation of financial protocols with Portugal. Additionally Portugal and Spain received 'pre-accession aid' from 1981 onwards. In the context of the Iberian accession negotiations, the Commission made proposals in 1984 to substantially increase the budgets for assistance to non-associated countries. Aid to these countries was brought under the budget heading for development in the 1985 budget. New proposals for increases in these budget lines were put forward despite a relatively low utilisation of existing resources under these budget headings. These included new aid resources to the Southern Mediterranean countries, motivated by the need to off-set the negative impact of the Mediterranean enlargement on the Southern Mediterranean. This resulted in a renegotiation of existing trade and co-operation agreements between the Southern Mediterranean and the EC, taking into account the export losses of these countries due to Spain's and Portugal's direct access to the common European market, in many products that would compete with those of the Southern Mediterranean (Commission 1985: 58).

The accession negotiations with Spain and Portugal also extended the reach of the EC's external relations with Latin America. In 1985 the Accession Treaty with Spain and Portugal was signed. This had a provision, annexed to the treaty, that Community aid to Latin America would be increased. This was deemed necessary because the aid programme to Latin America had remained fairly limited until then. In 1985 the budget of 268 million ECU, less overhead for aid to non-associated developing countries, was divided up on a geographical basis as follows: 75 percent for Asia, 20 percent for Latin America and 5 percent for non-associated African countries (Commission 1985: 328). This was agreed despite the fact that in committee the debate had been very animated with several Spanish members of the European Parliament (MEPs) expressing their wish for a 50/50 distribution, a position that Spain advocated at the same time in the European Council.

In 1988 the European Parliament insisted on increasing resources for aid programmes. The budget article concerning aid for developing countries in Latin America and Asia was split into two separate headings, 65 percent for Asia and 35 percent for Latin America. Following a debate in the European Parliament on aid to Asia and Latin America, the Parliament called again for more appropriations in the 1989 budget for 'economic assistance'. The Parliament also stated that Asia and Latin America should be differentiated and that a separate co-operation scheme should be set up for each of the two geographical areas. In this resolution the European Parliament also stated that financial and technical co-operation should be strictly poverty-oriented so that it would be the poorest countries and the poorest sectors of the population that would benefit most.

To sum up, in the 1980s three major features can be distinguished as main developments in the EC external co-operation programme.

- First, the proportion of aid through the budget increased and there was a proliferation in the number of budget lines, defined on the basis of either thematic or regional parameters.
- Secondly, the available resources, through the budget, for Latin America, and the Mediterranean increased exponentially, as a consequence of the enlargement of the Community towards the South (Greece, Portugal, and Spain).
- Thirdly, external co-operation became a major area in negotiations on the budget between the three Community institutions: the Parliament, the Council, and the European Commission.

9. Beyond 1989: Emphasis on the Near Abroad

The events in 1989 leading up to the fall of the Berlin Wall had an energising effect on the EC in almost every aspect of its existence. The visionary editor of *Agence Europe*, Emanuele Gazzo, noted in April 1990:

> The extraordinary upheavals that have taken place in Eastern Europe (and to the East of Europe) have deeply influenced world politics... The events in question coincided with a particularly active and sensitive phase of the EC's evolution... But the pressure of events – in other words, the unavoidable imperative of necessity – combined with the pressure of public opinion... demands an acceleration of movement. When history accelerates, stopping means going backwards... The acceleration is facilitated by the existence of favourable political, economic and psychological conditions, but this might rapidly change and Europe might then miss an historic opportunity. (*Agence Europe*: 5234)

In 1992 the Maastricht Treaty translated these prophetic words into the establishment of the EU. This treaty, and subsequent treaties, would dramatically increase the scope for European integration. It established a common foreign, security and defense policy, the European Monetary Union, and a further integration of many policy areas, including development co-operation.

10. The Legal Basis for the EU's Development Aid Policy

The Maastricht Treaty (1992) provided a legal basis for EU development co-operation. As a result development co-operation is clearly and fully integrated into the *acquis communautaire* (the legal provisions already negotiated in earlier European treaties). The responsibility in this policy area is shared with the member states. In order to further define Community responsibilities, the Maastricht (1992) and Amsterdam Treaties (1997) set out the principles of the four C's:

- *Coherence* between policies that have an impact on third countries and the objectives of development co-operation;
- *Complementarity* between member states and Commission activities in development;
- *Co-ordination* of actions between member states and the Commission;
- *Consistency* between the policies of the Common European Security and Defence Policy (ESDP) and development co-operation.

The objectives set out in the Maastricht Treaty were: (i) promoting social and sustainable development; (ii) the campaign against poverty; and (iii) the integration of developing countries into the world economy. In 2000 the European Commission presented a policy paper, and in a subsequent joint statement by the Council and the Commission the overarching objective was specified as 'the reduction, and ultimate eradication of poverty'. The Convention on the Future of Europe, a new body, which negotiated a Draft Constitutional Treaty during 2002-2003, included the objective of the 'eradication of poverty' as the overarching objective within a separate chapter for development co-operation and as one of the objectives of the EU's external policies.

For the first time, the Maastricht Treaty gave the EU responsibility for the Common European Security and Defence Policy (ESDP) – a responsibility that was established at an intergovernmental level in the so-called 'second pillar' of the Treaty. Whereas development co-operation was the responsibility of the European Community ('pillar I') and could be carried out by the European Commission, the ESDP remained within the scope of the European Council, the assembly of EU Member States ('pillar II'). In later treaty updates the Common Foreign Defence Policy (CFDP) was included – and extended the scope of the EU to military matters. In both foreign and defence policy, the entry point for greater EU common action has been in areas closely linked to existing development co-operation and emergency action. The reason for this has been both the availability of financial resources and the mandate, as well as public support for action in these areas. However, this has also carried the danger that distinctions between the policy areas were blurred.

This blurring has been compounded by a new legal heading that was created in the Nice Treaty, signed in February 2001, which entered into force on February 1, 2003. The new heading in the treaty was called: Co-operation with Third Countries (Art. 181a, TEC). The purpose of this chapter was aimed at ensuring a legal base for assistance with countries from the former Warsaw Pact (de Witte, 2001: 127). The Portuguese presidency in 2000 had acknowledged that a separate legal treaty would be justified, given that the 23 regulations and decisions on pre-accession aid and macro-financial assistance to former Eastern Bloc countries adopted since 1993 were made on a dubious legal basis.[12] The introduction of this chapter provoked an extensive debate as to its applicability – even though there is no legal difference of opinion on its scope. An article published by Bernd Martenczuk, member of the legal services of the European Commission and therefore a legal expert from the 'inside', argued unequivocally that 'Article 181a (EC) does not apply to co-operation with developing countries' (2002: 406).[13]

In the EU Constitutional Treaty, signed in 2004, the confusion was remedied and the provisions between developing countries and non-developing countries were distinctly separated. Case law and a legal opinion of the Council have further contributed to a clear interpretation of Article 181a with a view to maintaining a clear distinction between the two legal provisions and recognising the specific goals and objectives of the EU's development policy.[14] The Constitutional Treaty further provides a legal basis for the EU's humanitarian assistance aimed at relief operations in natural and man-made disasters. This legal basis is given in a separate Treaty article and its clarity is legally uncontested. An opinion by the Council Legal Services (2005)[15] unequivocally stated that: 'Article 181a empowers the Community, within its sphere of competence, to adopt "economic, financial and technical co-operation measures" with third (non-developing) countries.' A European Parliament legal opinion (2005) came to a similar conclusion.

The clarification of the legal basis for development co-operation was subject to prolonged negotiations, in which the European Parliament and the European Convention played a critical role. The reason for the prolonged confusion was the interest the Commission had in a broader definition of its mandate in external relations, and an extension of the use of the Community mandate in development policy (and its resources) for a wider mandate in external relations. The new relations with the former Eastern Bloc countries were used as leverage in an attempt to widen the mandate based on the strong foundation provided in EU Development Co-operation, as is explained below.

While the agreements defining the areas of co-operation with third countries in the treaties have been significant, the difficulties of the EU moving forward have also become visible, particularly with respect to the Common Foreign, Security and Defence Policy (CFSDP). The European Commission was not given a role in the implementation of the CFSDP. Soetendorp (1994: 104) highlighted the following concerns:

> The outcome of the year-long negotiations on the treaty of Maastricht raises therefore the question as to whether the willingness of the member states to act in international affairs as a single foreign policy actor has reached its limits. The willingness to share national sovereignty is an imminent condition for the capacity of the EC to effectively manage common foreign policies.

Several attempts were undertaken to clarify the many open ends left by the Maastricht Treaty. Both in the Treaty of Amsterdam and in the Treaty of Nice, member states failed to introduce a reform of the administrative and institutional structures that might match the political ambitions expressed in the treaties. In the Amsterdam treaty (1997) the principle was introduced that development co-operation should be consistent with CFSDP, a principle that has since gained increasingly more ground. It was agreed that the general secretary of the Council would also become the high representative of CFSDP. In 1999 Javier Solana was appointed to this post. The attempts to increase the profile of the CFSDP without a clear programme to support activities in this area have affected EC development co-operation policy which is often used as a substitute.

Within this context an understanding of the relations between the different components of the EU's external relations is crucial. The key policy principles that define the relationship between the external policy areas are the principle of 'coherence' (Art. 178 TEC) and the principle of 'consistency' (Art. 3 TEC), which in the context of the EC treaties have a legal significance. The principle of coherence sets out that those EU policies with an impact on developing countries should be 'coherent' with development objectives. Its meaning is described in Council resolution 8631 on coherence adopted in 1997 (van Reisen, 2000: 40-41), a Parliament resolution of 2000, and a Commission working document on the same subject in 2001. It should be noted that this principle identifies a hierarchical relation in which development objectives should be given serious consideration in any other EU interventions affecting the poorest countries, including trade, agriculture, and migration policy. The principle of 'consistency' is defined as the need for the various components of the EU's external policies, including development co-operation, to broadly support overall policy objectives towards third countries. The different components of the EU's external policy are all equal and one policy field is not considered superior to any other. The Draft Constitutional Treaty also respects the separation of these two principles.

Yet despite the clear distinction between coherence and consistency in the treaties, the meaning and use of these two concepts is often confused. There has been a trend to define the framework only in terms of 'consistency' leaving no independent room for the notion of 'coherence'. For instance, the Convention on the Future of Europe, which prepared the Draft Constitutional Treaty, initially did not specifically contain the concept of 'coherence' and proposals were introduced to make EU development co-operation subordinate to foreign, security, and defence policy objectives. Ultimately the convention accepted that the principle of 'coherence' was distinct from 'consistency', and that this was part of the *acquis communautaire*, and should be included into the Draft Constitutional Treaty. The Draft Constitutional Treaty includes the notion that all EU policies affecting developing countries should take the development objectives into account ('coherence').

While the treaty is clear on the relationship between the different components of the EU's policies, since 9/11 the Council has sought to give a higher priority to the EU's security policy and some parts of the EU have advocated for a stronger defence policy for the EU, all other components of the EU's external policies including development co-operation being subordinate to the EU security and defence policy. However, at present the EU's development policy is clearly included as an EU competence in all the treaties, whereas the EU's Common Foreign, Security and Defence Policy remains part of the intergovernmental arrangement provided in the Maastricht Treaty. Development policy remains the strongest area of the EU's external policy in terms of competence, resource allocation, and administrative capacity for implementation.

11. Towards Eastward Enlargement: Greater Emphasis on the 'Near Abroad'

While the formal basis for development co-operation became more poverty-focused, the EU's development co-operation was steered away from the poorest countries as a consequence of the change in geo-strategic priorities from 1989 onwards. The fall of the Berlin Wall was followed by a rapid shift of European attention towards the east. Aid allocated to Eastern European countries increased exponentially, as large aid packages were agreed (initially for Poland and Hungary) and were swiftly opened up for other Central European countries through the PHARE programme. Following the collapse of the Soviet Union in 1991 equally large aid packages were arranged for the independent countries of the former Soviet Union.

While in subsequent years a great deal more attention and aid was given to the countries of the former Eastern Bloc, EC aid to Southern countries and regions did not diminish in absolute terms. In 1989 a comprehensive new ten-year agreement with the ACP countries was signed. With Spain as the 'bridge' or self-declared advocate for Latin America and the Mediterranean, France for the ACP, Italy for the Southern Eastern European countries and former Yugoslavia and Germany for Eastern Europe, on the whole the political reality of EU's membership base ensured that a certain balance in the EU aid programme's global reach remained. All the same, the result of the increased emphasis on neighbouring foreign countries (the so-called 'near abroad') has been very noticeable. All of the top ten recipient countries of EC aid in 1999 were neighbouring countries.[16]

If pre-accession aid is excluded and only ODA is taken into account a clear trend emerges between 1989 and 2004. Whereas in 1989 five of the poorest countries were top recipients of EU aid, in 2000 the five top recipients were all among the near abroad in the Mediterranean and Eastern European region and this trend persisted in 2003 and 2004. This trend was significantly different from all DAC top five priority countries, which in 2003 and 2004 were Iraq, DRC, China, India, and Indonesia. The EU's tendency to favour the near abroad results in a distribution of disbursements per income group that is increasingly unreflective of the incidence of poverty in recipient countries. While in 1990 the share of EC aid to low-income developing countries was 70 percent, in 2001 this had declined 38 percent (BOND, 2002).

Thus it is clear that the neighbouring 'ring' around the Union has gained increasing importance. The new high profile issues on the political agenda, such as security and migration, have further contributed to this trend.[17] The 2004 enlargement did not change this preoccupation of the EU with its neighbours, particularly because the new member states had an interest in playing a role as a bridge to the region to their east, which had thus far lacked the support of the EU. The focus on the 'new abroad' is currently being formalised in the European Neighbourhood Policy (ENP). This will be implemented through the European Neighbourhood and Partnership Instrument (ENPI), which will replace the current TACIS and MEDA programmes from 2007 onwards, and will draw on "substantially increased funds" (Reisen 2005: 20-21). The ENPI will govern relations with the EU neighbours.[18] The majority of these are also classified as developing countries under the OECD Development Assistance Committee (DAC). Aid to these countries can, therefore, be classified as ODA. Furthermore, candidate countries negotiating potential accession with the EU will continue to benefit from assistance to give support to required reforms. From 2007 this will be administered by the new Instrument for Pre-accession Assistance.[19]

It is increasingly clear that the weight of the new member states in the EU Council is influencing the EU development policy, but their lack of capacity in this area forms a constraint. The problem of the limited public interest in development aid in the accession countries as well as the need for an active political involvement of advocates for North-South co-operation in new member states urgently needs to be addressed. A so-called 'Presidency Fund' supported by the Irish Government as a gesture to new member states following their entry during the Irish Presidency was set up and is managed by the European NGO network Eurostep.[20] It has the aim to enhance the capacity of civil society in new member states to strengthen European development policy. Subsequent EU presidencies are contributing to the fund.

12. Reform of Institutional Arrangements Affecting the EU's Development Policy

Following the introduction of the European Monetary Union and the eastward enlargement, political and public pressure has mounted to demonstrate that the EU is a global player, and can act independently from the United States. However, the incapacity of the EU to translate these aspirations in legal, institutional, and financial terms that would allow a stronger CFSDP has created increasing pressure on European development co-operation for resources and institutional capacity to be used in support of common external actions, other than development purposes.

The first change – a technical institutional change which would have major political implications – was the setting-up of the Common Service for External Relations (SCR or Service Commune Relations Exterieure) as a shared unit for the various Directorates General (DGs) dealing with external relations. This was a first step to divorce development policy (remaining in DG-Development, then called DG8) from the implementation of the development programmes. In

2000 Javier Solana was appointed Secretary General of the Council and high representative for ESDP. The appointment of Solana by the Council, intended to strengthen EU unity within in the context of the ESDP, provided a direct challenge to the external mandate of the European Commission. How the Commission could retain its influence in external relations was one of the most pressing questions that the Prodi Commission had to address when it was designating posts and portfolios in 1999. A key question in this context was the division of responsibilities between external relations on the one hand and development co-operation on the other hand.

The Prodi Commission renamed the Directorates General, and DG8 became DG-Development. Prodi also decided to award the Commissioner for Development, Poul Nielson, with the portfolio for all developing countries, including ACP, Asia, Latin America, Southern Africa, and the Mediterranean. However this was mostly a paper portfolio, given that the policy for countries in Asia, Latin American, and the Mediterranean came under the responsibility of the Directorate General for External Relations under the British Commissioner Chris Patten. Furthermore, the relations with Central and Eastern Europe were located in a new Directorate General for Enlargement. The earlier established SCR was moved within the Directorate General for External Relations, under the responsibility of the Commissioner for External Relations. Additionally trade policy with ACP countries was removed from DG-Development and went to a new DG dealing with all regions. The DG for External Relations (DG-RELEX) now managed the implementation of all aid to developing countries. DG-RELEX was also administratively in charge of programming and policy to the Mediterranean, Latin American, and Asian regions. DG-Development was no longer in charge of ACP trade policies (these had moved to DG-Trade). This was one of the major aspects of its programme with important significance on EU policies towards LDCs. Additionally DG-Development was not in charge of the policy and programming of development programmes in Asian, Latin American, and Mediterranean countries. Lastly DG-Development had no administrative influence over the implementation of any of the development programmes. Nevertheless, on paper at least, the development Commissioner's political responsibility covered all of the Commission's development programmes.

In reality the mismatch between portfolios and responsibilities for the Directorates General was setting the scene for a potential disaster. The Commissioner for development was politically responsible for development co-operation but had no administrative structures to ensure the implementation of his policies. The Commissioner for external relations, politically in charge of external relations, had the actual responsibility for the implementation of all development policies. The Commissioner for development, Poul Nielson, did not choose to publicly identify the problems that would arise from this structure. In his response to questions asked in the European Parliament he stated:

> The new Commission structure for external relations will give the Development Commissioner the lead role for development policy and development co-operation in all third countries. The Development portfolio will combine responsibility for development and humanitarian aid and will give greater coherence to the Commission's activities in this field ... There will be a single development policy towards all developing countries (European Parliament 1999).

The Commissioner was proven wrong. The Common Service for External Relations was replaced by a new organisation, which was given the name EuropeAid. A board of Commissioners, of which Commissioner for External Relations Chris Patten was the chair, supervised this new structure. The Commissioner for development was left with the post of director general of EuropeAid, and was stripped of all responsibilities for any policy-setting towards regions other than the ACP. While the programming towards the ACP countries was being decentralised to European delegations in developing countries, Nielson's Directorate General was left with few staff, even fewer tasks, and arguably became an empty shell that merely upheld the rhetoric that development co-operation still existed as a separate independent policy area in the European Commission. Just before leaving office a candid Commissioner Nielson acknowledged to the European Parliament: 'The CEO for EuropeAid was a joke. It was a bad joke' (2004).

The question remains how this Commissioner lost all powers to implement development policies. The answer lies in the heavy pressure exercised to mainstream the EU's development policy into external relations, in a response to the competition created between the European Commission and the Council in external relations, following the creation of a post of high representative of the EU Common Foreign and Security Policy in the Council. While the high representative, Javier Solana, had the advantage of power – being close to the CSFP decision-making process in the Council – the Commission potentially had the advantage of resources. These resources for external actions were primarily given in the budget lines for development co-operation. It is these resources that the Commission sought to give itself greater influence in the broader external area.

Meanwhile, a reorganisation of the Council in 2002 followed the trend to bring development aid closer to external policy objectives when the Development Council was abolished. This body had existed independently since the creation of the EU. The public justification for this change was given as the need to 'enhance the efficiency of the institution on the eve of an unprecedented increase in the number of Member States of the Union', as stated in the Presidency Conclusions of June 2002, somehow linking the abolition of the Council to the EU's enlargement. The link between the two events was not further explained.

During the deliberations on the abolition of the Development Council (a decision never formally put on the agenda but taken over lunch), several member states expressed concerns over the excessive remit of the new Council and asked questions about the effectiveness of such a merger. According to the terms of the Seville decision, each government would be represented at the different meetings of the General Affairs and External Relations Council by the minister or state secretary of its choice. Development ministers are seriously disempowered by this decision. With little opportunity to meet at the EU level, it has been reported that development ministers of member states are increasingly hesitant to attend EU Councils – given the limited scope for tangible impact on policy decisions. There have also been indications that this trend would have serious repercussions on the political level of representation given by member states in the area of development co-operation. It is hardly surprising therefore that the development ministers in member states are increasingly critical of the EU's development programmes and do little to defend the development policy of the EU as a whole, despite the sizeable extent of development resources allocated through the European Community.

A new Commission, led by President José Manuel Barroso, took office in 2004, making the institutional set up for development even worse. The board of EuropeAid, jointly established to represent the external DGs, was abolished and the agency came directly under the Directorate General for External Relations with Commissioner Benita Ferrero-Waldner, now in charge of policy towards Asia, Latin America, and neighbouring countries as well as implementation for all developing countries. The new Commissioner for development co-operation, Louis Michel, no longer had a say in EuropeAid and is now only in charge of the Directorate General for Development Co-operation and ECHO, the service for humanitarian assistance. Ferrero-Waldner proclaimed her mission immediately after her inauguration with a public statement at the unveiling of a poster campaign promoting EuropeAid across Europe, pointedly called: 'Would you leave it to chance? We don't.'[21]

Meanwhile the inter-institutional competition between the Commission and the Council remains, particularly with regard to negotiations on an EU External Action Service (EAS). Intended as a new institution on external relations jointly managed by the Council and the Commission, this was proposed and agreed without much deliberation at the final negotiations of the Constitutional Treaty. Even though the Draft Constitutional Treaty has not been ratified, negotiations on the set up of the EAS have begun – as part of a legal provision provided in the draft treaty allowing for negotiations to begin following the signing of the treaty and irrespective of its ratification. Its outcome will determine the future role of the Commission for external policy.

The reforms in both the Council and Commission are being pursued as technical changes, designed to increase the efficiency and effectiveness of the institutions – particularly in the face of enlargement. As internal reforms requiring no changes to the treaties of the EU, they are seen as internal decisions to two institutions. However, these reforms will inevitably have wide-ranging political implications for the role of development and humanitarian policy within the EU.

13. The Contradictory Trends in the EU's Policies

While the institutional and administrative set up was moving to eradicate development co-operation from the Commission's organigramme, the Cotonou Agreement (2000) and policy papers professed a greater commitment to poverty eradication. Cotonou established poverty eradication clearly as the principal objective and assigned a greater role to the participation of civil society as well as reinforcing the political dimension of relations between the ACP countries and the EU. It also included a process for renegotiation of the framework for trade relations with the EU – to be negotiated before 2008.

The first fully-fledged policy on development co-operation for all developing countries was adopted by the three EU institutions in 2000, which stated that: 'the main objective of Community development policy must be to reduce and, eventually, to eradicate poverty.' The Communication also identified that the 'policy frameworks in different regions' should be 'aligned'. At the same time, the rival idea, that EU development policy should be focused on and limited to Africa, seemed to gain ground in the allocation of money and implementation structures. This was expressed during a debate in 2003, when the Commission stated in the Budget Committee that development policy was no longer a basis for its activities in Asia and Latin America, although MEPs did not accept that view. In that year, the Commission changed the budget nomenclature and removed Asian, Latin American, and Mediterranean countries from the chapter on development co-operation and re-introduced these under a chapter of external relations. This is consistent with the way development has been communicated by the Commission, which, for several years, has focused on the website of the DG for development exclusively on ACP countries. Additionally, during the preparations for the review of country strategy papers DG-RELEX has refused to accept general guidelines for all developing countries, and stated that it would have separate guidelines for Asian, Latin American, and Mediterranean countries (Eurostep: 2003). All this suggests that the tension between exclusive regionalism (focused on Africa) and EU multilateralism (focused on a global approach to all developing countries) is still very much alive within the EU.

In the meantime, advocating the need for a global approach to developing countries, the Commission has proposed that the (still separate) funds for ACP countries in the European Development Fund are included in the Community Budget. If this were to be the case, resources for the ACP countries would no longer be 'ring-fenced' in the future. A report offering justifications to the French government for going along with this proposal stated:

> In today's European Union, it is ... the integration of the EDF [resources allocated for ACP countries] into the community budget which will make it possible to assign a more central role to co-operation with ACP countries with regard to political choices (Bocquet and Viallon, 2003: 29).

What explains the apparent contradictions in the proposals by the Commission? An internal explanatory note from the Commission prominently features the concept of 'flexibility' – arguing that budgeting of resources for the ACP would allow greater flexibility over the funds. Flexibility in this context appears to mean that development resources can be more easily used for non-development areas such as security, defence, and migration. While the EU is clearly committed to the Millennium Development Goals as the main international framework for development policy, seen in the context of the Paris Declaration on the harmonisation of aid, 'flexibility' has become the key objective – almost to the extent that it has become an end in itself.

The principle of flexibility served as the rationale to prevent a definition of poverty objectives in the development co-operation budget lines (Reisen, 2002). This was also the major rationale for a renegotiation of the legal instrument that governed EU co-operation with Asia and Latin America. In 2002, the Commission proposed a very loose legal instrument, justifying this on the grounds that in that way Asia and Latin America could be dealt with under one set of guidelines. Spanish opposition in the European Parliament focused on the need for specificity in regional co-operation – as it had first demanded in 1988. Commissioner Patten, in charge of negotiations on the legal instrument, threatened to withdraw the proposal, an unprecedented way of exerting pressure, ultimately leading to the early death of the proposal altogether.

The Commission also paved the way for further flexibility in the EU's development policy to incorporate non-development objectives in the development programmes, in another new instrument negotiated under the Financial Perspectives for 2007-2013 – the Development Cooperation Instrument (DCI). The initial proposal mixed assistance to developing and non-developing countries and lacked a clear legal basis, which has been resisted by the European Parliament.[22] The negotiations on this important legal instrument have been concluded and the legislation is now based on the existing treaty articles for development co-operation. These negotiations on the remit of the legislation stalled the overall progress on the multi-annual finance agreement for the EU for over a year.

A new direction was taken in the 2005 policy statement adopted by the Commission, the Council, and the European Parliament confirming the Millennium Development Goals as the main framework for the EU's development policy, and giving clear emphasis to the objective of poverty eradication. While it extends to all developing countries, the policy statement provides a strong new direction in terms of bringing the EC and member states together in one overall framework. Called the 'European Consensus on Development' it expresses the wish that this might provide a compromise solution for the EU's development policy in coming years.

The new Consensus is complemented by bold new agreements on financing EU aid. In preparation for the UN Financing for Development Summit in Monterrey in 2003 the EU committed itself to jointly increasing aid to €39 billion by 2006, equivalent to 0.39 percent of the joint GNP of the 25 member states. In May 2005, in preparation for the 2005 World Summit, EU ministers from the 25 member states agreed to a new collective target of 0.56 percent for 2010. If achieved, this would provide an additional €20 billion in aid by that time. The EU 25 also set 2015 as the date for reaching 0.7 percent.

14. Conclusions: Enlargement and Development: Is there a Future?

Development co-operation has been one of the major policy areas for the EU since its inception. The relations between the EU and the developing world are rooted in three major historical circumstances: Europe's colonial past, the politics of the Cold War, and the creation and expansion of the EU. The 2004 enlargement of the EU, incorporating ten new members, was a unique event that will not only change the nature of the EU, but also its relations with the South.

The various actions taken by the European institutions and the member states intended to prepare the EU for enlargement brought great pressure to improve on both the quality and independence of the EU's development co-operation, subordinating it to the objectives formulated by the EU's external relations policies and the common foreign and security policy. At the same time the legal basis for development co-operation in the EU treaties was strengthened. In the area of development co-operation there was thus an increasing discrepancy between legal definition, political rhetoric, and reality. While the general tone of this chapter has given little room for optimism, there are some positive observations that can be made.

First, every enlargement of the EU has so far increased the scope for development co-operation – both in terms of regional coverage as well as the kind of approaches adopted. The specific experiences in the international arena of the acceding member states have proven to be valuable assets for the expansion of the EU's activities abroad and development co-operation has played a vital part in forging and enhancing these new links. The accession countries, with their specific ties and history related to the east and elsewhere, might again prove a valuable asset for a broadening of the Community's actions abroad.

Secondly, it has been recognised since the inception of the EU that its prosperity is dependent on and closely associated with the EU's ability to co-operate with countries of the South. The EU needs the South, it needs energy, raw materials, primary products, and minerals; the EU needs the labour forces of the South, the export markets they provide, and as locations for foreign direct investment. But the EU also needs the South to promote the values on which it was founded – the European values of social democracy, the promotion of human rights, and accountable and transparent governance. Finally, the EU needs the South if it wants to fulfil its aspirations of becoming a global player. If the EU rejects the notion of a unipolar world that is dictated to by the United States it will need to seek alliances with the South.

Thirdly, the South has always had its own strategies towards the EU, recognising it as a key player and potential ally in international affairs. This chapter has shown that this was an important part of negotiations in all earlier enlargements, and the competition between previous rivals has given space to the South to negotiate its own agenda with the EU. In that context it is important that the development policy of the EU is not just described in terms of a continuation of its colonial past, but also as a new beginning of a multilateral approach towards developing countries. With the eastward enlargement there is now an opportunity for the countries east of the enlarged EU to be included in such a policy.

The recognition of this potential will not necessarily lead to a European development policy that is focused on development and poverty eradication. This chapter has demonstrated that EU development co-operation has, in the new millennium, been continuously under the pressure of subordination to the EU's Common Foreign and Security Policy and of being linked to other external priorities, notably, migration, defence, and security. In the medium to longer term there is a danger that the commitment to the poverty-oriented development policies of the EU is seriously undermined. The lack of a tradition of development policy, a development administration, and of ministerial-level political representation in the new member states are impediments to a strong future for the development agenda in the enlarged EU. This will have some influence on current member states, particularly those whose development policies are already weak or dominated by national political and commercial policy interests. It will surely be more difficult for member states with strong development policy traditions to promote these values and approaches effectively within the Union. Already it is apparent that the pro-development group of 'likeminded' member states in the Council has weakened because of opposition by a coalition of member states lacking a firm national development policy.

Nevertheless, it is likely that the EU's development policy will remain an important aspect of the EU's external relations. Public opinion polls show consistently that European citizens value EU development co-operation when focused on poverty eradication, and the Constitutional Treaty reflects this priority. The newly adopted 'European Consensus on Development', and the scope now set out for the new legal Instrument for Development Co-operation (DCI), demonstrate that development will remain an important area within the enlarged EU, even if contradictory trends compete with a poverty-focused development policy. While the EU development policy will have to adapt to regional priorities and thematic concerns of the new member states, experience has also shown that it is more than likely that the new member states will become increasingly important actors in international development. As members of the EU, the new member states will absorb the European consensus on development, a consensus that has been prominently on its agenda since its inception.

Notes

1 The author would like to thank Carl Greenidge, Ambassador Harry Dyett, Guido van Hecken, and Simon Stocker for their extensive advice on this chapter. I would also like to thank Andrew Mold who helped in editing the chapter. The author is solely responsible for its content. Parts of this chapter are based on research being undertaken for my Ph.D. thesis and are being published in "The Logic of Coincidence. Agenda-setting in EU development policy", by EEPA, Brussels.

2 These policies were prepared in extensive studies undertaken during World War II, conducted by the US Council on Foreign Relations, which brought together internationally-oriented corporate and financial interests, and top US State Department planners (Chomsky, 1994:83). At first, it was assumed that Germany (though not Japan) would survive as a major power centre. The so-called 'Grand area' was initially to be a non-German bloc, which was to initially incorporate the Western Hemisphere, the Far East, and the former British Empire. The British Empire was to be dismantled (along with other colonial systems) and subsequently incorporated under U.S. control.

3 In figures: 23 percent of French imports originated from its colonies, and 32 percent of the imports from the colonies originated from France in 1956. Between 1952 and 1956 the average annual growth of the French economy increased by 5.5 percent, and a significant part of this growth was attributable to its trade with the colonies. The French colonies were connected to France through a monetary and economic union, and, therefore, the question of the future of these relations posed some serious questions.

4 The constitutional reform after World War II intended, among other things, to give greater powers to the French colonies – the support and participation of whom had been crucial for the successes of the army of the Free French. The Fourth Republic, which emerged from this constitutional renewal, transformed the French empire into the French Union, originating from the Conference of Brazzaville (1944). The French Union was directed by the president of the Republic who presided over the National Assembly and the 'Conseil de la République', two chambers of Parliament, to which the colonies had direct access through deputies and senators representing the colonies.

5 Kubursi A. and Mansur S. , 'The Political Economy of Middle Eastern Oil', in: Stubbs R. and Underhill G., (eds.) Political Economy and the Changing Global Order, London: MacMillan, 1994, pp. 318-321. Kubursi and Mansur argue that the United States and Saudi Arabia had a strategic understanding in which profits made from exports to Europe were reinvested in the US, so as to avoid further devaluation and erosion of the dollar, as inflation induced by the Vietnam war eroded the value of the dollar. See also M. Hubbert (1982); 'Techniques of Prediction as applied to the Production of Oil and Gas', in: Gass S., (ed.), Oil and Gas Supply Modelling, National Bureau of Standards Special Publication 631, Washington DC, 1982, p.140-141.

6 For more details, see van Reisen (forthcoming), 'The Logic of Coincidence, Agenda-setting in EU Development Co-operation', doctoral thesis.

7 During the negotiations these fears seemed well-founded, as observed by Guyanan Ambassador to the EEC Lawrence E. 'Bonny' Mann: 'The Community was at one stage demanding the right to be consulted by any ACP state which contemplated taking measures in the trade field which would affect the interests of any EEC Member State. This in effect ... could have the result of requiring ACP finance ministers trotting up to Brussels to discuss in advance their proposed annual budgets with the Commission – a departure from sanity of altogether intolerable proportions' (cited in Dyett 1998:45).

8 Programmes were adopted by the United Nations General Assembly in 1974 and 1975. Faber, G., op. cit.; See also: Dyett, op. cit, Grilli, op cit., Roon, van, ibid, op cit. Stevens, C., Renegotiating Lomé, in: EEC and the Third World: a Survey, ODI, IDS, 1984.

9 The British floated a proposal for integrating the EDF into the Community budget during the negotiations on the Lomé I Convention. In 1973 the European Parliament also agreed that the EDF should be incorporated into the EC Budget. The Commission issued a memorandum on EDF budgeting in April 1973 in which it supported some form of 'budgetisation'. On the other hand some developing countries looked on the arrangement of the EDF outside the budget as a 'safety valve' and saw the EDF Committee as a 'political representation on their behalf' (Dyett 2002). The European Council rejected proposals for integrating the EDF into the budget. Since that time the European Commission has included the EDF in its pre-budget proposals and since 1977 the European Parliament has included the EDF in the annual budget – even though the Parliament has no authority over it.

10 The European Development Fund is a five-year fund containing the financial resources designated by a particular Convention as agreed between the Community and the ACP. It operates outside the Community budget. All EC members contribute to the Fund with voluntary contributions. In 1970, when the EC was endowed with its own resources, the powers of the budgetary authority were shared between the Council and the Parliament. However, as the EDF is outside the budget, the European Parliament does not have any powers over the EDF or its disbursements. Additionally, the principle of 'annuality' does not apply to the EDF and on average the implementation of the fund takes 12-13 years instead of intended five years. Member states do not transfer the resources to a central fund but retain them in their national budgets, so the slow disbursement of the funds reduces the available resources for development aid in European member states. In earlier research on this matter, I observed that: 'In this way approximately €3 billion annually leaves the EU budget for development co-operation and never reaches developing countries – a figure which is a staggering 50 percent of total CEC aid. This constitutes approximately 10 percent of ODA from the EU as a whole' (Reisen 1999: 93-109) These conclusions were corroborated by DG-8 Director General Philip Lowe in a speech on January 19, 1999 to the Development Committee and Poul Nielson, then the Danish minister for development co-operation, on the Danish television news, January 27, 1999.

11 Data: European Commission (2000) Courier, September, Special Issue, Cotonou Agreement, p. 12; Grilli, Enzo R. (1993), The European Community and the Developing Countries, Cambridge: Cambridge University Press, ,, p. 99, for per capita calculations; author's calculations for 1995 and 2000, data from http://www.census.gov/cgi-bin/ipc/idbagg

12 Ex-Art. 235 and Art. 308 of the TEC were used, which is very broad: "If action by the Community should prove necessary to attain, in the course of the operation of the common market, one of the objectives of the Community and this treaty has not provided the necessary powers, the Council shall, acting unanimously on a proposal from the Commission and after consulting the European Parliament, take the appropriate measures." A 1996 legal opinion of the Court of Justice ruled that provisions being an integral part of

an institutional system based on the principle of conferred powers, cannot serve as a basis for widening the scope of Community powers beyond the general framework created by the provisions of the Treaty as a whole. The Presidency argued that because of the systematic use of Art. 308 for co-operation with non-developing countries, and the fact that the existing articles only covered co-operation with developing countries, a new legal basis was required for non-developing countries (De Witte 2002: 217-8). See also: Presidency Note, CONFER 4711.00, Brussels, 22 February 2000.

13 Martenczuk argues that Art. 181a applies to those countries for which previously recourse was necessary to the very broad Art. 308 EC. The central objective of Art. 181a was: "not to create a new Community competence, but to provide for a simpler procedure that was previously exercised on the basis of Article 208 EC.(p. 406)." Art. 181a differs from Art. 179 in terms of procedure.

14 For details on the analysis see http://constitution.eurostep.org

15 Council of the European Union, Opinion of the Legal Services, Commission proposal for a Council Regulation establishing an instrument for Stability – legal basis – scope of Community competence, 8095/05 Jur, 15 April 2005 . Council of the European Union, Opinion of the Legal Service, Jur 176, 26.05.2000 also defines Art 177-179 as applying to all developing countries.

16 The OECD Development Assistance Committee (DAC) regularly decides whether a country is eligible for ODA (Official Development Assistance) or for Official Assistance (OA). This list is regularly revised, and is organised on objective needs-based criteria. It includes all low and middle income countries, except those that are members of the G8 or the European Union (including countries with a firm date for EU admission; i.e., Bulgaria and Romania). OECD DAC 'European Community's aid at a glance', http://www.oecd.org/dataoecd/12/1/1935386.pdf [accessed 4th August 2006].

17 See for instance: Council of the European Union (2003) 'European Security Strategy. A Secure Europe in a Better World?' 12 December, p. 12.

18 This includes Algeria, Armenia, Azerbaijan, Belarus, Egypt, Georgia, Israel, Jordan, Lebanon, Libya, Moldova, Morocco, Syria, Tunisia, Ukraine and the Palestine Authority.

19 This covers candidate countries (Turkey and Croatia) and potential candidate countries (Albania, the Former Yugoslav Republic of Macedonia, Bosnia and Herzegovina, Serbia and Montenegro, and Kosovo).

20 For further information see: http://www.presidencyfund.org.

21 Statement by Benita Ferrero-Waldner on her objectives as lead Comisssioner on development co-operation, given at the unveiling of a poster campaign launched in airports across Europe.

22 The first proposal from the Commission was called the 'Economic Co-operation and Development Co-operation Instrument', clearly prioritising economic co-operation over development co-operation. The original proposal was based on the articles concerning developing and non-developing countries and included a regulation for economic co-operation with industrialised countries. The European Parliament refused to consider the proposal and judged it un-amendable. After the UK presidency had presented a new text that clearly defined the legal base and split the co-operation between developing and non-developing countries, the European Parliament adopted a decision to amend the Commission proposal. For details see: Eurostep briefings at www.eurostep.org.

References

Bocquet, Dominique and Viallon, Stéphane (2003), La Budgétisation du FED, Une Étape dans la modernisation de l'Aide. Rapport pour le Ministre de l'Economie, des Finances et de l'Industrie, Paris.

Bretherton, Caroline and John Vogler (1999), *The European Union as a Global Actor*, London: Routledge.

Chomsky, Noam (1992), *What Uncle Sam Really Wants, The Real Story*, Tuscon, Odonian Press.

Chomsky, Noam (1994), *World Orders Old and New*, New York: Columbia University Press.

Commission of the European Communities (1985), 'Nineteenth General Report on the Activities of the European Communities', Brussels – Luxembourg.

Commission of the European Communities (2000), 'The European Community's Development Policy', Communication from the Commission to the Council and the European Parliament, Brussels.

Commission of the European Communities (1981), Fourteenth General Report on the Activities of the European Communities in 1980, Brussels – Luxembourg.

Council of the European Union (2000), Conference of the Representatives of the Governments of the Member States, Presidency Note, CONFER 4711/00, Brussels, 22 February.

Council of the European Union (2003), *European Security Strategy. A Secure Europe in a Better World*, Brussels.

Department for International Development (DFID) (2001 revised), 'Working in Partnership with the European Community', Institutional Strategy Paper, London.

Dyett, Harry (1998), *ACP Diplomacy. The Caribbean Dimension*, Georgetown, Guyana: Lahama Gardens.

Dyett, Harry (2002), personal note to the author dated 20 July 2002.

European Commission (2003), 'Flexibility versus systemic constraints of the EDF system'. DG-Development Paper for the DEV DG's meeting, DEV/A/1/D (2003), Brussels 13 June 2003.

European Commission (2005), 'The European Consensus on Development', Communication, Brussels.

European Parliament (1999), 'Questionnaire for Nominee Commissioners with special responsibility for Development Co-operation and Humanitarian Aid'. Reply from Commissioner designate Poul Nielson, Brussels/Strassbourg.

Eurostep (2003), 'IGC Toolkit', Brussels.

Gorbachev, Mikhail (1996), *Memoirs*, London: Bantam.

Grilli, Enzo R. (1993), *The European Community and the Developing Countries*, Cambridge: Cambridge University Press.

Lanning, G. and M Mueller (1979), *Africa Undermined, A History of the Mining Companies and the Underdevelopment of Africa*, Middlesex: Penguin Books.

Martenczuk, Bernd (2002), 'Co-operation with Development and Other Third Countries: Elements of a Community Foreign Policy', in: Griller, Stefan, and Wiedel, Brigit (eds.) *External Economic Relations and Foreign Policy in the European Union*, Wien, New York: Springler, pp. 385-417.

Mollet, Howard and van Reisen, Mirjam, et. al., (2002), *Tackling Poverty in Asia*, London: BOND.

Ortoli, François-Xavier (1975), President of the commission of the European Communities, Address to the European Parliament on 18 February 1975, in *Commission of the European Communities, Eight General Report of Activities of the European Communities 1974*, Brussels-Luxembourg.

Ortoli, François-Xavier (1976), President of the commission of the European Communities, Address to the European Parliament on 10 February 1976, in *Commission of the European Communities, Ninth General Report of Activities of the European Communities 1975*, Brussels-Luxembourg.

Reisen, Mirjam van (1999-2000), *EU 'Global Player', The North-South Policy of the European Union*, Zeist: International Books.

Reisen, Mirjam van (2002), Directing EU Policy Towards Poverty Eradication: From Commitments to Targets to Results, ECDPM Discussion Paper No. 35, Maastricht.

Reisen, Mirjam van (2002), '*Tackling Poverty: A Proposal for European Union Aid Reform*', London: BOND.

Reisen, Mirjam van (2005) 'To the Farthest Frontiers: Women's Empowerment in an Expanding Europe', Brussels: Eurostep and Social Watch.

Soetendorp, Ben (1994), 'EC/EU as a single foreign policy actor', in: Carlsnaes et al. (eds.) *European Foreign Policy*, London: Sage, pp. 103-119.

Uribe, Armando (1984), 'Le Général de Gaulle et l'Amerique Latine', in Institut du Droit de la Paix et du Développement et Institut Charles de Gaulle, *De Gaulle et le Tiers Monde*, Paris: Editions A. Pedone.

de Witte, Bruno (2001), 'Clarifying the Delimitations of Powers. A Proposal with Comments', in European Commission *Europe 2004 Le Grand Débat: Setting the Agenda and Outlining the Options*, Brussels, pp. 121-129.

3 European Development Policymaking: Globalisation and the Post-Lomé World

Marjorie Lister

1. Introduction: Globalisation and Development

Globalisation – the process of creating an integrated global economy, polity, and society – is an inescapable theme of much of today's academic literature. In fields ranging from cultural studies to economics, sociology, and politics, scholars address questions of what globalisation is, how it is occurring and who benefits and who loses out. In development studies the analysis and categorisation of different regions or groups of countries such as the richer countries of North America and Western Europe, the formerly socialist countries of Central and Eastern Europe, and poorer countries of Africa and Asia has been central, with the aim of getting the poorer regions to 'modernise' or catch up to the living standards and development levels of the richer ones.

Previous models or schools of thought of development studies divided the world into 'haves' and 'have-nots' for the liberals, or in dependency terms, into the powerful and developed 'centre' and the weak and marginalised 'periphery'. From the perspective of globalisation, there is a distinction to be made between the countries and individuals who are richer and more powerful in the new globalised world system and the others. That is, some countries or individuals can be categorised as the 'globalisers' – those who have agency and actively make the decisions creating globalisation – and the 'globalised' who are powerless onlookers 'or just a mere prop in the play being staged' (Ki-Zerbo, 2001). For Professor Ki-Zerbo, Africa as a whole fell into the powerless and 'globalised' category; which, up until now, also fits most of the rest of the developing and post-socialist world.

This chapter addresses the changing environment produced by globalisation and how it affects the international development agenda, the concept of a 'Third World', and the post colonial approach to international politics. Furthermore, it analyses the positions of the eastern and central European states *vis-à-vis* the developing countries in the European Union's panoply of external relations and compares their experiences. Finally, in the new globalising international system both Central and Eastern Europe and the developing countries are known as 'partners' of the European Union (EU). In practice, what does this mean?

2. The End of Development?

Traditionally, development studies aimed at understanding and improving the lot of the global poor and disadvantaged, but met with mixed success. Over the past three decades, the Lomé Conventions and subsequent Cotonou Agreement between the European Union and 77 African, Caribbean, and Pacific (ACP) states were emblematic of this disjuncture between high development aspirations and limited positive, measurable development performance (Lister, 1997). Since the 1980s the whole project of international development and the discipline of development studies have been called into question. For some, the development agenda failed because it could not prevent the increase in global poverty and inequality, coupled with the destruction of the environment (Amin, 1997). The French post-structuralist author, Bruno Latour, succinctly expressed the anguish of the failure of the West's attempt to develop the Third World: 'We might have done it; we thought we could do it; we can no longer believe it possible' (quoted in Lister 1998: 377). In theoretical terms, the failure of development thinking to transcend the limitations of the dependency and modernisation schools (representing socialist- and capitalist-based approaches respectively) led in the 1990s to a period of stagnation and introspection in development studies (Scott, 1996). Ankie Hoogvelt (2001) argued that not only was 'developmentalism' (i.e., the pro-development international agenda) dead, the disappearance of a definable Third World had caused the disappearance of development studies as a discipline. Development studies, she contended, had no coherent identity and no pretensions to being an academic discipline in its own right. Development studies had fragmented and virtually dissolved into area studies, gender studies, environmental studies, and international political economy.

Nevertheless, the reported death of development studies is premature. The fragmentation of development studies lamented by Hoogvelt could instead be considered an enrichment of the field as insights from area studies, geography, gender, and environmental studies and elsewhere are incorporated. The literature of development studies, including numerous journals as well as books, is burgeoning rather than decreasing and academic departments are successfully recruiting talented students at both undergraduate and post graduate levels. Professional organisations and study groups are active in producing papers, holding conferences, and creating networks.

While some disciplines such as economics become more and more rarefied,[1] development studies have kept a more grounded and empirical focus. Its interdisciplinarity and openness to incorporating new ideas and approaches constitute its strength rather than its weakness. The explanations, for instance, of the relative post-war economic success of the southeast Asian 'tiger' countries like South Korea, Taiwan, and Singapore are not merely due to the single factor of economic neo-liberalism as contended by politicians such as Ronald Reagan, but to a variety of causes ranging from government leadership to education, culture, social policies, and export strategies (Broad, Cavanagh and Bello, 1995).

Another source of strength both for the global development agenda and, secondarily, for the development studies discipline, is the widespread public support for (if not always deep knowledge of) development objectives as revealed in numerous opinion polls (Lister, 1997; Spur, 1995; European Commission, 1999). This support is also evidenced in the financial contributions from the public and governments for development objectives. Even the EU-ACP relationship, which has frequently struggled for political attention and legitimacy, and the Euro-Mediterranean Partnership which has faced considerable criticism (Joffe, 1999), have continued into the third millennium whilst carrying with them a mixture of political, developmental, and other objectives.

To return to the central theme of this section, some scholars like McMichael have contended that the development era is indeed over. The end of the development era, with its emphasis on state-centred development and 'modernisation', was identified by McMichael as having occurred sometime in the post-war period, around the 1970s according to his timeline (McMichael 2000). Its demise, he argued, took place in the wake of the debt crisis and the popular disillusionment with traditional development thinking. The development project was then replaced, McMichael contended, with the globalisation project. The dominant idea of globalisation was the rule of the free market at the global level. Nevertheless, McMichael himself backtracked from this position, noting subsequently that the development project had perhaps changed rather than disappeared (McMichael, 2000: 54).

In summary, the death of development argument is unconvincing: governments, NGOs, and the public continue to take an interest in development aid and in international development targets for reducing hunger, poverty, and illiteracy. Neither has the development agenda completely collapsed into the mere management of crises in Africa or former Yugoslavia or the mere management of exclusion (Amin, 1997; Hoogvelt, 2001). The European Union, for instance, bolstered its development credentials with the signing of the Cotonou Agreement in 2000, an extension of its longstanding Euro-African partnership for development with the ACP group. The EU also hosted the Third United Nations Conference on Least Developed Countries in 2001, promoting special trade concessions in 'everything but arms' for 49 of the world's poorest states. At the same time, conferences such as the World Food Summit Plus 5 of 2001, Earth Summit Plus 10 of 2002; the Beijing Plus 10 conference and the Millennium Development Summit of 2005 (the latter attended by an unprecedented number of heads of state and government) continue to put forward development objectives at the global level.

3. Third World or Globalisation?

> *The emergence of the Third World, the assertion of its independence, and its collective awareness of the historic role it has to play will appear as major facts in the history of the twentieth century.*
> ***Edgard Pisani – speech to United Nations Conference on the Least Developed Countries, Paris, 1-4 Sept. 1981.***

The Third World has always been an ill-defined or ambiguous concept. It signified a political unity desired by the developing countries, but also a convenient lumping together of the poorer countries by outsiders. In Cold War terms, the Third World meant the countries that were neither part of the Western nor Eastern camps, the so-called 'grey areas'. Many academic authors struggled to get to grips with the concept of the Third World and its implications. To Clapham, for example, the Third World was defined by its economic, cultural, and social peripherality – and their political repercussions (Clapham, 1985). Although this formulation failed to put politics as firmly at the centre of the 'Third World' idea as it belonged, it did express the commonality of weakness, marginalisation, and poverty which characterised much of the developing world. For reasons of political 'correctness', the negative stereotype of being third rate or third class led many authors to abandon the concept entirely, although it still persists extensively in journalism, in popular usage and in many academic texts.

The emergence of 'Third World politics', or the Third World as a political force, was considered by European Development Commissioner Pisani (quoted above) as one of the key facts of the twentieth century. The apparent power of the Third

World as a voting bloc in the UN General Assembly, with its demands for political, economic, social and cultural equality, and fair trade, challenged the thinking of decision-makers in the developed countries, especially in the 1960s and 1970s. However, it has been argued – in parallel to the death of development thesis – that as we enter the new millennium, 'the Third World as such no longer exists' (Hoogvelt, 2001: xi). The Third World appears to have lost its political coherence by acceding to Western neo-liberal orthodoxies and becoming fractionalised into competing regions and states.

Alternatively, the Third World, it can be contended, has not disintegrated; it has been globalised. This signifies that, since the end of the Cold War, more states have become poor and marginalised, vulnerable to external political and economic conditions. Notably, the formerly socialist countries have left their 'Second World' status and now entered the 'Third World'. Like the poorer Third World countries they depend economically and politically on the richer, developed countries. In addition, within all states both 'First World and 'Third World' conditions exist (Thomas, 1999). For instance, the expansion of low-paid, sweatshop garment industry jobs in developed countries such as the United States has been compared to Third World conditions (McMichael, 2000). Thus the answer to Caroline Thomas' question, 'where is the Third World now?' would seem to be – everywhere.

4. The *Post* Post-colonial Phase?

According to the EU's green paper, which prepared the way for the Cotonou Agreement of 2000, "the colonial and post colonial period are behind us" (European Commission, 1997a). Europe's relations with the developing world would henceforth be based on a new international environment. But to what extent is this picture of non-colonial Europe true? Europe still has dependencies, although they are greatly reduced in number from the high point of the colonial empires: 20 territories with varying legal status are covered by the Cotonou Agreement. And some of them, like the Falkland Islands, are the subject of post-colonial dispute. Thus, Europe's colonial period is not entirely over.

The end of the post-colonial phase is also difficult to establish. Post colonialism is a particularly broad concept or approach to contemporary social and political conditions. On one hand, it refers to events from the colonial period and its aftermath, but on the other it also refers to viewing the present in terms of the effects of the colonial experience. Emerging in the 1980s, post colonialism became largely a discourse of identity, aiming to restore self-esteem to the colonised peoples (Hoogvelt, 2001). Post-colonialism is also often associated with the work of the Palestinian-American philosopher Edward Said. Said insisted on the importance of the political dimension of imperialism in understanding not only politics but also literature and philosophy. He argued that 'the political dimension of imperialism governs an entire field of study, imagination, and scholarly institutions' (Said, 1991: 13-14).

In contemporary politics, the grievances of Zimbabwe's President Mugabe, for example, against the British government, or the political struggles of East Timor cannot be fully understood without reference to the colonial and post-colonial experience. Nevertheless, an alternative perspective on developed-developing country relations is currently emerging that places less emphasis on the colonial period and could therefore more nearly be called *post* post-colonial. According to this perspective, current levels of development are not based on colonial or post colonial legacies, but depend largely on the quality of national governance.

This mode of thinking is enshrined not only in the declarations of national equality between the EU and ACP states stretching back to Yaounde 1 in 1963, but even more explicitly in the Cotonou Agreement of 2000 which places the primary responsibility for maintaining positive conditions for development on the ACP side (Cotonou Agreement, preamble). Furthermore, the ACP states were intended to be responsible for their own development strategies: 'the partnership shall encourage the ownership of the development strategies by the countries and populations concerned' (article 2). In a similar vein African presidents like Uganda's Museveni and Gambia's Jammeh have acknowledged that many of their continent's problems are not the fault of Europe, but of Africa's own making.

In 1976 William Zartman argued that the Lomé Convention was a step on the road to real decolonisation and political development for Africa (Zartman 1976). But by 2000, with the influence of *post* post-colonial thinking in the Cotonou Agreement, few scholars saw the new system as particularly favourable to the African, Caribbean, and Pacific side. Cotonou in fact represented the loss or rolling back of some of the key benefits of Lomé I, including contractually guaranteed levels of aid, non-reciprocal trade concessions, special trade provisions for commodities, and an interest in addressing the problems of commodity-dependent economies (Raffer, 2001).

5. Enlargement and Development

An important part of the end of the Cold War, with its division of the world into Western, Eastern, and Third World camps, and the subsequent rise of globalisation, is the change in the status of Eastern and Central Europe. They have shifted since 1989 from socialist to transitional, or even developing countries as argued above, and many are now set to join the developed world through the European Union. The last major enlargement of the EU with the addition of ten new members – Poland, Hungary, the Czech Republic, Slovakia, Slovenia, Latvia, Lithuania, Estonia, Cyprus, and Malta – occurred in May 2004. However, the overall mood of the EU at the time of this enlargement was sombre, with a notable lack of public enthusiasm for the project. Yet the importance to the EU of this new millennium's enlargement would be hard to overstate. Just as the 1980s have been termed 'the lost decade for development' the failure of the EU to act more swiftly to reunify Europe in the 1990s could be called 'the lost decade for enlargement'.

Timothy Garton Ash compared the 2004 enlargement to a wedding party 'delayed for fifteen years by the meanness and prevarication of the bridegroom (EU)' (2002). The lack of public interest from Western Europe, the complex and costly bureaucratic regulations imposed on the prospective new members, notably some 80,000 pages of EU legislation, the miserly regional aid allocated to the new members after joining (around half of the levels for existing members), and limited benefits to their farmers suggested the EU was less than fully committed to a successful enlargement process (*The Times*, 2002). Even the emergency aid granted by the EU to the candidate members following the floods of 2002 was originally not new funding, but reallocated from other projects (Benoit, Guerrera, and Wright 2002). A new aid fund of 500 million euros was allocated only after intense public criticism of the EU's stinginess (Dombey, 2002). Nevertheless, the 2004 enlargement did not dim other European countries' interest in EU membership. Romania and Bulgaria joined the EU in January 2007. Membership talks with Croatia and Turkey opened in 2005, and Macedonia was granted candidate member status at the end of that year.

Four areas of comparison below illuminate the differences and similarities in EU policy towards Central and Eastern Europe and the developing countries. These are EU power, the importance of political versus economic links, the policies' effects on the core EU political system, and the disappointment of the partner countries with their relationship to the Union.

6. The European Union as a Powerful Attractor

The extent of the EU's external influence has often been doubted. The EU is not a state, its actions are often dismissed as not amounting to foreign policy, not coherent, and not influential (Ginsberg, 2001). In terms of its Mediterranean partnership, for instance, the EU has succeeded in paying the piper but not in calling the tune. That is, although Europe is the biggest donor to the region its political influence in the Middle East peace process is far outstripped by that of the United States.

In respect to both the cases of developing countries and Eastern and Central Europe, the powerful attraction and influence of the EU is undeniable. As the world's largest trade bloc and, collectively with the member states, as the world's largest aid donor, the EU is the rich countries' club almost every government in Europe wants to join – or, in the case of the ACP group, at least to have as a partner. Thus, the EU's often-discussed powerlessness and lack of superpower status is belied by its great influence in Central and Eastern Europe, and with its African, Caribbean, and Pacific partners in the Cotonou Agreement.

For both Central and Eastern Europe and the developing countries, relations with the EU have become overtly more political. For Africa, relations with the EU extend back to the Treaty of Rome, to its various annexes dealing with developing countries, and the Part IV Association which prefigured the Yaounde and Lomé Conventions. Links between Europe and the ACP were always post-colonial and political links, despite the convenient fictions often invoked by the European Commission that the Conventions were solely economic, neutral, or non-political (Lister, 1988). Under the Cotonou Agreement the political element has been explicitly recognised, enhanced, and turned from a vice into a virtue.

In contrast, relations between the EU and Eastern and Central Europe were not mentioned in the Treaty of Rome. Links between the EU and Central and Eastern Europe evolved only gradually under the common commercial policy and originally aimed only at defending Europe's trading interests. During the Cold War, relations between Eastern and Western Europe were often strained. Not until 1990 did association agreements signed with Eastern and Central European countries call them 'partners' and begin to talk about shared values and close political relations (Grilli, 1993).

Ultimately, the Central and Eastern European countries accepted for membership in the EU will achieve levels of power and influence in the organisation's structure and policies immeasurably greater than those of the developing world.

For these countries, the challenge is to make membership – including aid from the EU's structural funds – as positive as it has been for previous new EU members such as Spain, Greece, and the Republic of Ireland. The high degree of relative importance attached to the Central and Eastern European countries can be, to a large extent, gauged by the levels of aid allocated by the EU. In 1999-2000, middle income countries received more aid than the least developed and low income countries together. The top ten recipients of ODA from the EU (1999-2000 average) were in descending order, Poland (which received more than twice the amount of any other country), the Czech Republic, Romania, the Former Yugoslavia, Morocco, Bosnia and Herzegovina, Hungary, Slovakia, Ex-Yugoslavian states, and Egypt (Development Assistance Committee, 2002).

Although per capita aid comparisons for different regions are not normally provided by the EU (see European Commission, 2000; European Commission, 2002a), EU figures for 1996 showed EU aid per capita as US$ 0.7 for low income countries, US$ 1.4 for middle income countries, and US$ 4.5 for Central and Eastern Europe and the former Soviet Union. The EU's relative generosity to the countries of Central and Eastern Europe and the former Soviet Union is in itself commendable. But it sat uncomfortably next to the European Commission's and Council's formal policy statement on development which emphasises the importance of poverty eradication and directing aid to low income countries (European Commission, 2002b, European Union, 2005). Nevertheless, in keeping with this policy objective, the percentage of EU aid devoted to the least developed (poorest) countries did rise from 32 percent in 2000 to a high of 44.5 percent in 2003, before falling back slightly to 43.7 percent in 2004 (European Commission, 2005: 16).

7. Effects on the Structure of the EU – Constituent Policies

Policies that affect the ground rules of the structure and functioning of the EU are known as constituent policies (Wallace 1996). To what extent have the relations of the EU with the other regions examined here had effects on the structure of the EU itself? In the case of development policy, effects were felt primarily at the stage of negotiating the Treaty of Rome. In 1956 France made the association of its colonial possessions an essential condition of membership of the European Community. France got its way: the Association for developing countries was established and France joined the Community. British accession to the European Community in 1973 resulted in the enlarged system for developing countries known as the Lomé Convention, but not in any fundamental changes to the structure of the Community.

The constituent effects on the EU of its relations with Central and Eastern Europe are more complex and far-reaching. In order to create a solid Union of 25 member states instead of the previous 15, a constitutional convention was launched in 2002. Chaired by Valery Giscard d'Estaing, it sought to make the fundamental changes needed to create a constitution for Europe for the next 50 years. Key topics under consideration included a common foreign policy, tax harmonisation, power over national budgets, the respective powers of the European Parliament, national parliaments and council of ministers (*The Economist*, 2002). The convention completed its proposed constitutional treaty in late 2003, but referendums in France and the Netherlands in 2005 rejected the document. However, it is possible that a revised constitution could win acceptance in the future.

8. Disappointment

Many ACP countries have been disappointed with the mixed results of their three or more decades of partnership with the EU and with Western development aid in general (Lister, 1997). As Morrissey et al. point out in chapter 8 of this volume, the current negotiations under the Cotonou Agreement for regional free trade areas between developing countries and the EU, scheduled for completion in 2008, could well increase levels of disappointment as some regions or categories such as least developed countries receive more favourable treatment than others.

Likewise, Eastern and Central European candidate members of the EU (as well as Turkey) have been disappointed at the slow pace of membership negotiations, strict conditions for membership, and the lack of full membership benefits upon joining. A Eurobarometer poll found that support from the citizens of Central and Eastern European countries for joining the EU averaged 59 percent, but ranged from just 33 percent in Latvia and Estonia to 80 percent in Romania (which was not included in the first wave of entrants). Only 49 percent of existing EU citizens supported the expansion of the EU (European Commission, 2001).

9. Partnership: An Elusive Goal?

The meaning of partnerships among sovereign states has long been a subject of some perplexity, given the number of widely different international partnerships in operation (Lister, 1988; Raffer, 2002). Nevertheless, the usage of this terminology is virtually universal today, having flourished, for example, in the EU's lexicon ever since it replaced 'association' to designate EU relations with developing countries in the first Lomé Convention of 1975. At present 'partnership' can be applied to almost any inter-state relations – from the close links between EU partner states, the relations between Europe and the US in NATO, NATO's Partnership for Peace with Central and Eastern European states, to the US plans for partnerships with poor countries in Africa (Lister, 1999b). The dissemination of the contemporary discourse of 'partnerships' between countries is a part of the process of globalisation.

Adjectives such as 'uneven', 'unequal', or 'asymmetrical' can be added to 'partnership' to indicate its often unbalanced nature in practice. Even more graphic is the description of partnership as stemming from the model of the partnership of the horse and its rider (Lister, 1988) or the Orwellian model of partnership where the stronger party (the EU) makes all the decisions and the weaker one (the developing world) is largely a historical burden (Raffer, 2001). In any case, relations of equality seem much rarer in contemporary interstate partnerships than those of inequality. Despite the vagueness of the term 'partnership' and the difficulty of defining it precisely (Maxwell and Riddell, 1998), it does express for many people an ideal of equality, equity, and harmonious cooperation. This ideal, for example in the case of the Lomé Convention, is 'known by everybody never to have existed but to be necessary to create' (Sebegnou, 1999). In the case of the Euro-Mediterranean Partnership between the 27 members, the terminology and the ideal of partnership can be juxtaposed against the problems of inequality between the wealthy and powerful EU states and the poor countries of the southern Mediterranean littoral. Instead of partnership, the basic power configuration in the region is one of European hegemony with Europe as the centre or hub of the system and the outlying Mediterranean countries as the spokes (Joffe, 1997; Joffe, 1999).

Francis Fukuyama emphasised the importance of trust in building social capital and promoting economic development (Fukuyama, 1995). He argued that prosperity depends not only on free market economics and democratic government, but also on an underlying social condition of trust. High trust societies such as Japan and Germany experience greater economic development than those where social trust is rarer. But Fukuyama's argument could be further extended beyond national societies to international relationships or regimes. That is, international regimes based on trust, or at least based on predictable and consistent patterns of state behaviour (Lister, 1997), for example between the EU and US or between EU member states, could be expected to perform better than those based on lower levels of trust. According to this expanded version of Fukuyama's model, under conditions of international trust, for instance around the Mediterranean basin, economic prosperity would be a more likely outcome.

In discussing partnership, it is impossible to ignore an ambitious recent African initiative. In July 2001, five African states – Nigeria, South Africa, Algeria, Senegal, and Zambia – launched the New Partnership for Africa's Development (NEPAD). Its intention is to use peer pressure to evoke policy change in African countries, to turn its back on the unsuccessful history of loans and aid to the continent while developing a more successful partnership with the international community. This does not mean NEPAD rejects aid from the developed world; rather it rejects unproductive aid and the debt burden it caused (NEPAD, 2001).

NEPAD aims at creating a new Africa-led development agenda for Africa. It seeks to build a comprehensive policy framework for the socio-economic renewal of Africa (Obasanjo, 2002). The new partnership's priorities are: peace and security; democracy and good political, economic and corporate governance; regional cooperation and integration; capacity-building; policy reform and increased investment in key sectors such as agriculture and human development; and mobilising resources through a variety of means such as increasing domestic savings and investment, and external capital flows (NEPAD, 2004). NEPAD plans to cooperate closely with the European Union, to hold biannual meetings between its executive committee and the European Commission, and to consider other development issues such as how to coordinate the new initiative with the instruments of the Cotonou Agreement (Mouradian, 2001).

Already a number of questions have been raised about the partnership, including the potential membership, means of accountability, relations with the African Union, proliferation of institutions and the top-down nature of the agreement, which has had little public or civil society input (Maxwell and Christiansen, 2002; De Waal, 2002). Although hopeful about the future of NEPAD, Alex De Waal argued at an early stage that, 'the initiative can easily be read as either Africa's best hope or another futile grand plan' (De Waal, 2002: 475). So far, the successes of NEPAD include increasing its membership to 20 countries by 2003 (NEPAD, 2003) and attracting EU funding for its peacekeeping operations in Africa (Anyazawa, 2004). NEPAD has also gained the attention and the financial support of the developed G8 countries. President Obasanjo, chairperson of the NEPAD Heads of State and Government Committee emphasised NEPAD's accomplishments: 'In response to NEPAD, the G8 countries have not only produced the G8 Africa Action Plan, they have reversed the downward trend in development assistance ... Africa features prominently in high-level investor conferences instead of featuring only on television screens as a centre of conflicts, natural disasters, and human misery' (Obasanjo, 2002: 11). NEPAD's African Peer Review Mechanism, which assesses member countries' development performance, was initiated in 2003. Widely seen as the most important instrument of the organisation, so far 26 countries have participated in the review process (Oyuke, 2006).

10. Conclusion

For the EU, globalisation has several meanings. On one hand, it means becoming a global actor, taking on a larger political role as its 'richer but inevitably more complex relations with the rest of the world' unfold (European Commission, 1997b: 36). Globalisation also means more international economic integration, but without ending the inequalities between the rich and the poor, 'the globalisers' and 'the globalised' (Ki-Zerbo, 2001). For the EU, the advent of its single currency, the euro, the external potential of the single market, and the Union's ability to act cohesively in international fora such as the World Trade Organization (WTO) potentially offer it great power.

The effects of globalisation on the EU's existing development and external policies are extensive. Globalisation also means facing global-level problems, including poverty-alleviation, development, failures in governance, conflict, gender inequality, and environmental mismanagement. But addressing these as global problems does not necessarily mean the death of the international development agenda, including aid, nor the demise of regional partnerships such as the Cotonou Agreement.

Not only the end of development, but also the demise of the Third World as a cohesive political force have been widely discussed. The idea of the Third World as a political and geographical unity is certainly greatly diminished. Developing countries participate in organisations as varied as the North America Free Trade Area (NAFTA), the Association of South East Asian Nations (ASEAN), and NEPAD. But the fragmentation of the developing world has not achieved the end of the conditions of poverty and marginalisation which characterised developing countries and peoples during the Cold War period.

It can be argued that 40 years after most of the developing countries attained independence, the post-colonial approach to politics and society has now been superseded. Initiatives like the Cotonou Agreement and the NEPAD stress that the ownership (i.e., responsibility) for development programmes lies mainly with the developing countries, not with the former colonisers. Yet the relationship, for instance, between Britain and the 54-member Commonwealth, or the basis of the

Cotonou Agreement are impossible to understand without reference to the colonial period. The post-colonial perspective on slavery and on political and economic dependency is still valuable to complement an emerging perspective of globalisation.

The changed status of Eastern and Central European countries from socialist to developing or transitional countries is one of the outstanding features of post-Cold War politics. A comparison of the respective experiences of the developing countries and the Central and Eastern European candidate members of the EU shows the powerful influence of the Union on these regions, the increasing politicisation of relations in both cases, the effects of these external relationships on the internal structure of the EU, and the disappointment these relations have often occasioned. Whether the changes in aid programming, the regional free trade areas scheduled to emerge under the Cotonou Agreement, or the full EU membership achieved for ten Central, Eastern, and Mediterranean European countries in 2004 will eradicate past disappointments remains to be seen.

The 2005 British EU Presidency oversaw the formal reaffirmation of the principles of partnership and political dialogue with developing countries. Perhaps more importantly, these principles were supplemented by a commitment to increasing aid volume to 0.56 percent of gross national income by 2010 and 0.7 percent by 2015, as well as improving aid effectiveness (European Union, 2005). But EU plans to increase pressure on poor countries to implement anti-terrorism and migration control measures (Bounds, 2006) and to pursue regional trade agreements following the failure of the WTO Doha Round have attracted substantial criticism (Oxfam, 2006).

In this era of globalisation, creating a real partnership for development constitutes a significant challenge. From NATO's Partnership for Peace to the New Partnership for Africa's Development, 'partnership' is the international discourse of choice. Yet the term is most remarkable for its flexibility in operation, and for its aspirational qualities. 'Partnership' appeals to an ideal of equity, equality, and harmonious cooperation among states and peoples which has to be realised in practice.

Note

1 For example, the failure of economic theories to apply successfully to real world situations was evidenced in the disastrous collapse of the Long Term Capital Management hedge fund in 1998, despite the contribution of two Nobel prize-winning economists to its management.

References

Amin, Samir (1997), *Capitalism in the Age of Globalization*, London and New Jersey: ZED Books.

Anyazawa, J. (2004), 'EU gives for Peace Plan', April 15, www.nepad.org.

Benoit, B, Guerrera, F, and Wright, R. (2002), 'EU nations agree aid as floods hit north', *The Financial Times*, 19 August, p. 5.

Bounds, A. (2006), 'EU under fire for attaching strings to aid', *Financial Times*, August 7, p. 6.

Broad, R., Cavanagh, J. and Bello, W. (1995), 'Development: The Market is not Enough' in Frieden, J. and Lake, D. (eds) *International Political Economy*, 3rd ed., London and New York: Routledge and St. Martin's Press.

Clapham, Christopher (1985), *Third World Politics*, London and Sydney: Croom Helm.

Cotonou Agreement (2000), 'ACP-EU Partnership Agreement signed in Cotonou on 23 June 2000', *The Courier*, Brussels, special issue, September.

De Waal, Alex (2002), 'What's New in the "New Partnership for Africa's Development?"', *International Affairs*, vol. 78, no. 3, July, pp. 477-492.

Development Assistance Committee (2002), 'Development Cooperation Review: European Community', Paris: OECD.

Dombey, D. (2002), 'Commission plans flood relief for central Europe', *Financial Times*, 29 August, p. 5.

The Economist (2002), 'Europe's Constitutional Convention', vol. 364, no. 8282, July 20-26, pp. 31-32.

European Commission (1997a), *Green Paper on relations between the European Union and the ACP countries on the eve of the 21st century*, Luxembourg: Office for Official Publications of the European Communities.

European Commission (1997b), 'Agenda 2000: 1. For a Stronger and Wider Union', COM (97) 2000 final, vol. 1, Brussels, 15 July.

European Commission (1998), *The Future of North-South Relations*, Luxembourg and London: Official Office of Publications of the European Community and Kogan Page.

European Commission (1999), 'Europeans and Development Aid', *Eurobarometer*, Report no. 50.1, Brussels, 8 February.

European Commission (2000), 'Communication from the Commission to the Council and the European Parliament: The European Community's Development Policy', Brussels, COM (2000) 212 final, 26 April.

European Commission (2001), 'Public Opinion in the Countries Applying for European Union Membership' in *Eurobarometer*, Brussels, December.

European Commission (2002a), *Annual Report 2001 from the Commission to the*

Council and the European Parliament ON the EC Development Policy and the Implementation of the External Assistance, Brussels, COM (2002) 490 final, 12 September.

European Commission (2002b), 'The European Community's Development Policy – Statement by the Council and the Commission', October 15, available at www.europa.eu.int/comm/development/lex/en/council20001110_en.htm

European Commission (2005), *Annual Report 2005: The European Community's Development Policy and the Implementation of External Assistance in 2004*, Luxembourg, Office for Official Publications of the European Communities.

European Union (2005), 'Joint Statement by the Council and the Representatives of the Governments and Member States meeting within the Council, the European Parliament and the Commission on European Development Policy' 20 December, available at www.europa.eu.int/comm/development/body/development_policy_statement.

Fukuyama, Francis (1995), *Trust: The Social Virtues and the Creation of Prosperity*, London: Hamish Hamilton.

Garton Ash, Timothy (2002), 'The grim wedding', *The Guardian*, June 27, p. 19.

Ginsberg, R. (2001), *The European Union in International Politics*, Oxford and Boston: Rowman and Littlefield.

Grilli, E. (1993), *The European Community and the Developing Countries*, Cambridge: Cambridge University Press.

Hoogvelt, A. (2001), *Globalization and the PostColonial World*, 2nd ed., Houndmills: Palgrave.

Joffe, G. (1997), 'Southern Attitudes towards an Integrated Mediterranean Region', in Gillespie, R., (ed.), *The Euro-Mediterranean Partnership*, London and Portland OR: Frank Cass.

Joffe, G. (1999), 'The Euro-Mediterranean Partnership Initiative: Problems and Prospects', in Joffe, G., (ed.), *Perspectives on Development: The Euro-Mediterranean Partnership*, London: Routledge, 1999.

Ki-Zerbo, J. (2001), 'Porto Alegre or Davos?', *The Courier*, no. 186, May-June 2001, pp. 9-10.

Lister, Majorie (1988), *The European Community and the Developing World*, Aldershot: Avebury.

Lister, Majorie (1997), *The European Union and the South*, London and New York: Routledge and St. Martin's Press.

Lister, Majorie (1998), 'The European Union's Green Paper on Relations with the African, Caribbean and Pacific Countries', *Oxford Development Studies*, vol. 26, no. 3, pp. 375-390.

Lister, Majorie, ed. (1999), *New Perspectives on European Union Development Cooperation*, Boulder and Oxford: Westview Press.

Maxwell, Simon. and Christiansen, K. (2002), '"Negotiation as Simultaneous Equation": Building a New Partnership with Africa', in *International Affairs*, vol. 78, no 3, July, pp. 477-492.
Maxwell, S., and Riddell, R. (1998), 'Conditionality or Contract: Perspectives on Partnership for Development', *Journal of International Development*, 10, March-April, pp. 257-268.
McMichael, P. (2000), *Development and Social Change*, 2nd ed., Thousand Oaks: Pine Forge Press.
Mouradian, A-M, (2001), 'Europe Supports the African Renaissance', *The Courier*, no. 189, Nov-Dec, pp. 10-11.
NEPAD (2001), 'The New Partnership for Africa's Development', October.
NEPAD (2003), 'Report on the Expanded NEPAD/G8 Dialogue Meeting on 10 November in Paris', available at www.nepad.org.
NEPAD (2004), 'NEPAD in Brief', April 15, available at www.nepad.org.
Obasanjo, O. (2002), 'Statement of H.E. Chief Olusegun Obansanjo, President of the Federal Republic of Nigeria and Chairperson of the NEPAD Head of State and Government Implementation Committee', in NEPAD, *Annual Report 2002: Towards Claiming the 21st Century*.
Oyuke, J. (2006), 'NEPAD Reviews Taking Too Long, Say Experts', *The East African Standard* (Nairobi), 28 April, 2006, available at www.allAfrica.com/stories/200604270853.html.
Oxfam (2006), 'Oxfam warns of threat of regional trade deals for poor countries', August 4, available at Oxfam.org/news/pressreleases2006/pr060804_wto.
Raffer, Kunibert (2001), 'Cotonou: Slowly Undoing Lomé's Concept of Partnership', European Development Policy Study Group, Discussion Paper no. 20, February.
Said, Edward (1991), *Orientalism*, London: Penguin, pp. 13-14.
Scott, C. (1996), *Gender and Development*, Boulder and London: Lynne Rienner.
Segbenou, R. (1999), 'About the ongoing negotiations', contribution to internet forum; forum-e@ue-acp.org, 1 September (M. Lister trans).
Spur (1995), 'Only 1 in 10 people would support cuts in ODA', November/December.
Thomas, C. (1999), 'Where is the Third World Now?' *Review of International Studies*, December, pp. 225-243.
The Times, Editorial (2002), 'Seams Showing', 9 August, p. 23.
Warakaulle, C. (2002), 'In and Out', *The World Today*, vol. 58 no 7, July, pp 16-17.
Wallace, W. (1996), 'Government without Statehood: The Unstable Equilibrium', in Wallace, H. and Wallace, W., (eds), *Policy-making in the European Union*, 3rd ed., Oxford: Oxford University Press.
Zartman, I.W. (1976), 'Europe and Africa: Decolonization or Dependency?' *International Affairs*, January, vol. 54, no. 2, pp. 326-343.

4 Clash of Civilisations or Intercultural Dialogue? Challenges for EU Mediterranean Policies

Roderick Pace

1. Introduction

Since Samuel Huntington published his theory that world politics in the post-Cold War era should be understood from the perspective of a 'clash of civilisations', it has become customary when discussing Mediterranean politics to refer to this theory. Huntington's theory (Huntington, 1993; 1998) has a measure of appeal because it is simple, compressing a very complex reality into a simplified and comprehensible framework of world politics. It achieves therefore what is expected of theory. But as is the case with many other theories it has also proved to be controversial. Does it have explanatory value? Is it reductionist in its simplicity? Questions like these and others, which strike at the core of Huntington's premises, are clearly warranted. However, for the purpose of the present analysis, Huntington's theory is addressed because it is often cited to explain contemporary events in the Mediterranean region, particularly since the latter is a *point of contact*, or alternatively as others see it, a *fault line* between the world's three main monotheistic religions and the civilisations/cultures that they have given rise to.[1]

What explanatory relevance does Huntington's theory have for Euro-Mediterranean relations? Significantly, the European Union (EU) has attached importance to the 'dialogue of cultures' and the need for developing stronger links between the civil societies on both sides of the Mediterranean. This was supposed to be one of the main innovations of the Barcelona Process which was initiated in 1995. This dialogue was intensified after the terrorist attacks of September 11, 2001 and following the attacks carried out in Turkey, Morocco, Madrid, and London. Following decisions taken by the Euro-Mediterranean foreign ministers in successive meetings in 2002-2004, the Anna Lindh Euro-Mediterranean Foundation for the Dialogue Between Cultures was established. This foundation, whose main aim is to promote dialogue between cultures and to contribute to the visibility of the

Barcelona Process, has its headquarters in the Alexandria Library in conjunction with the Swedish Institute in Alexandria, Egypt. The EU accepts that cultural and civilisation cleavages exercise a strong influence on the politics and the trans-national relations of the Mediterranean region, though it is reluctant to concede the 'logic' of a 'clash of civilisations'. By and large, the governments of the Muslim states of the region share the same view.

Indeed, following the events of September 11, 2001 the governments of the Euro-Mediterranean region proclaimed that the attacks should not be equated with Islam. This was reassuring in so far as it showed that the political elites of the countries on the Mediterranean littoral shared a similar world view about the motivations behind these terrorist attacks. The late Edward W. Said, critical of Huntington's theory and of those who claimed that September 11 proved it, had this to say: 'The carefully planned and horrendous, pathologically motivated suicide attack and mass slaughter by a small group of deranged militants has been turned into proof of Huntington's Theory.' He further described the 'clash of civilisations' as a gimmick (*Said*, 2001). That said, however, religious identity and 'anti-Western' sentiments remain heightened in many strata of Muslim societies, and the latter sentiments have also intensified in the wake of the war in Iraq. For example, a public opinion survey in four key Islamic countries found that the people there identified more with religion, claiming to be Muslims above all, than with nationality. The same survey found that following the events of September 11, 71 percent of those questioned in Egypt, the most populous Arab country, singled out the 'Western cultural invasion' as a very serious problem (Moaddel, 2003). A much discussed and controversial opinion poll carried out by Gallup in December, 2001 and January, 2002 in nine Islamic countries found amongst other things that only 12 percent thought that the 'West' respects Arab or Islamic values.[2]

The aim of this chapter is to further expand on the above arguments, to explore whether indeed a 'clash of civilisations' explains relations in the region, and to review some of the salient efforts pursued in the Mediterranean region to encourage the dialogue of cultures. The analysis is divided in three sections:

1. A review of the EU perspective of the Mediterranean region;
2. A discussion of some of the more salient theoretical ways of analysing international relations in the region; and
3. Some implications for EU policies.

2. The EU's Perspectives of the Mediterranean Region

The Mediterranean region is crucial for the EU. Any instability there can spill over and affect the EU itself. Lacking the means and often the will to conduct a military-based foreign policy towards the region, the EU has traditionally opted to act as a 'civilian power'.[3] But in recent years the limitations of this policy have increasingly become apparent and since 1993 the EU has been developing its Common Foreign and Security Policy (CFSP) and the Common European Security and Defence Policy (ESDP). If and when it is fully developed, the CFSP and ESDP may enable the EU to play a more credible role in meeting the region's security challenges and in helping resolve its long-standing problems since it will have the capabilities of deploying peacekeeping forces and of gathering information on regional threats.[4] The Mediterranean security challenges can be grouped together under two main headings – 'hard' and 'soft'.[5] Both sets of security challenges are interconnected. They are separated here only for analytical purposes and because each requires different responses: military means being the most efficacious in the case of 'hard' threats, non-military responses in the case of 'soft' threats.

With respect to the 'hard security' questions, the likelihood of a North-South confrontation seems remote; South-South crises are more likely. The main hard security regional threats perceived by many European governments are the proliferation of weapons of mass destruction and international terrorism.[6] The presence of US and North Atlantic Treaty Organization (NATO) naval and military forces in the region provide a credible defence shield. However, long-term reliance on the US is not a cherished goal for many European governments. This explains the effort to develop the CFSP and ESDP which, if achieved, will enable the EU to take on more of the military burden of its own security, including in the Mediterranean region. The main question in this case is whether the EU's actions will match its rhetoric. However, it must also be added that challenges such as the proliferation of weapons of mass destruction and terrorism cannot be met by military means alone but require North-South collaboration, the sharing of information, diplomatic effort, and confidence-building measures.

It is when dealing with the Mediterranean 'soft' security challenges, involving mostly non-military measures and where the EU is using its 'civilian power' approach, that the EU is more likely to encounter a number of cultural cleavages in its relations with its Mediterranean partners. This is where notions of a 'clash of civilisations' (within the parameters discussed in this chapter) or of different cultural values may become more relevant. It is important to keep this in mind since the EU's 'civilian power' approach is also likely to remain the most widely used approach in the foreseeable future. Furthermore, the relevant EU external policy instruments, namely the Euro-Mediterranean Partnership (EMP) and more recently the European Neighbourhood Policy (ENP), are both based on the liberal world view that regional stability is enhanced by encouraging democracies and market economies. This 'Western' liberal model clashes with some of the views of Islamic 'fundamentalists', who are in opposition in most of the Mediterranean Muslim states. But it also clashes with the authoritarian governments of these countries who accept economic liberalisation (to varying degrees) but not democracy since the latter entails their loss of political and economic power. Yet the evidence does not suggest that the liberal model and Islam are intrinsically incompatible (El Fadl et al., 2004).

3. The EU's Policy Response

The EU's main response to its Mediterranean security challenges is the decade-old Euro-Mediterranean Partnership launched in Barcelona in 1995. This was followed by the Common Strategy towards the Mediterranean region adopted by the Feira European Council (Common Strategy, OJ L183 2000). In 2004, the EU launched the new Neighbourhood Policy (ENP), which reinforces the Partnership without displacing it. The Euro-Mediterranean Partnership succeeds previous EU policies pursued since the early 1970s. It consists of initiatives gathered under three main 'baskets' comprised of political and security issues; economic and financial co-operation; and social, cultural, human, and civil society matters. It was agreed from the start that progress in the three areas had to be 'balanced', i.e., that the partners would aim towards simultaneous and even progress on all three fronts (Barcelona Declaration, 1995). This is still the main policy objective as was reiterated by all the partners in April 2002 during the Fifth Mediterranean Foreign Ministers' meeting held in Valencia.

Actual achievements on the ground, however, have been much less impressive. Progress in the economic sphere clearly seems to be running smoothest, though there are still problems of proper implementation. At the mid-term Euro-Mediterranean conference of foreign ministers held in Crete at the end of May 2003, a total of 35 foreign ministers participated as a result of the impending EU enlargement, compared 27 ministers at the previous conference. The conference led to no substantial new initiative (Mid-Term Euro-Mediterranean Conference, Crete, 2003). Nor was progress made with regard to the Euro-Mediterranean Charter for Peace and Stability. Similarly at the meeting which was held in Barcelona on

27-28 November 2005 to mark the tenth anniversary of the Barcelona Declaration, only two political leaders from the 10 partner countries attended, namely the prime minister of Turkey and the president of the Palestinian Authority. The representatives present approved an anti-terrorism code of conduct and agreed on a work programme for the next five years, but failed to adopt a common declaration.

Overall there has been a general failure to achieve meaningful progress in the whole of the political and security basket of the Euro-Mediterranean Partnership and only limited results have been registered in the cultural/civil society one. In the meantime, a reasonable amount of progress has been achieved in the economic area, consisting of the conclusion of the bilateral free trade accords between the EU and all the Mediterranean partners except Libya (which has the status of observer). Relations with Libya are likely to improve as the country continues to move out of its international isolation. Libya wishes to develop relations with the EU but does not want to join the Euro-Mediterranean Partnership.[7]

For the free trade area to be completed, the main challenge lies in concluding free trade agreements between the southern littoral states themselves. To make this feasible, the southern Mediterranean countries need to establish (among other things) a common system of rules of origin and on fair competition, so as to make it easier for these countries to increase their export potential by taking advantage of cumulative rules of origin.[8] The longer-term implications of this are that as one stage leads to another in the evolution of the Euro-Mediterranean free trade area, a substantive part of the EU internal market legislation may have to be extended to the Mediterranean partners. This increasingly appears to be a more realistic possibility.

The launching of the so-called Agadir Initiative on May 8, 2001 aimed at creating an Arab Mediterranean Free Trade Area, initially comprised of Tunisia, Morocco, Egypt, and Jordan, is a positive step. The initiative has received the EU's constant support and encouragement. On January 11, 2003, the four Arab countries initiated a formal free trade agreement in the Jordanian capital of Amman. Then on February 25, 2004 at a ceremony in Agadir, attended by Commissioner Chris Patten, the four countries formally signed the agreement, which should have gone into effect at the beginning of 2005 but to date has not. The Agadir free trade area, should it come into being at some future date, will comprise a total population of around 100 million. The initiative is an open-ended one, and other Arab League member states are free to join it when they are ready to do so. In addition, attempts have been made from time to time to try and reinvigorate the Greater Arab Maghreb

Union (AMU), which aims at closer economic integration between Algeria, Morocco, Tunisia, Libya, and Mauritania. Since it was launched in 1989, the AMU has been stifled by a number of adverse developments, beginning with the deteriorating relations between Algeria and Morocco, later by the internal situation in Algeria itself, and the UN embargo against Libya. In 2003, an attempt was made to re-launch the organisation, but a summit of leaders of the organisation scheduled for 23-24 December 2003 had to be postponed primarily because of a dispute between Algeria and Morocco over the Western Sahara (Arabic News, 2003)

The failure of the AMU and the lack of progress on the Agadir free trade area are very serious since South-South free trade agreements are envisaged in the 1995 Barcelona Declaration as an important step towards the creation of the Euro-Mediterranean free trade area. It is argued that such South-South trade arrangements could improve trade and the economic prospects for the countries of the region (MENA, 2002: 57-60). However, the potential adverse social and environmental ramifications of economic restructuring and trade liberalisation could also be significant unless mitigating action is taken (SIA-EMFTA, 2005). Nevertheless, since economic growth has picked up in the last two years[9] after a long period of decline, stagnation, or low growth (1985-2005) a window of opportunity has opened up for the countries of the region to tackle the challenge of poverty alleviation, particularly unemployment (for which the Arab Mediterranean countries are notorious) (Iqbal, 2006). One other clear issue that emerges from the lack of meaningful progress on South-South integration is what Stephen Calleya has underscored as the main Achilles' heal of progress in the region, namely the lack of drive on the part of the Mediterranean countries to engage in self-help (Calleya, 2005). The EMP, the EU Neighbourhood Policy, and the 'tailor-made' Action Plans signed within this policy, provide the opportunities and the incentives but it is the Mediterranean partners that must grasp them.

4. The Underlying Principles

The underlying rationale of EU policies links political stability in the southern Mediterranean states to these countries' economic performance. In the past, sluggish economic growth was blamed for the lack of foreign direct investment (the Mediterranean region is the world's second worst performer on foreign direct investment, after sub-Saharan Africa) while Africa as a whole receives a dismal 3 percent of world flows (UNCTAD, 2005: 39-52). Other factors include bad governance worsened by authoritarian rule, a lingering bias towards import substitution and state intervention, and bureaucratic bottlenecks (Nabli, 2005). The rate of economic growth, though positive, has been insufficient to meet the demands of the fast growing, relatively young population of these countries. The Marseille-based research centre Forum Euro-Méditerranéen des Instituts Economiques (FEMISE) estimates that in order to maintain unemployment rates as they are the region has to create 35 million new jobs between 2000-2015 (Radwan and Reiffers, 2005). According to the Commission this can only be achieved by a sustained annual GDP growth rate of six to seven percent whereas the annual rate in the 1990s was a mere four percent (Rabat-Skhirat, 2005). By employing an assortment of bilateral, multilateral, and multi-level approaches, the aim of the Barcelona Process was to encourage faster economic growth to meet such targets. In addition the Barcelona Declaration envisaged that economic restructuring, trade liberalisation, regional integration, and the accompanying political reform, would eventually entangle the region in a cobweb of economic, political, and cultural relations and interdependencies which together would have a stabilising effect.

This approach requires two simultaneous and obviously well co-ordinated policies to be followed by the Mediterranean Partners, namely democratic and economic transition, both considered to be mutually reinforcing. There is a belief that economic reform will attack the root cause of the region's socio-economic problems, which in turn are the source of its political turbulence, while democratisation will underwrite the economic reforms and ensure their resilience in the long-term. Such approaches to creating peace and stability are based on the controversial liberal notion that 'democracies are less likely to go to war'.

The second approach suggests that the establishment of free market economies in each of the partner countries will result in irresistible pressure to set up democratic political institutions. This approach is more gradualist and confident that a free market economy will precipitate democracy by a kind of 'invisible hand' process. The two approaches discussed entail the importation and assimilation by the Muslim societies and their cultures of a substantial amount of Western or liberal values. Most governments in the Mediterranean partner countries are prepared to accept the economic liberalisation part of the 'formula' but are reluctant to accept or take a longer-term view of the introduction of democratic freedoms. It is also argued that Islamic culture resists such changes. In the political domain, Huntington has already claimed that Islamic culture explains in large part the failure of democracy to emerge in much of the Muslim world (Huntington, 1998: 29). However the advances made on the democratic front in Albania, Turkey, Malaysia, and Indonesia as well as the more timid developments in some of the Arab countries show that democracy and Islam are not incompatible.

In the economic domain, Mediterranean Muslim countries have shown a strong tendency towards grafting imported economic models onto their societies. For example, in the immediate post-colonial era, governments pursued to varying degrees a state-centric economic development path, an economic model imported from Europe which was based on import substitution. In the mid-1980s when the limitations of this approach began to be realised, they embarked, again at various speeds and to varying degrees, on a liberalisation process. What many have identified as the main factors retarding the region's economic development – such as bureaucratic bottlenecks, corruption, patronage, political tensions, a deficit in the rule of law, trade barriers, and a host of other problems linked to bad governance – are not intrinsically related to Islam. Indeed Islamic culture has lived without serious problems alongside many of the main approaches to organising the economy, whether it was a command or centrally planned approach, a liberal one or a mixed economy. As Bernard Lewis points out, in Islamic societies the Western notion of 'secularism', or better still *la cisme*, and the dichotomy of church and state, do not exist except in Turkey. In sum: 'Correct Islam is defined not so much by orthodoxy as by orthopraxy. What matters is what a Muslim does, not what he believes' (Lewis, 1993: 178).

Differences in economic practice between Islamic and Western societies are thus often exaggerated. Take for example the case of financial institutions and in particular in Islamic banking. The Sharia (Islamic Law inspired by the Koran) prohibits the granting of interest and loans. Thus Islamic banks have to resort to 'Sharia-friendly' practices such as paying dividends on investment accounts but not on current accounts and sharing profits when they provide capital to investors. Islamic banking is not a widespread phenomenon in the Arab world and some key countries still do not permit it (Wilson, 2002: 143-163). Although its practices are different from Western banking, its objectives are the same. But going beyond Islamic banking, the economic values of Islamic movements – such as respect for private property, promotion of good fiscal management, and the discouragement of corruption are clearly compatible. No serious objections of a religious nature have been raised against privatisation or liberalisation, although there is a tendency towards autarky in some Islamic economic programmes. Trade union rights, social security, and equal pay for equal work are also compatible with the Sharia. Differences are encountered in some cases as in the right of woman to choose their own occupation (Baderin, 2003: 176-212). In sum, the evidence so far does not appear to suggest that there are wide value differences between Islam and the West that make the adoption of a liberal economic model based on a market economy and private property impossible in Islamic states, though some difficulties cannot be ignored.

Within the political domain of Euro-Mediterranean relations, it can be argued that the partners' reticence regarding democratic reform seems to owe more to considerations of internal power politics than to a clash of cultural or civilisation values. EU measures aimed at encouraging the growth of civil society encounter problems because the governments of the partner states are apprehensive that 'uncontrolled' growth and expansion of civil society may lead to increased pressure for pluralism and more democratic and accountable political institutions. Furthermore, as Yom (2005) observes, the civil society approach is defective. First, because analysts have reached little consensus in defining civil society in the Arab context. Secondly, the recent expansion of the associational sector, seen in the West as positively encouraging the growth of civil society, is more a function of autocratic rulers' strategy of controlled liberalisation rather than its objective weakening, which means that Arab states remain robust in their will and capacity to repress (Yom, 2005).

The EU has also been somewhat ambivalent on promoting democracy and human rights. Despite inserting so-called democracy clauses in the new generation of association agreements of the Euro-Mediterranean Partnership, its actions on this front certainly do not match its rhetoric. Expectations were high that the EU could use its economic strength in the region to promote democracy and human rights more strongly, particularly in the wake of the publication of the *Human Development Reports* by the United Nations Development Programme (UNDP) and the Arab Fund for Human and Social Development. Amongst other things, these reports harshly criticised the poor state of democracy in most of the Arab world and called for concrete measures to achieve positive change (UNDP, 2002; 2003; 2004). Taking the lead from this report, and in reply to criticism of the EU's perceived ambivalence, the European Commission issued a Communication in 2003 on 'Reinvigorating EU Actions on Human Rights and Democratisation with Mediterranean Partners – Strategic Guidelines' (Com 2003 294 final, 21.05.2003). In this Communication it listed a number of actions designed to promote human rights in third countries. Although the Council concurs with the Commission's proposed actions, it has stated clearly that the 'principal role of the (democracy) clause is to provide the EU with a basis for positive engagement on human rights and democracy issues with third countries' (EU Council, 2005 point 3.5). In other words, the EU's Mediterranean partners are unlikely to be punished for their reticence in introducing human rights unless they commit human rights violations on a massive scale. The EU's Neighbourhood Policy may indeed close this lacuna since the 'action plans' negotiated with each of the Union's partners on a bilateral basis include a number of reforms which the partner has to achieve in return for enhanced privileges in the EU (such as increased aid, deeper integration in the internal market, and more participation in EU programmes).

A third goal of the Euro-Mediterranean Partnership is to promote mutual understanding between civil societies in Europe and the Arab world. This entails strengthening the inter-cultural and inter-religious dialogue, the role of the media in promoting dialogue and mutual understanding as well as the development of human resources in the cultural field. Since 1995, the Euro-Mediterranean Partnership has also hosted the Euro-Mediterranean Civil Forum. The Community's TEMPUS programme on higher education has also been extended to the Mediterranean partners since 2003. Although EU financial support for these initiatives under the MEDA instrument have often been criticised for being insufficient, nevertheless they do represent a substantive development over previous EU policies in the Mediterranean region. Then there is the 'Action Programme for the Dialogue between Cultures and Civilisations' approved at the Fifth Meeting of the Ministers of Foreign Affairs held in Valencia between the 22-23 of April 2002 as well as the Anna Lindh Foundation in Alexandria charged with further promoting this dialogue. Finally, the Euro-Mediterranean Parliamentary Forum (Pace et al., 2004), which has now been developed further into a Euro-Mediterranean Parliamentary Assembly (EMPA) adds a parliamentary dimension to these initiatives.[10]

5. Is there a Clash of Civilisations in the Mediterranean Region?

It has already been argued that there has been an increased tendency to read a 'clash of civilisations' into most adverse developments in the Mediterranean region. The temptation is difficult to resist because the Mediterranean region, in addition to being the point of contact between the world's three most important monotheistic religions – Judaism, Christianity, and Islam – is also the home of many terrorist organisations that claim an Islamic basis. On the European side, not all political leaders readily subscribed to the notion of a 'clash of civilisations', as was amply testified by their public reactions to the events of September 11 and their criticism of a statement by Italian Prime Minister Silvio Berlusconi on September 27, 2001 to the effect that the 'West' is superior to Islam.[11] Nonetheless, a dialogue of civilisations is a *sine qua non* in the Mediterranean region in order to strengthen mutual confidence and preempt the manipulation of religious sentiment by extremists. In this respect the Mediterranean region is not so different from other regions of the world where civilisations and cultures co-exist side by side.

The 'clash of civilisations' has often been intelligently manipulated by authoritarian governments to block political reform by claiming that basic human rights and democratic freedoms are 'incompatible with Islam' since Islam has a solution for everything and is not in need of the implementation of 'western democratic rights'. Such claims can also at times be defended on the basis of 'cultural pluralism'. Meanwhile, in Europe, the diversity and heterogeneity of Muslim opposition movements and what they are really opposing in their respective countries are either poorly understood or purposely misconstrued. Though undeniably there are cultural and civilisation cleavages in the Mediterranean region, their veracity needs to be examined closely.

One can start with Huntington's theory itself. It is clear that his theory seems to challenge the classical realist perception of world politics based on the centrality of the nation-state, claiming that while states were and continue to be important protagonists in international relations, the other important actors have been 'civilisations'. His approach is still a realist one, paradoxically both accepting and rejecting the centrality of states in foreign affairs, replacing states by civilisations or 'macro-states'. He accepts that civilisations are dynamic, changing, and adapting, and that they can also lose the struggle for survival, in this respect he undertakes a brief survey of world history showing that many civilisations have lost out to their competitors and disappeared (Huntington, 1993: 24-25; 1998: 43-45). The writer identifies three phases in the history of civilisations: a first phase in which they had no contact at all and evolved separately; a second phase characterised not only by intense inter-civilisational contact but also the unidirectional impact of Western civilisation over the rest, which commenced around the seventh century AD; and a third phase beginning in the twentieth century whose main features are 'intense, sustained and multidirectional interactions among all civilisations' (Huntington, 1998: 53). Huntington's other main contribution is that he banishes Fukuyama's rashly optimistic judgement that the 'end of history' ushered in the universalisation of Western civilisation. Lastly, his central thesis is that world politics from here onwards will be increasingly characterised by clashes along the fault lines that separate civilisations. He summarised it thus:

> In the emerging world, the relations between states and groups from different civilisations will not be close and will often be antagonistic. Yet some inter-civilisational relations are more conflict-prone than others. At the micro level, the most violent fault lines are between Islam and its Orthodox, Hindu, African and Western Christian neighbours. At the macro-level, the dominant division is between 'the West and the rest', with the most dominant conflicts occurring between Muslim and Asian societies on the one hand and the West on the other. The dangerous clashes of the future are likely to arise from the interaction of Western arrogance, Islamic intolerance and Semitic assertiveness. (Huntington, 1998: 183)

This pessimistic assessment spells out a very catastrophic scenario for the world and the Mediterranean region in particular, where the Islamic and Western civilisations meet and interact. The theory's credibility is enhanced by the perceived radicalisation of Muslim societies and the rise of the so-called Islamic fundamentalist movements. From the moment that these were singled out as the main threat to stability in the region, the 'clash of civilisations' appeared deterministically inevitable. Huntington's assessment clashes markedly with that of Latouche (1996). While the former perceives the world as a clash of civilisations competing 'freely' in the world, Latouche sees Western civilisation as a destructive force of all other cultures across the globe (Latouche, 1996). For Latouche the game is as good as won. For Huntington it has just started.

Huntington's main assessment however needs to be addressed. Historically, the realities in the Mediterranean region show evidence of a mixture of co-operation and conflict that is probably neither better nor worse than the co-operation and conflict in other regions, not least within Europe itself. Conflict and co-operation, war and trade have been an essential feature of the Mediterranean for millennia. The radicalisation of politics exhibit patterns of development experienced elsewhere. It is doubtful whether the manner in which the civilisations which border the Mediterranean are currently adapting to the global changes, to the global culture, and to each other differs markedly from previous epochs. It is true that the risks are higher today because the technology of war is more destructive. But this counts for all the other regions of the world as well. In addition many of the conflicts in the Mediterranean region not only predate Huntington's theory but owe more to other sources such as nationalism, the struggle for power and interests, and the problems generated by the penetration of the 'global culture' rather than to a 'clash of civilisations'. More terrorist attacks by so-called Muslim fundamentalists have been directed at targets within Muslim countries than at targets outside of them.

Furthermore, the differences differentiating the Mediterranean region's civilisations are not so glaring as some make them out to be. Religious leaders have frequently referred to the many commonalities between the three monotheistic religions, which need not be repeated here. Besides, proximity does not necessarily breed contempt. It can also lead to mutual influences. As Fernand Braudel pointed out 'civilisations continually borrow from their neighbours, even if they reinterpret and assimilate what they have adopted' (Braudel, 1995: 29). A civilisation may also stubbornly reject or resist assimilating a particular import, sometimes after a long period of hesitation and experimentation. It may also reject some of its own values, a rejection which may be lasting or short-lived. This means that civilisations evolve and assume a shape such that they are never wholly new but never quite the same as before (Braudel, 1995: 29-30). Braudel's assessment of civilisations shows their dynamic nature, a point with which Huntington would also agree. Historic evidence supports this since it can be shown that every civilisation or culture that has made its impact in the Mediterranean region seems to have left its mark on those around it and those which succeeded it, from pre-history down to the present. Indeed, although some civilisations (such as the ancient Greek, Roman, Carthaginian, and Arabic) have disappeared their influences have been grafted onto those that succeeded them.

Thus, although misunderstandings and prejudices may still exist on both sides of the Mediterranean littoral, influences have indeed been criss-crossing the region and mutually influencing the countries and civilisations. Throughout the post-war period Islamic countries have been 'importing' a number of elements of the 'global culture' and assimilating them because they are essential to the continued economic development of their societies. This in itself may have created a crisis in a culture long accustomed to the idea that Islam has the answer to everything. The process of the globalisation of the world economy and the growth in communication networks imply that as the Mediterranean countries liberalise their economies and integrate more in the global system, the more they will have to adopt to this 'global culture'.

This point can be illustrated by reference to the economic changes that the Mediterranean Muslim countries have had to confront. Beginning first with the financial and economic crisis of the 1980s, largely instigated by the collapse of oil prices, it is clear that this has led them to gradually abandon post-colonial economic policies, which they had imported from Europe, in favour of more market-oriented ones. This shift has led to the importation and assimilation of liberal economic principles that have long-term economic and cultural effects on the region in general. For example, in the fiscal field the historic preference for customs duties as a source of public revenue had had a long-standing distorting effect on government incomes in the region while at the same time constituting a significant barrier to South-South integration. However, the adoption of value-added tax (VAT)[12] was not only positive because it is a more efficient tax system leading to more effective fiscal policies if properly implemented, but also because it facilitates North-South and more importantly South-South economic integration amongst the Mediterranean non-EU countries. The oft-criticised 'Western-imposed' economic models, promoted by the International Monetary Fund, the World Bank, and the European Union do not only lead to economic changes but also instigate cultural changes in the long term. Furthermore, increased integration in the regional and global economies requires the adoption of other measures such as competition laws, business law to improve the business environment, copyright and data protection, consumer protection laws, the establishment of regulatory authorities, and eventually health and labour standards if these states wish to protect their citizens against the worse excesses of globalisation while increasing their attractiveness to FDI.

Change, whether slow or rapid, is bound to provoke reactions, particularly when traditional values and principles have to temporarily or permanently make way for new or imported ones. But it would be a mistake to conflate the populist protest movements in the southern Mediterranean countries with a more fundamental reaction to 'Western' imports in their cultural milieus, as has often been done in the past. Western analysis of the Islamic movements has confusingly been prone to make such false judgements, often leading to policy failures. The so called fundamentalists have shown no aversion to adopting technological innovations in the Muslim societies and many of the socio-economic values and rights which they foster are similar to the ones that many of us have been enjoying in the West for decades. Obviously there are values that raise disagreements, such as the position of women in Islamic society. But even in this case the argument can be made that the differences may not be as wide as some would depict them to be. One cannot generalise about Islamic movements. But although broadly speaking they are critical of the 'West', the main purpose of resorting to Islam seems to be to criticise and oppose their authoritarian governments, which have also resorted to Islam to justify their policies, because they have failed in building more egalitarian societies (Zoubir, 1998: 123). It is claimed that in Algeria, the Front Islamique du Salut FIS and other main Islamic movements did not repudiate political pluralism (Zoubir, 1998: 147-150). It is interesting for example that the government that is spearheading political and economic reforms in Turkey in preparation for eventual EU membership is headed by the Justice and Development Party of Recep Tayyip Erdogan, which is an Islamic party. That said, one must also bear in mind that Turkey is already a secular state in which religion and politics have been separated since the founding of the modern Turkish Republic.

Similarly it would be detrimental to a clear assessment of the actual challenges posed by the present international conjecture to equate international terrorism with 'Islamic fundamentalism' even when the terrorists themselves may employ Islamic slogans or appeal to Islamic unity. It would be like claiming that the terrorism that has been assailing some countries in Europe has the religious basis that it sometimes claims.[13] It is apt to recall in this context the words of Abdelouahed Belkeziz, secretary general of the Organisation of the Islamic Conference at the joint OIC-EU Forum on Civilisation and Harmony held in Istanbul February, 2002:

> The events in question (September 11th) have indeed nothing to do whatsoever with either the Western or Islamic civilisations ... to outstretch the implications of such a criminal individual act indiscriminately and attribute it to the followers of an entire faith or civilisation who are numbered in hundreds of millions is a totally unjustified tort if not a premeditated act of malevolence aimed at maligning Islam...(Belkeziz, 2002)

The discussion so far has served to establish that there seems to be no intrinsic incompatibility between Islamic principles and liberal democratic freedoms and economic principles. The cultural foundations of Islam are being shaken because it has for centuries been based on the belief that Islam has the answer for everything while the process of modernisation is leading to new dilemmas. It has also been argued here that the resistance to democratic reform most probably developed out of the interests of the elites in the region to maintain political power. This point is illustrated by the ups and downs of political reforms. It can be argued that some of these reforms have been introduced in order to placate strong internal pressures. In other words they may be no more than carefully aimed adaptations intended to ensure that regime change does not occur, at least in the foreseeable future, let alone countenance changes in a truly democratic direction. Consider in this respect that the same ruling elites (or their chosen successors) have been at the helm since or immediately after their countries' independence.

Electoral reform has had a mixed but generally sorry history. By and large the press is muzzled, controlled either by blatant censorship or self-restraint, the judiciary is not independent, the forces of law and order are often manipulated, the political opposition is outlawed and/or harassed, fundamental human rights are not respected (though some improvements have recently been registered due to international scrutiny), and the peaceful change of government is an anathema. The only democratic states in the region apart from those belonging to the EU, are Israel and Turkey, although some important improvements have still to be registered by both countries.

Naked repression has been discarded by the majority of the governments of the region, which due to the force of world public opinion have preferred to use other methods of control. Forms of representative government have been tried in many of them: Jordan has introduced municipal elections. Parliamentary elections in Morocco in 2002 and municipal elections in 2003 were mostly free. Elections to the Majlis al-Sha'abi Al-Watani in Algeria in May 2002 were also considered to have been reasonably well conducted – although the turnout at 46.2 percent was 19.4 percent down on the previous elections June 1997 due to a boycott by the main opposition movements including the FIS, who were banned from contesting. The election held in Algeria on April 8, 2004 was described by an observer of the Organisation for Security and Co-operation in Europe (OSCE) as 'one of the best-conducted elections, not just in Algeria, but in Africa and much of the Arab World' (Washington Post, 2004: 12). Some progress was also registered in Egypt where the first contested presidential elections were held in September 2005. President Mubarak was re-elected, with 88 percent of the vote while his two main challengers, the much harassed Ayman Nour and No'man Gom'a, obtained seven percent and three percent of the vote respectively. The government's interference in the November and December 2005 parliamentary elections was heavy handed and in January 2006 municipal elections were postponed for two years in order to block further electoral gains by the Muslim Brotherhood. In the Tunisian presidential and legislative elections, held in October 2004, President Ben Ali, in power since 1987 and running against three opposition candidates, won no fewer than 94.49 percent of the popular vote, with official turnout quoted as higher than 90 percent. Reports stated that there were indications that voter turnout figures were artificially inflated (US Country Reports on Human Rights, 2004). Indeed, in most of the Arab world, the electoral process leaves much to be desired. The only Arab 'state' to hold free elections is the Palestinian state. But when Hamas won a majority in the Palestinian Parliament in January 2006, after winning a similar majority in the West Bank municipal elections the previous month, a political impasse developed between the US and the EU, members of the Middle East 'Quartet' (the USA, EU, Russia and the UN) and the new Hamas-dominated Palestinian government.

The Arab stance towards economic and political reform remains an ambivalent and fragile one: in March 2004 an Arab League summit due to take place in Tunis had to be postponed primarily because of disagreements on the Middle East 'problem' but most of all because of a deeper discord on the issue of Arab reform. Two years later the evidence suggests that the drive for democracy has stalled throughout the Arab world (Fattah, 2006). Economic considerations must not be ignored when analysing the inertia in political reforms: in non-democratic societies, economic liberalisation and free market principles are often turned into opportunities for the ruling elites and their families and friends to muster important economic interests which in turn help to keep them in power. Power is further employed to decide how the resources of the economy are shared: and who gets what and when. A liberalised economy provides an ideal setting in the absence of real democratic control and institutional checks and balances for such patronage and clientalism to be employed.[14] This provides an added reason why ruling elites in the EU's Mediterranean partners are frightened by the EU's emphasis on human rights and democratic principles, realistically perceiving such a policy as a recipe for losing political control (EUROMESCO, 2002).

The war against terrorism also provides serious obstacles to the reform process. Following the events of September 11, the terrorist attacks in Morocco, Egypt, Turkey, Indonesia, Spain, and the UK the new policy emphasis on fighting terrorism seems to have been allowed to eclipse the priority of political reforms. An article published in the *Chicago Tribune* of September 4, 2002, drew attention to the fact that 'the terror war has US in dubious alliances' (Witt, 2002). The correspondent's main argument was that in securing the co-operation of many states in the global war against terrorism, the US had aligned itself with some of the worst human rights transgressors in the world. As Europe and the Mediterranean Basin states strengthen their efforts against terrorism, there is a danger that the whole exercise transforms itself into an alliance of convenience where under the pretext of fighting terrorism, some governments take the opportunity to attack their opposition – among them human rights activists – while Europe watches helplessly. This is apart from the danger to democracy posed by the introduction of anti-terrorist measures in the EU and other 'Western' democratic countries. Human rights groups have drawn attention to the enactment of new anti-terrorism laws and a reinvigorated campaign against extremists in many Muslim states after 9/11 and following terrorist attacks such as those that occurred in Egypt and Morocco, pointing out that these measures also erode human rights.[15]

6. Conclusions

This analysis has tried to demonstrate that there are reasonable doubts as to whether relations in the Mediterranean region can be characterised by a 'clash of civilisations'. I have argued that conflicts arising in the region that are attributed to cultural differences or a 'clash of civilisations' are no more than clashes of interest or worse a 'clash of ignorance', an expression employed by Said (2001). Since the region is a point of contact between the three principal monotheistic religions and their cultures, there are bound to be some frictions emanating from the different values that they espouse. However, within the Mediterranean context, proximity allows civilisations to borrow and assimilate from one another and to adapt to one another. It is significant that the civilisations on all sides of the Mediterranean region exhibit several common points, values that they have borrowed from each other, in addition to their well-known differences, which are too often exaggerated.

Many Muslim scholars argue that there do not appear to be major intrinsic obstacles in Muslim culture that make it incompatible or incapable of absorbing democratic values and the liberal market economy. On the other hand it appears that the main obstacles, or the rejection of certain liberal political and economic values, are linked to the political and economic aims of political elites and their opponents.

Reference has been made to the models of economic and political transition in the Mediterranean, the bottom-up model that is based on civil society, and the economic development model whereby the creation of market economies will create the conditions for the establishment of democratic institutions. I remarked that both processes may be at work, albeit to a limited and uneven extent in the Mediterranean region. Constant attention must be paid to the effectiveness of reforms. Gestures of political liberalisation do not necessarily mean anything unless real powers are transferred from current political elites to democratically accountable institutions. Economic restructuring is ineffective without the implementation of the norms of good governance that help create the right business and economic environment. A longer-term view of the effects of reforms that are introduced also needs to be taken.

Economic liberalisation without parallel progress on the democratic reform front leads to the creation of an unfettered economic regime for ruling elites to exploit by increasing their patronage. Thus incompatibility of cultural values may often be invoked to protect vested interests. In short care must be taken when attributing conflicts in the Mediterranean region to a 'clash of civilisations'. Of course since the term has entered the political discourse there is also the possibility of its manipulation – by terrorist groups or by European advocates of more radical policies towards the Arab world. Cultural conflicts exist everywhere and are not limited to the Mediterranean region. If left uncontrolled they can escalate. But this is not to say that every skirmish in the Mediterranean is one such conflict. Traditional values are being challenged everywhere by the process of globalisation as well as by economic liberalisation and the focus should therefore not be limited to the political domain.

Notes

1 For example, during the violent protests which erupted in some European and Muslim countries in the wake of the publication of the cartoons in the Danish newspaper *Jyllands-Posten* on September 30, 2005, frequent reference was made to a 'clash of civilisations'.

2 The 2002 Gallup Poll of the Islamic World consisted of a total sample of 10,004 people and was carried out in the following countries, with sample size indicated: Pakistan (2,043), Iran (1,501), Indonesia (1,050), Turkey (1,019), Lebanon (1,050), Morocco (1,000), Kuwait (790), Jordan (797), Saudi Arabia (754). Important aspects of the poll, including the sample size and composition have been criticised and its findings are probably relevant only as general indicators.

3 This signifies a marked shift in European attitudes considering that up until the 1956 Suez Crisis many European countries considered intervention in developing countries a policy tool they could utilise if necessary. This of course created a negative attitude among the populations of these countries towards Europe.

4 The old problems such as the Arab-Israeli question, Greek-Turkish rivalries, the Cyprus problem and the difficult relations between Algeria and Morocco amongst others, have a destabilising effect on the whole region and their peaceful resolution will obviously enhance the region's overall stability.

5 The term 'soft power' often contrasted to 'hard power', the latter referring to tangible military force, was originally introduced by Joseph S. Nye in 1990 (see Nye, 1990). It refers to the ability of a state to employ non-military means in order to induce other states to comply with its demands or to share its approach/ world view in confronting international problems.

6 The General Affairs and External Relations Council (GAERC) of the European Union adopted a declaration on the proliferation of weapons of mass destruction which was later endorsed by the European Council meeting in Thessaloniki on June 19-20, 2003. The EU's policy to combat terrorism was adopted by the European Council meeting in Seville on June 21-22, 2002 and recommendations were made by the GAERC on December 4 of the same year.

7 In a reply to an oral parliamentary question submitted by the Maltese member of the European Parliament (MEP), Simon Busuttill (H-0443/06, 17.05.2006), Commissioner Franco Frattini confirmed (13.06.2006) that following his talks in Tripoli in May 21-22, including a meeting with Colonel Gaddaffi, it was made clear to him that although Libya wanted to enhance co-operation with the EU and to help in controlling illegal immigration from its shores it did not wish to join the Euro-Mediterranean Partnership.

8 Because regional trade agreements cut tariffs only on goods originating in those states that have signed the agreement, rules of origin are used to determine which goods benefit from the tariff cut. In essence, they are used to avoid 'tariff jumping' – i.e., the illegal transhipment of goods from outside the region in order to take advantage of the lower tariffs between members of the agreement. For an empirical analysis of their importance for North African countries, and also how European rules of 'cumulation' can impact regional integration in North Africa, see Augier, Gasiorek, and Lai-Tong (2005).

9 According to a paper circulated by the European Commission at the Euro-Mediterranean ECOFIN Ministerial Meeting, Rabat-Skhirat, 19-20 June 2005, real growth in the Mediterranean partner countries averaged 4.5 percent in 2004, compared to 3.8 percent in 2003.

10 The website of the Euro-Mediterranean Parliamentary Assembly is www.europarl.eu.int/intcoop/empa/default.htm.

11 Silvio Berlusconi was reported to have said: 'We must be aware of the superiority of our civilisation, a system that has guaranteed well-being, respect for human rights – in contrast with Islamic countries – respect for religious and political rights... the West will continue to conquer peoples, even if it means a confrontation with another civilisation, Islam, firmly entrenched where it was 1400 years ago.' Radio Netherlands, 28 September 2001, available at http://www.rnw.nl/hotspots/html/italy010927.html.

12 Both as a result of pressures to improve fiscal yields and correct fiscal imbalances and as a result of pressure to remove customs tariffs in response to new World Trade Organization (WTO) agreements and free trade with the EU.

13 The most specific example of terrorism linked to a religious motive would perhaps be the IRA, an organisation with roots in the Catholic community in Northern Ireland. However even in this case it would be very difficult to establish a clear religious motivation for the terrorist actions of this group.

14 For a more detailed and thorough assessment of this side of the problem, see Murphy, 2001.

15 Arab Press Freedom Watch (APFW) (2003) 'The State of the Arab Media 2003: The Fight for Democracy', May, London, available at http://www.apfw.org/data/annualreports/2003/english/2003annualreport.pdf :
'Some Arab governments have used the euphoria of the so-called anti-terrorism policies that resulted from Sept.11 attacks on the USA to restrict freedom of expression. Extending emergency laws and applying what is described as national security measures on every aspect of daily life, is threatening freedom of expression and the march for democracy.'

References

Augier, Patricia, Michael Gasiorek and Charles Lai-Tong (2005), 'Rules of Origin – The Trade Effects', *Economic Policy*, vol. 20, no. 43, pp. 569-624.

Baderin, Mashood A. (2003), *International Human Rights and Islamic Law*, Oxford and New York: Oxford University Press.

Belkeziz, Abdelouahed (2002), speech to the 'OIC-EU Forum on Civilisation and Harmony – The Political Dimension', Istanbul, February, available at http://www.oic-un.org/Sg/Statements/2002/SG.EU.html.

Braudel, Fernand (1995), *A History of Civilisations*, London and New York: Penguin Books.

Calleya, Stephen (2005), *Evaluating Euro-Mediterranean Relations*, London and New York: Routledge.

Fattah, Hassan M. (2006), 'Drive for Democracy Stalls in the Arab World', *The New York Times*, 10 April.

Huntington, Samuel P. (1993), 'The Clash of Civilizations?', *Foreign Affairs*, vol. 72, no. 3, Council for Foreign Relations, New York.

Huntington Samuel P. (1998), *The Clash of Civilisations and the Remaking of World Order*, London and New York: Touchstone Books.

Iqbal, Farruk (2006), 'Sustaining Gains in Poverty Reduction and Human Development in the Middle East and North Africa,' Washington: The World Bank, available at http://web.worldbank.org/WBSITE/EXTERNAL/COUNTRIES/MENAEXT/

Khaled, Abou El Fadl with Jermey Waldron, John J. Esposito, Noah Feldman et al. (2004) in Joshua Cohen and Deborah Chasman (eds.), (2004), *Islam and the Challenge of Democracy*, Princeton and Oxford: Princeton University Press.

Latouche, Serge (1996), *The Westernisation of the World*, Cambridge: Polity Press.

Lewis, Bernard (1993), *Islam and the West*, New York and Oxford: Oxford University Press.

Moaddel, Monsoor (2003), 'Public Opinion in Islamic Countries: Survey Results', *Footnote*, vol. 31, no. 1, January, American Sociological Association.

Murphy, Emma C. (ed.) (2001), *Mediterranean Politics*, vol. 6, no. 2, special issue, Frank Cass.

Nabli, Mustapha K. (2003), 'Challenges to Private Investment in the Middle East North Africa Region ... and what the World Bank is doing', presentation Cairo, 5 February http://lnweb18.worldbank.org/mna/mena.nsf/Attachments/Cairo-Panel-PI/$File/Cairo-panelPI.pdf

Nye, Joseph S. (1990), *Bound to Lead: The Changing Nature of American Power*, New York: Basic Books.

Pace Roderick, Stavridis Stelios and Xenakis D. K. (2004), 'Parliaments and Civil Society Co-Operation in the Euro-Mediterranean Partnership', *Mediterranean Quarterly*, vol. 15, no. 1, winter.

Radwan Samir and Reiffers Jean-Louis (eds.) (2005), *The Euro-Mediterranean Partnership: 10 Years After Barcelona – Achievements and Perspectives*, Marseille: Forum Euro-Méditerranéen des Instituts Economiques (FEMISE), February.

Arabic News (2003) 'Maghreb summit postponed until indefinite time', available at http://www.arabicnews.com/ansub/Daily/Day/031223/2003122315.html

Said, Edward W. (2001), 'The Clash of Ignorance', *The Nation*, 22 October, 2001, available at http://www.thenation.com/doc/20011022/said.

Washington Post (2004) 'World In Brief: Algeria's President Wins with 83%', April 10, p. A 12.

Wilson, Rodney (2002), 'Arab Government Responses to Islamic Finance: The Case of Egypt and Saudi Arabia', *Mediterranean Politics*, vol. 7, no. 3.

Witt, Howard (2002), 'Terror War Has US In Dubious Allances' *Chicago Tribune* 4 September.

Yom, Sean L. (2005), 'Civil Society and Democratisation in the Arab World', *The Middle East Review of International Affairs*, vol. 9, no. 4, December.

Zoubir Yahia H. (1998), 'State, Civil Society and the Question of Radical Fundamentalism in Algeria', in Moussali Ahmad S., (1998) *Islamic Fundamentalism: Myths and Realities*, Reading: Ithaca Press.

EU Documentation

'Common Strategy of the European Council on the Mediterranean Region', (2000), 19 June *Official Journal of the European Communities*, L 183, 2000, pp 5-10.

Barcelona Declaration and Work Programme, (1995), *Bulletin of the European Union*, no. 11, 1995, pp. 136 forward.

COMMUNICATION FROM THE COMMISSION TO THE COUNCIL AND THE EUROPEAN PARLIAMENT: Reinvigorating EU actions on Human Rights and democratisation with Mediterranean partners – Strategic guidelines, Com 2003 294 final, 21 May 2003.

Council of the EU (2005) *EU Annual Report on Human Rights – 2005*, point 3.5., p. 33.

Presidency Conclusions, Mid-Term Euro-Mediterranean Conference, Crete, 26-27 2003, *Euromed Report*, 59, European Commission, Brussels, 28 May, 2003.

UNDP Reports

Arab Human Development Report 2002: Creating Opportunities for Future Generations, UNDP, Arab Fund for Economic and Social Development, UNDP, New York.

Arab Human Development Report 2003: Building a Knowledge Society, UNDP, Arab Fund for Economic and Social Development, UNDP, New York.

Arab Human Development Report 2002: Towards Freedom in the Arab World, UNDP, Arab Fund for Economic and Social Development, UNDP, New York.

Other Documents / Studies

Economic Trends in the MENA Region 2002, The Economic Research Forum for the Arab Countries, Iran and Turkey, Cairo and New York: The American University in Cairo Press, pp 57-60.

Colin Kirkpatrick, Clive George, Balsam Ahmad, Sergio Alessandrini, Carol Chouchani Cherfane, Raymond Colley, Lydia Richardson, Dirk Willem te Velde (principal authors) (2005), Preliminary Consultation Draft, *Sustainability Impact Assessment Study of the Euro-Mediterranean Free Trade Area*, Final Report on Phase 2 of the SIA-EMFTA Project, Impact Assessment Research Centre, Institute for Development Policy and Management, University of Manchester.

UNCTAD (2005) *World Investment Report 2005*, New York and Geneva.

US State Department (2005), *Country Reports on Human Rights Practices – 2004*, released by the US Department of State Bureau of Democracy, Human Rights, and Labor, 28 February, available at http://www.state.gov/g/drl/rls/hrrpt/2004/41733.htm.

EUROMESCO (2002), Report of Working Group 1, *Security and Common Ground in the Euro-Mediterranean Partnership*, Paper 17, June.

5 To Reciprocate or Not to Reciprocate? Is that the Question? – A CGE Simulation of the Euro-Mediterranean Agreements

Andrew Mold[1]

1. Introduction

After the post-Cold War expansion of the European Union (EU) to the east, Southern-tier members of the EU started to argue that this needed to be balanced by looking to the south as well. Many observers were particularly alarmed by the socioeconomic rift dividing Europe and North Africa. The European Commission noted that European-Mediterranean income disparities stood at 1 to 12 and would increase to 1 to 20 by 2010 if no measures were taken. The Commission also estimated that the Mediterranean countries' populations would grow from 220 million in 1995 to 300 million by 2010. North Africa's population explosion and lack of economic opportunity heightened European fears of massive illegal immigration that would destabilise Europe (Nsouli, 2006). The tragic events of 11 September 2001, and the terrorist attacks in Madrid in March 2004 only drove home further the importance of achieving greater economic and social prosperity within the Mediterranean region.[2]

Despite the depth of these concerns, however, up until now the treatment received by the region in international negotiations has arguably been less than generous. In this chapter, we will suggest that this has been the case of the Euro-Mediterranean agreements (EMAs), an undertaking made at the conference of Barcelona in June 1995 to create a free trade zone between the EU and the Southern and Eastern Mediterranean (SEM) countries by 2010.[3] Although the conclusions drawn here probably have a broader relevance for all the signatory countries of the EMAs (and we will frequently refer to the SEM countries collectively), this chapter focuses more specifically on the implications of the EMAs for three North African countries – Egypt, Morocco, and Tunisia.

The objectives of the Barcelona Declaration are broad and in fact go far beyond the establishment of a simple free trade area. These are:

1. To establish a common Euro-Mediterranean area of peace and stability based on fundamental principles including respect for human rights and democracy (political and security partnership),
2. To create an area of shared prosperity through the progressive establishment of free trade between the EU and its partners and among the Mediterranean partners themselves, accompanied by substantial EU financial support for economic transition in the partner countries and for the social and economic consequences of this reform process (economic and financial partnership), and
3. To develop human resources, promote understanding between cultures and rapprochement of the peoples in the Euro-Mediterranean region, as well as to develop free and flourishing civil societies (social, cultural, and human partnership).[4]

In its totality, then, the EMAs represent an ambitious attempt to integrate the Southern and Eastern Mediterranean countries firmly into the economic and political sphere of influence of the EU.

After more than a decade since the Barcelona process was initiated, however, most analysts concede that progress has been painfully slow. Although some partner countries have progressed much faster than others in dismantling their trade barriers (Tunisia being the most obvious example),[5] the original prospect of a fully fledged free trade area by 2010 is now virtually out of reach (Dombey and Khalaf, 2005). More importantly, despite a general improvement in indicators of macroeconomic stability, economic performance has generally been disappointing, and overall living standards in Euro-Mediterranean countries have failed to converge towards EU levels. Indeed, on average, and for most of the partner countries, GDP per capita of the region adjusted for purchasing power parity has actually declined relative to the EU since 1995 (Nsouli, 2006). Even though most social indicators (such as life expectancy and literacy rates) have continued to improve over the last decade and, in relative terms, poverty rates in the region remain low compared to other developing regions, there are few compelling reasons to attribute this to the Euro-Mediterranean agreements. Rather, it is more probably the result of a combination of a relatively equal distribution of income, high levels of international remittances, and government employment, which cushion the impact of a relatively sluggish economic performance (Adams and Page, 2003). Unemployment continues to be a serious problem in all countries of the region, and migratory pressures are still very much in evidence.[6] Progress has been below par for all parties concerned, to say the least.

Why this is so has been the subject of much debate. Some blame the SEM countries themselves for the lack of resolve to tackle their structural problems. Is it possible, for example, that the long transition periods for implementing liberalisation and other measures has undermined the will of the North African countries to reform? Nsouli (2006) argues that the slowness in moving ahead with the association agreements may partly have reflected the fact that some countries were not ready to take full advantage of the partnership in the first place. With a combination of unstable macroeconomic conditions, high external debt, heavy reliance on trade taxes, excessive regulation, and weak social safety nets, some partner countries may not have perceived strong gains from rapidly pursuing free trade with the EU, and even less from liberalising trade within the region.

While not wishing to negate the importance of these underlying problems of economic structure and governance, it is also possible to argue that the design of the EMAs themselves has been flawed and is in fact far less generous on paper than the rhetoric of a Euro-Mediterranean partnership would suggest. This is mainly because the degree of economic integration with the EU that was initially on offer under the EMAs was rather limited. Despite some studies which suggest a quite considerable scope for expanding agricultural exports from North Africa (e.g., Muaz et al., 2004; Mold, 2003), agricultural produce and fisheries were excluded from the original agreements. Moreover, under the previous bilateral cooperation agreements of the 1970s, the EU had already unilaterally removed its protection on manufactured goods. The EMAs thus constituted a *de facto* opening of the SEM countries to industrial imports from the EU (Kuiper and van Tongeren, 2004: 2).

Given the relative lack of international competitiveness of SEM industry,[7] the spectre quickly arose of a possible sharp contraction of domestic industry and further rises in unemployment in a region where unemployment already constitutes a serious social problem. There have been similar concerns regarding whether the amount of financial support to deal with the adjustment costs (the *mise-au-niveau* programmes) was sufficient. Understandably, this situation undermined the resolve of the SEM countries to fully implicate themselves in the reform process. Moreover, it was generally felt that the original agreements were selective, in the sense of leaving off the agenda such important areas for the SEM countries as the free movement of labour (even though this was provided for in the Barcelona Declaration). As the UN's Economic and Social Commission for Western Asia (UN, 1999: 10) noted, 'it is issues such as these that lie behind the groundswell of dissatisfaction manifest within the SEM region'.

To some extent, such scepticism on the part of the SEM countries was clearly warranted. Early on in the process, even generally enthusiastic proponents of the EMA (e.g., Hoekman and Djankov, 1996) recognised that the liberalisation process might be welfare-reducing in the short to medium term. Reading between the lines, there has been sufficient caution in most of the studies to suppose that the long-term benefits may well not materialise. According to some critics, as a response to the profound problems of the region the EMAs might not only prove to be insufficient, they may even aggravate some existing problems. Thus Joffe (2000: 40) for example warned that

> under present plans, the danger is that the alternative will be that enclave economies will be created in South Mediterranean states, designed to serve the European market and that the national economies will merely become states of the European Union without experiencing genuine economic development and the prosperity which should accompany it.

In 2004, the European Commission responded to such criticisms by introducing a new European Neighbourhood Policy (NP). The Neighbourhood Policy (which also applies to non-Mediterranean neighbours of the EU) was intended to complement rather than to replace the Barcelona process for the Euro-Mediterranean countries. In particular, via its national action plans, which are negotiated with the EU, the NP provides a bilateral mechanism to leverage accelerated structural reforms and offers additional rewards in the form of closer integration into the EU single market (e.g., by adopting common technical norms and standards, rules for protecting intellectual property rights, and competition and consumer protection regulations). Nonetheless, on one of the key revindications of the North African countries – a greater opening to their agricultural exports – little movement has been made. Indeed, the EMAs do not mention any calendar for tariff elimination on the whole agricultural sector. While a few concessions have been included for specific products, the EU has remained inflexible on sensitive products such as beef meats, milk, wheat, sugar, flowers, and rice.[8]

Against this backdrop, in this chapter we will argue that the key challenge is to provide economic opportunities to the North African and other Euro-Med partner countries that go beyond the simple elimination of trade barriers between the two groups of countries. The EU's programme of financial support (MEDA) to accompany the reform of economic and social structures is an explicit recognition of this, but in its present form it is argued here that it is inadequate in scope and depth. The EU also needs to re-examine the whole case for reciprocity as the major driver of reform – trade liberalisation in itself is neither a sufficient nor necessary condition for the kind of structural change required in the North African economies. That requires a deeper rethink on the part of the partner countries on both sides of the Mediterranean. Finally, at a time when the EU is also pursuing an ambitious set of trade agreements with the ACP countries (see chapter 8 on the EPAs), the success or failure of the EMAs may also be taken as an indicator of the desirability of this kind of agreement. In short, there is a lot at stake not only for the SEM countries, but also for the EU itself with regard to the way in which it uses trade as the main instrument in its development policy. The current analysis begins with a short review of the previous experience of trade liberalisation in the SEM countries.

2. The Historical Experience of Liberalisation in the Region

There is an important precedent to the EMAs in the guise of the bilateral cooperation agreements signed with the European Community by a number of SEM countries in the 1970s. These agreements, which included Algeria, Morocco, Syria, Jordan, Lebanon, Egypt, and Tunisia, granted a series of preferential trading arrangements for each of these countries. They included the following basic points:

- Customs duties on industrial products were phased out one year after the signature of the agreements;
- All quantitative restrictions were abolished at the same time, except for agricultural products and some textiles and clothing products; and
- Selected agricultural products were subject to tariff concessions (Inama and Jachia, 2000: 2).

From the point of view of the SEM countries, these agreements had several advantages over the current EMAs. In exchange for the aforementioned concessions, little was required of the Mediterranean countries other than granting the European Union most-favoured nation (MFN) status. Indeed, SEM countries were even entitled to introduce new customs duties and/or taxes having an equivalent effect to customs duties or quantitative restrictions where such measures are necessitated by development of local industries or development issues in general. In other words, it could be argued that the bilateral agreements were both more flexible in content and more generous in spirit than the subsequent EMAs.

Did these earlier agreements achieve their objectives? Only to a limited extent. Exports of some products from the region to the EU did increase quite sharply in the 1970s and 1980s. But although some countries like Tunisia and Morocco were allotted fairly generous quotas with regard to products such as textiles, they were often unable to fully use those quotas, finding themselves gradually undercut by more efficient, lower-wage countries from outside the region, such as China. Moreover, duty-free access to the EU was to some degree an 'empty concession' since manufacturers needed high quality, expensive European fabric and technical aid in order to manufacture products acceptable to European consumers. Because of the reciprocal granting of duty-free imports of EU fabric to the Maghreb, this arrangement was highly favourable to European textile companies (White, 2001: 67).

The other fundamental problem with the co-operation agreements of the 1970s was that, by leaving out agriculture products, the SEM countries were deprived of important export markets. Before the second enlargement of the EU (Greece in 1981, and Portugal and Spain in 1986), the EU still had a significant deficit in certain kinds of agricultural products where the SEM countries have an important comparative advantage – olive oil, tomatoes, wine, citrus fruits, etc. But the gradual assimilation of Spain and Portugal into the Common Agricultural Policy (CAP) raised the degree of agricultural self-sufficiency to unprecedented levels (from 51 to 98 percent in citrus fruits, for example, and 88 to 109 percent in olive oil), implying a loss of export markets for the SEM countries. In other words, SEM countries have found themselves in direct competition with the subsidised agriculture of Southern Europe (White 2001: 76).[9] Moreover, the application of protectionist measures on agricultural products by the EU was highly discretionary, making it difficult for SEM countries to develop coherent export strategies. In 1976, for example, Italy invoked safeguard clauses against the importation of Tunisian olive oil. Similarly, in 1996, shortly after the EU signed a partnership agreement with Morocco, French farmers implemented a safeguard clause against Moroccan tomatoes.

To sum up, then, the previous experience of bilateral trade agreements with the EU has hardly been encouraging. Bolbol (1999: 12) is particularly critical of these earlier agreements:

> A cynical but correct view would argue that the European Union knew that even with zero tariffs, Arab industrial products could never compete on European markets, and where they could, as in textiles and agriculture, the competition would be curtailed by quantitative controls. Not that the

European Union had not done that: it restricted Morocco's and Tunisia's agricultural quotas when they threatened Portugal and Spain and Egypt's when it threatened Turkey – not even a full European Union member. In other words, the European Union's one-sided trade policy ensured that it would remain the main beneficiary.

The European Commission for its part now argues that the fundamental Achilles' heel of these earlier agreements was not the partial and selective liberalisation of access to the EU market, but the lack of reciprocity, in the sense that the agreements provided no incentives or momentum for domestic reform (much as it is currently argued by the European Commission that the non-reciprocal Lomé/Cotonou Agreements did not provide the impetus for reform in the ACP countries, and thus need to be replaced by the EPAs). Whether this argument is valid or not will be the subject of the simulation exercise in section 4 of this chapter.

3. Potential Comparative Advantages of the SEM Region

One of the principal objectives of the EMAs is to facilitate the integration of the SEM countries into the global economy. Yet it is neither immediately obvious that the EMAs are the best way to achieve this objective, nor that these countries necessarily need to integrate themselves further into the world economy at the present time. It is true, of course, that their tariffs on imports are high in international terms (see table 3). Nevertheless, to use this as evidence of the 'closed' nature of their trade regimes is to confuse policy measures with policy outcomes. Relatively speaking, their trade to GDP ratios are in fact quite high (table 1).[10]

Table 1 Trade to GDP Ratios, 2003*

Algeria	63.3	Tunisia	90.3
Egypt	45.3	Turkey	58.6
Israel	81.4	Middle East & North Africa	61.6
Lebanon	51.8*	High income OECD	42.2*
Jordan	114.6	World	47.6*
Morocco	68.7	United States	23.4*

Source: World Bank Development Indicators on CD-ROM (2005).
* indicates figures for 2002

Of course, this is due in part to the importance of some SEM countries as exporters of oil and other primary products. But it also reflects the relative success of some countries in the region to promote manufacturing exports (particularly Tunisia and Turkey). Moreover, to the extent that openness to trade is lower than it might be, this structural characteristic should be seen (in part at least) as a logical reaction to the protectionist policies adopted in the past against SEM exports in the industrialised countries, particularly in Europe. In such a context, it was hardly surprising that many SEM countries adopted inward-oriented development strategies in the region during the post-war period.

One recurrent argument of this chapter is that greater openness to international trade has not always been advantageous to the SEM countries and is not necessarily the best vehicle for resolving the deep-seated structural problems of the SEM countries. In its dealings with developing countries, the European Commission has tended to increasingly treat trade as the principal catalyst of change. But it could be argued that by deepening the dependence of the SEM countries on external trade, the EMAs may simply intensify the vulnerability of these countries to external shocks.[11] Successful integration in the world economy requires more than simply applying tariff cuts – it implies a creative search for developing competitive niches. Unfortunately, for various reasons that are explained below, the EMAs may make it more, not less, difficult for the SEM countries to develop those niches.

Traditionally, the countries of the region have tended to rely on natural resource exports and, in particular, on mineral and petroleum products. This is still true for a number of the SEM countries. For Algeria, Egypt, and Libya, oil represents around 45, 25, and 76 percent of export earnings respectively. Even for Morocco, a country that has successfully decreased its dependency on mineral exports, phosphate still represents around 12 percent of total export earnings (Mold, 2003). The economic arguments regarding the dangers of relying on mineral and petroleum exports are well versed and need not be repeated in detail here.[12] Suffice it to say, in the SEM countries, this pattern of exports has had a number of negative consequences, including overvalued exchange rates (the 'Dutch disease' phenomena), instability of earnings, and environmental degradation. Less commented upon is the impact that it has had on democratic control. As an easily accessible source of income, these resources have meant that governments in the region have generally remained unaccountable to their respective populations. Political participation has remained low and governments have remained unresponsive to pressure from below (UNDP, 2004). Moreover, the tax base has remained weak, something which will have important repercussions when taxes on trade with the EU are finally eliminated under the EMAs.

Diversification towards other sectors should therefore be a priority for the governments of the region. Exports are currently excessively concentrated in products of a low or negligible technological content. Unfortunately, the SEM countries are caught in the awkward situation of falling between two stools – they face fierce competition in low-skilled labour intensive manufacturing from more populous Asian countries, yet do not possess the necessary workforce required to specialise in more skill-intensive manufacturing (Karshenas, 2001; Lall, 2000). With the entry of Poland, the Czech Republic, and Hungary into the EU, Eastern Europe also represents a significant competitive threat to the SEM countries. To show this, Mold (2003) calculates the simple correlations of the indices of revealed comparative advantage, based on data from the International Trade Centre (ITC). These correlations give a broad measure of the degree to which the export structure of countries overlap, and therefore an idea of the potential for competitive clashes. The correlations are surprisingly high in a number of cases for Morocco, Tunisia, and Turkey, in particular with the lower income countries of Eastern Europe (Bulgaria and Romania). The less diversified economies of the EU (Portugal and Greece) are also potential competitors. In addition, as the SEM countries gradually loose their preferential advantages in the EU markets through preference erosion, they will find their export markets under even greater competitive pressures. This is particularly true in textiles, where a large proportion of the regional workforce in manufacturing is concentrated.[13]

Despite these points, it would be wrong to fall into an attitude of complete despondency regarding the future perspectives of these countries as exporters of manufactured and industrial products. An interesting analysis of relative comparative advantages at a regional level is provided by Wood and Mayer (1999). These authors regress data regarding relative factor endowments of land and human capital on the share of manufactured exports vis-à-vis primary exports. Although the results are subject to certain limitations, the regression analysis does suggest that the share of manufactured products in total exports in the MENA region is about what would be expected, given the current endowments of human capital and land (figure 1).[14] The expansion of manufacturing exports was particularly rapid during the 1980s (Haddad, 2000). In Turkey, the share of manufacturing in total exports increased from about 27 percent in the 1980s to almost 69 percent in 1990; in the case of Tunisia, it increased from 35 percent to 69 percent, in Morocco from 26 percent to 53 percent, in Syria from 6 percent to 40 percent, and in Egypt from 11 to 66 percent (Karshenas, 2001: 71).

Figure 1 **Export Structure (Manufactured/Primary) by Region, 1990**

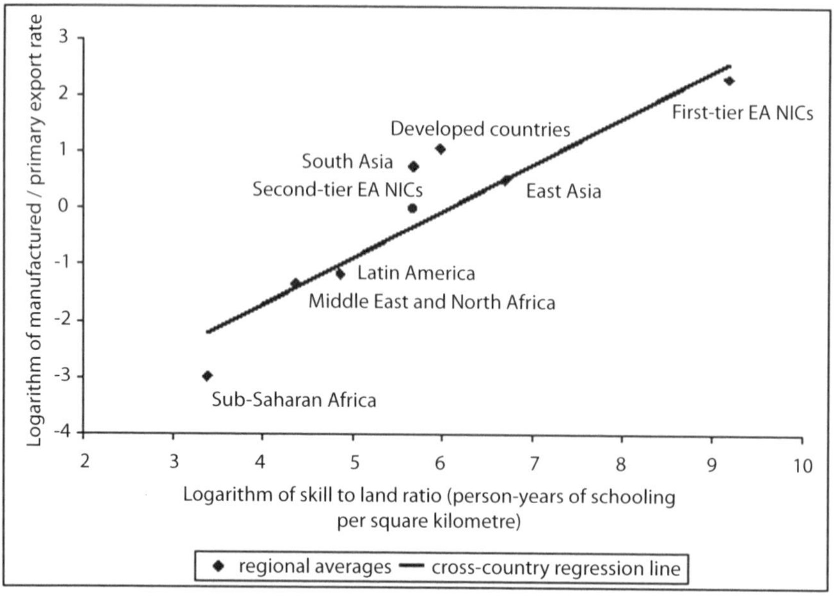

Source: Wood and Mayer, 1999: 14

Other SEM countries may have a comparative advantage under a free trade regime in agricultural and other primary products, but it is a line of specialisation that is currently being blocked due to the EU's protective policies in agriculture. The idea that some SEM countries could specialise more in agricultural products may at first sight seem counterintuitive – after all, with the exception of Morocco, these are all countries which have accumulated large agricultural trade deficits (see table 5). Moreover, one of the binding constraints on agricultural production is the shortage of water (rather than the lack of cultivable land per se): in recent years, the countries of the Mahgreb have been particularly vulnerable to drought. As Karshenas (2001: 78) points out, however, these constraints should not

> preclude the possibility of restructuring agricultural output and trade towards more export oriented products. The efficiency gains resulting from such restructuring may even give rise to a lower agricultural trade deficit while maintaining the current per capita food consumption levels.

To some extent, the apparent weakness of these countries in agricultural production is anyhow more illusory than real. It is more the result of a combination of poorly applied domestic policies and the closing off of the European market to agricultural imports rather than due to an intrinsic comparative disadvantage.[15] There may, in other words, be significant potential for the expansion of agricultural production in some countries of the region, particularly in the cases of Syria, Morocco, and Lebanon where water resource constraints are less binding (Mubarak, 1998). An empirical analysis carried out by Muaz et al. (2004), focused on the scope for expanding horticultural exports. For the five crops studied (strawberries, grapes, dates, green beans, and sweet melon) the researchers estimate that meeting the EU demand will result in 119,000 new job opportunities, an economic profit to Mediterranean partner country producers and exporters of US$ 498 million, and a value added to the economies of the five countries of US$ 756 million.[16]

Nor does such an agricultural expansion threaten in any significant way agricultural production in the EU. Even in the case of products which are considered 'sensitive' by Southern Europe, the overall scale of production in all the SEM countries is usually of little relative significance. In the case of olive oil, for example, Spain produces around half of the total world production (at around 1.1 million tons of a total of 2.4 million tons in 2003). This volume of production is almost 18 times higher than the production of SEM countries such as Tunisia and Turkey (60,000 tons each).[17] This vastly superior production is also apparent in the volume of exports of fruits and vegetables from Europe vis-à-vis North African production (Mold, 2003). Given the limited size of the agrarian flows, it is not surprising that the European Commission itself does not consider the SEM countries as a threat to EU farmers (Kuiper and van Tongeren, 2004: 1).

Against this backdrop, the insistence of the EU to cling to its protectionist agricultural policy has been a source of constant frustration to the SEM countries. Critically, what liberalisation has occurred has primarily involved products for which poorer farmers in the southern Mediterranean countries have no comparative advantage. Crops like olives (and olive oil), grapes, tomatoes, wine, and apples, for example, are well suited to the southern Mediterranean climate and can be produced more cheaply there, but are not freely allowed into the European market as trade is regulated through quotas. For example, Jordan's climate means that it can produce crops like beans, tomatoes, strawberries, sweet peppers, roses, and carnations competitively, but the EU has put limits on its imports of these crops by the use of tariffs, quotas, or timetables (Oxfam, 2005).

The attitude of the EU on this issue also contrasts starkly with the more generous treatment received by the Central and Eastern European countries (CEEC) in their negotiations with the EU in this area, which did provide detailed provisions granting CEEC farmers preferential access to EU markets (Ghesquiere, 1998; Hoekman and Djankov, 1996). The imbalance of resources is also patently clear when comparing the funds dedicated to agricultural policy and the funds made available under the MEDA scheme. Projected expenditure under MEDA for 2002 was €600 million, compared with €39,570 million set aside for EU agricultural policy (plus an additional €4,330 million for rural development). In other words, the total MEDA programme represented a mere 1.4 percent of the resources dedicated to support European farmers.

Thus the nature of the liberalisation has so far been imbalanced and inequitable. Yet agricultural development is clearly a priority for the SEM countries. Throughout the region, poverty has driven large numbers of rural workers towards urban centres. Cities like Cairo, with 16 million inhabitants, have been, in the words of the city's governor, Abdel Reheem Shehata, 'completely overwhelmed by rural migration'.[18] As far as possible, European policy should facilitate rural development on the southern shore of the Mediterranean, not impede it as has been the case up until now.[19] As Chahberli and El-Said (2000: 16) comment:

> Despite the resource constraints ... the region still enjoys a great potential for agricultural production given the abundant agricultural skills acquired over many generations (water harvesting techniques, soil conservation, etc.). Its geographical diversity makes it possible to produce commodities that do not necessarily make it a direct or unfair competitor to its main trading partners (especially the EU).

4. Trade Creation and Diversion within the SEM Region

Apart from the immediate objective of increasing trade between members, regional trade agreements are increasingly being sold as an instrument (or even the instrument) for accelerating poverty reduction. This is patent in the way in which the European Union has vigorously promoted regional trade agreements with developing countries over the last decade or so, ostensibly with the objective of promoting faster growth and poverty reduction. The underlying logic for this approach is quite straightforward – free trade is good for growth; growth is good for poverty; regional agreements create more trade; therefore regional agreements are useful as a policy tool for reducing poverty. Yet most professional economists acknowledge, if pressed, that free trade provides a relatively small contribution to overall growth of an economy. Typical empirical analyses put forward estimates in the range of two to three percent of GDP, disappointingly low if one considers that these gains are spread across the whole implementation period of the free-trade regime (Dunkley, 2004).[20]

The popular emphasis on free trade agreements as a way of accelerating economic growth and helping to resolve the problems associated with widespread poverty may therefore be largely misplaced. As Paul Krugman (1994) has asserted,

> 'the growth of living standards essentially equals the growth rate of domestic productivity – not productivity relative to competitors, but simply domestic productivity. Even though world trade is larger than ever before, national living standards are overwhelmingly determined by domestic factors rather than by some competition for world markets.'

This does not mean that trade policy is unimportant. But the enormous emphasis evident in contemporary discourses on trade policy as a way of lifting countries out of poverty may be exaggerated.

The traditional perspective on measuring the welfare impact of forming a regional trading block is based on the seminal work of Viner (1950), who distinguished between trade-creating and trade-diverting effects. The intuitive idea behind this approach is that a regional trading agreement should promote trade between member countries, but not at the expense of reducing trade with more efficient (i.e., lower cost) trading partners outside the agreement. A priori, therefore, orthodox trade theory leads to an agnostic stance regarding the potential benefits of regional trading agreements, because there is no guarantee that trade creation will indeed be higher than trade diversion. An important critique of the traditional theoretical framework was provided by Cooper and Massel (1965). Cooper and Massel point out that a developing country may value industrialisation as an end in itself, so that it is willing to give up a certain amount of achievable national income for this end. In other words, $1 worth of home-produced industrial output is weighted as more valuable than $1 worth of imports of industrial product, a weighting which market pricing does not reflect. Free trade between the partners may, on the other hand, raise the problem of an unacceptable share-out of common industries, and the possibility of 'de-industrialisation'.[21]

This danger is certainly inherent in the EMAs. The fact that the MFN tariffs of most SEM countries are, on average, high (more than 25 percent in Jordan or Egypt) points to large trade diversion effects and shifting losses that will have to be borne by the SEM countries (Tovias, 2000: 158). This is particularly true of the countries at the eastern end of the Mediterranean, which have a relatively low share of imports originating from the EU, resulting in even higher levels of trade diversion (Ghesquiere, 1998:3). Lebanon, for instance, is highly dependent on budgetary revenue from import duties and its agreement is seen as yielding a positive result only if accompanied by foreign investment and technology transfers to its services sector. For Egypt and Jordan, the relatively low share of imports originating in the EU also results in substantial trade diversion. Trade diversion is also likely to be intensified by European rules of origin, which undermine the potential to source from third countries (Augier et al., 2005).

Table 2 Simulation of the Impact of Trade Liberalisation with the EU on Algeria, Egypt, Morocco, and Tunisia, 1995 (in Millions US$)

Country	Gains from Trade Creation	Losses from Trade Diversion	Net effect on Welfare
Egypt (a)	87.6	307.8	-220.2
Egypt (b)	35.2	307.8	-272.6
Morocco	204.7	266.2	- 61.5
Tunisia	104.7	363.0	-258.3

Source: Tovias (2000)

A study into the impact of the EMAs on the economies of Egypt, Morocco and Tunisia is provided by Tovias (2000), using a partial equilibrium model. The results were not at all encouraging (table 2). Although generally relatively small, the net welfare effects of the EMAs were clearly negative. The largest loss would be for Tunisia, with a fall of welfare due to net trade diversion equivalent to 1.5 percent of GDP. For Morocco, the EMA would cause a net fall of trade of US$ 61.5 million, resulting in a net welfare loss equivalent to -0.2 percent of GDP. Finally, in the case of Egypt, the corresponding loss would be -0.5 percent.[22]

Of course, as well as all the standard limitations of partial equilibrium analysis (see chapter 8), this kind of analysis does not include dynamic effects due to greater competition or scale economy effects. But a recent critical review of the literature on trade liberalisation by Deraniyagala and Fine (2001: 810) reaches the conclusion that the theoretical arguments on these dynamic effects are often based on questionable assumptions and, moreover, are generally not backed up with empirical evidence. It should not, therefore, be so surprising that policymakers frequently take an agnostic view of claims by economists that dynamic benefits may outweigh static gains (or losses) several fold.

5. A CGE Simulation Scenario

Summary of previous studies

An alternative way of estimating the potential costs and benefits to the kind of partial equilibrium analysis cited above is by using a computable general equilibrium (CGE) model. These models have been used extensively to gauge the possible impact of trade liberalisation. However, in recent years there has been a critical (and probably well-deserved) reassessment of the utility of these modelling techniques.[23] Crucially, the results of the CGE models of trade liberalisation depend on a set of assumptions about demand- and supply-side responses to trade liberalisation. By building optimistic responses into the models (particularly with respect to what are called 'Armington elasticities', which determine the relative elasticity of substitution between alternative sources of supplies for traded commodities), and by not making the underlying assumptions sufficiently explicit, these models run the risk of producing a kind of self-fulfilling prophecy – in other words, providing the results that the modeller is searching for. As the World Bank (2000: 50) concedes,

> [These models] have the major weakness that they are not usually fitted to data as carefully, nor are they subject to the same statistical testing as econometric models. The cost of the microeconomic detail is a complexity that makes rigorous econometric estimation impossible.

One particular area of concern for the analysis of the impact of liberalisation on the SEM countries is that CGE models tend to assume that there will be full pass-through of tariff changes to import and domestic prices. However, the SEM economies are characterised by market imperfections, such as monopolistic power by importers, price rigidities in domestic markets, and other government interventions. If these rigidities are large and sustained, the effects on consumer welfare could be lower than estimated by CGE models, because of lower changes in domestic prices. At the same time, the effects on domestic production would also be lower than estimated by the models (SIA, 2006: 15).

A number of summaries of previous CGE studies into the impact of the EMAs on the North African economies have been carried out elsewhere (e.g., SIA, 2006; Kuiper, 2004; Mold, 2003), so it is not our intention here to repeat these assessments. However, a few of the most salient results are worth highlighting. Comparisons between the different simulation results is not easy, due to differences in the scale of tariff reductions, treatment of non-tariff barriers, harmonisation of standards, and how the models deal with loss of tariff revenue, exchange rates, investment decisions, long-run productivity gains, and technology transfer. But the broad conclusions are fairly consistent. The majority indicate that the change in economic welfare is generally positive but small. In the EU, welfare is estimated to rise by about 0.2 percent of GDP, with little difference between the short and long term. Most of the results for welfare changes in SEM countries lie in the range minus one to plus two percent of GDP. The average change estimated is a rise of about 0.8 percent, which corresponds to about three or four month's economic growth at typical rates (SIA, 2006: 17).

Thus it is probably fair to say that the results from CGE modelling hardly provide a resounding endorsement of the EMA process. Indeed, even in studies that report a positive static welfare gain from the trade effects, when one reads between the lines the overall results are far less impressive. For instance, in one of the earliest studies Rutherford et al. (1993) estimated static welfare gains for Morocco in the range of 1.5 to 2 percent of GDP. But the adverse budgetary revenue impact was projected at two percent of GDP after 12 years, more than sufficient to wipe out any gains through enhanced trade (and bearing in mind the fact that the static gains are one-off increments in GDP, whereas the revenue effect will be permanent). Likewise, under fairly generous assumptions, Konan and Maskus (1997) estimate that free trade between Egypt and the EU would result in a welfare gain of only 0.2 percent of GDP.[24]

It is also important to note that even the most optimistic studies show that in absolute terms the share-out of potential benefits accruing from the EMA is highly unequal. Using a computational general equilibrium model for the case of Tunisia, for instance, Brown et al. (1997) estimate that, although in relative terms the welfare impacts are marginal, in absolute terms *the gains are eight times larger for the EU than for Tunisia*, the principal beneficiaries being the economies of France, Italy, and Spain. An analysis by Alessandri (2000) arrives at a similar conclusion, with gains accruing to the EU that are more than three times larger than for Turkey, six times larger than Morocco, and 45 times larger than the gains for all the other countries of North Africa combined (where absolute gains are considered negligible). The author concludes "the actual agreements – due to their bilateral nature – tend to create a core-periphery system; the EU captures bigger gains because it is the only subscriber able to freely access all the involved national markets". Although the magnitude of these estimates could be called into question, there seems little doubt that the lion's share of the potential benefits of the EMAs will accrue to the European exporting firms.

Model specification and closure

If so many previous CGE simulations have been carried out into the potential impact of liberalising trade on the North African economies, why repeat this analysis here? Two reasons stand out. One is the inclusion in the Global Trade Analysis Project (GTAP) version 6.0 of tariff data that includes tariff reductions due to preferential market access. Previous versions of GTAP did not include data on preferential tariffs, and this typically resulted in an overestimate of the potential gains from trade liberalisation for preference-receiving countries. This is particularly the case for the North African countries which, as we have seen earlier, already benefited from preferential market access to the EU. A second reason is the inclusion, for the first time with GTAP 6.2., of Egypt in the GTAP database. As the largest economy in the region, Egypt accounts for too much of the North African economy to be ignored.

The standard GTAP model used in this exercise is a static, multiregional, multi-sector, CGE model that assumes perfect competition and constant returns to scale. Input-output tables reflect the links between sectors. This assumes that investment adjusts endogenously to changes in savings, although the trade balance can vary, so that at a national level the change in exports need not equal the change in imports. Real exchange rates are implicit in the model and are assumed to be fully flexible. In the labour market it is assumed that the amount of skilled and unskilled labour is fixed and cannot move between regions (although it can move readily between sectors). In line with standard neoclassical assumptions, wage rates are assumed to be flexible (see Hertel, 1997, for a full description of the GTAP model).

In order to allow a more precise view of the impact of liberalisation on the industrial sectors, our own model involves a 20-sector aggregation derived from the standard 57-sector GTAP aggregation.[25] Sixteen of these are industrial sectors, and in addition a distinction is made between processed and non-processed agriculture. Finally, fuel and services are aggregated into separate sectors. The share of each of these sectors in total value-added for each country (ranked in descending order) is shown in annex table 7. Five regions are defined in the model – Egypt, Morocco, Tunisia, the EU-25, and the rest of the world (ROW). As a baseline, we use the GTAP model to simulate the impact of a 100 percent reciprocal reduction in tariffs, excluding the agricultural sector.[26] In addition, the kind of socio-economic context discussed in earlier sections lead us to adopt a non-standard closure for the model. Firstly, it is assumed that countries will have to substitute losses in tariff revenue with an equivalent value tax on consumption.[27] Secondly, in view of the high unemployment rates in the region (especially for unskilled labour), we modify the standard closure for wages according to a Keynesian-type assumption, and assume that wages are fixed over the short run for the North African economies.

The scale of the asymmetry in the tariff cuts can readily be appreciated in table 3. Even prior to the simulation exercise, it is patent that there is very little to be gained from the EMAs on the part of the Egyptian, Tunisian, and Moroccan

Table 3 Pre-simulation Percent Ad Valorem Tariffs on Imports Egypt, Tunisia, Morocco, and ROW, 2001

	EU tariffs on imports from...				*Tariffs on imports from EU....*			
	Egypt	**Tunisia**	**Morocco**	**ROW**	**Egypt**	**Tunisia**	**Morocco**	**ROW**
1. Agriculture	6.48	7.87	2.45	6.8	8.13	27.96	73.53	10.45
2. Processed agriculture	22.11	3.5	42.27	18.26	15.78	48.81	40.31	17.57
3. Fuel	0.01	0.00	0.03	0.02	14.18	3.98	7.31	1.24
4. Textiles	0.12	0.14	0.19	4.73	52.03	36.71	17.77	8.41
5. Wearing apparel	0.21	0.08	0.09	6.43	387.54	49.9	19.09	10.04
6. Leather products	0.07	0.10	0.04	5.94	35.95	44.41	14.51	8.17
7. Wood products	0.10	0.01	0.14	0.78	13.88	35.02	18.5	4.92
8. Paper products, publishing	0.51	0.03	0.02	0.39	17.2	34.99	16.04	4.25
9. Petroleum, coal products	0.02	0.00	0.00	1.76	14.54	20.3	4.19	5.1
10. Chemical, rubber, plastic products	0.25	0.02	0.04	2	12.67	21.37	5.55	4.22
11. Mineral products, nec	0.21	0.03	0.06	2.82	21.65	31.77	14.47	7.2
12. Ferrous metals	11.52	0.00	0.00	4.25	14.49	7.68	3.14	5.18
13. Non-ferrous metals	0.05	0.01	0.00	0.88	19.61	10.39	6.27	4.62
14. Metal products	0.17	0.04	0.03	2.01	24.85	31.76	16.47	6.26
15. Motor vehicles and parts	0.4	0.04	0.00	6.33	44.08	26.06	8.55	8.01
16. Transport equipment nec	0.19	0.11	0.00	1.67	6.19	7.02	5.42	2.59
17. Electronic equipment	0.09	0.15	0.17	0.97	9.23	0.27	4.92	3.56
18. Machinery and equipment nec	0.08	0.04	0.17	1.24	12.9	11.58	8.02	4.63
19. Manufactures nec	0.05	0.07	0.04	1.4	22.45	17.3	21.78	7.17
20. Services	0.00	0.00	0.00	0.01	0.00	0.00	0.00	0.01

Source: GTAP database, version 6.02

economies in terms of better access to the EU market. In contrast, the scale of the cuts on tariffs on imports from the EU is very considerable indeed.[28] Notice also that, with the exception of Tunisian products, the average tariff imposed on EU imports of processed agricultural products from the North African economies is much higher. This can be seen as vindicating commonly made criticisms of EU policy regarding tariff escalation (i.e., imposing higher tariffs at the higher stages of processing so as to protect domestic manufacturing industries).

Results of simulation exercise

Table 4 summarises the results in terms of per capita welfare for the different model closures and scenarios in terms of the comprehensiveness of the tariffs cuts. These summary results from the simulation reveal a number of important things. First, the welfare results hinge significantly on the type of closure specified. Under a full liberalisation scenario, GTAP's standard closure does provide welfare gains for two of the three North African countries, but except in the case of Tunisia, the gains can be considered negligible. Under an arguably more realistic closure assumption (unemployment of unskilled labour and tax replacement of lost tariff revenue), the situation changes quite significantly. The simulation that most closely mirrors the current state of liberalisation (i.e., excluding agricultural liberalisation) produces an exceedingly high welfare loss of -3.06 percent for Morocco, but also with a major decline for Egypt (-1.33 percent).[29]

Table 4 Results of Simulation in Terms of Percent Change In Per Capita Welfare (Equivalent Variation of Household Income)

	Standard closure		Non-standard closure	
	Without agriculture	With agriculture	Without agriculture	With agriculture
Egypt	*-0.60*	*-0.55*	*-1.42*	*-1.33*
Morocco	0.18	0.10	*-2.80*	*-3.06*
Tunisia	*-0.04*	0.94	*-1.54*	*-0.31*
EU	0.03	0.03	0.03	0.03
ROW	0.00	*-0.01*	0.00	*-0.01*

Source: Simulation results

Secondly, the oft-made claim that with the inclusion of agriculture, welfare impacts would be significantly different is not borne out by the simulation analysis. This is to some extent unsurprising – although North Africa may benefit from the expansion in certain crops, the region is a net food-importing region (table 5). The removal of subsidies from European agriculture is also unlikely to benefit North African economies, for the very same reason. Although Morocco's agricultural trade is more or less evenly balanced (with a small surplus with the EU), that is not the case for Egypt and Tunisia. The 2001 data in the GTAP database reveals that approximately 25 percent of the total trade deficit is due to imported foodstuffs. But in actual fact most of that deficit does not accrue through food imports from the EU, but rather is due to imports from outside the region. Despite very legitimate concerns about the future of small-holders and agricultural workers in the North African countries (Oxfam, 2005), it would thus be wrong to overestimate the impact of EMAs on North African agriculture. The key conclusion is that it is not the exclusion of agriculture, per se, which causes the seriously imbalanced welfare impact of the EMAs, but rather reciprocity itself.[30]

Table 5 Pre-simulation Net Balance in Food Trade, Egypt, Morocco, and Tunisia, 2001

	Egypt	Morocco	Tunisia
In millions US$ 2001			
EU	-274.6	16.9	-200.1
World	-3475.2	-2.1	-578.2
As % share of total trade deficit			
EU	7.4	-1.0	11.6
World	25.8	0.1	24.6

Source: GTAP 6.02 database

In this sense, there is a lot in these simulations to support the 'deindustrialisation' hypothesis that was noted in the introduction (table 6). Most of the manufacturing sectors contract under the EMAs. The most notable case here is Tunisia, where manufacturing output declines in 15 of the 18 defined industrial sectors, the only exceptions being for textiles and apparel. Both Morocco and Egypt are also affected negatively by the same phenomenon. To gauge the relative import of these shifts, it is important to refer to the annex table 7 where the pre-simulation output of each sector is listed by its relative contribution to total output. For Morocco, for instance, the processed agricultural sector represents 20 percent of total industrial output. Consequently a fall of -6.8 percent in output is highly significant for the Moroccan economy. Similarly, in Egypt the estimated -11.6 and -26.7 percent fall in the output of textiles and wearing apparel respectively would have a major impact on an industry which contributes around 23 percent of total industrial output. This is especially so in the case of an industry which is so labour intensive as wearing apparel, and there are consequently important implications for employment.[31]

Table 6 Percent Change in Output by Sector

	Egypt	Morocco	Tunisia	EU	ROW
1. Agriculture	-1.4	-1.4	-4.7	-0.0	0.0
2. Processed agriculture	-1.1	-6.8	-0.9	0.0	0.0
3. Fuel	0.7	-7.7	-3.9	-0.0	0.0
4. Textiles	-11.6	41.9	7.2	1.7	-0.3
5. Wearing apparel	-26.7	49.9	49.0	0.7	-0.5
6. Leather products	-11.8	-30.1	-6.2	0.4	0.0
7. Wood products	-1.4	-19.9	-14.2	0.1	0.0
8. Paper products, publishing	-2.7	-23.6	-14.3	0.1	0.0
9. Petroleum, coal products	0.4	-7.6	-7.6	0.1	-0.0
10. Chemical, rubber, plastic products	1.9	-12.8	-7.8	0.0	0.0
11. Mineral products, nec	-1.2	-13.5	-23.1	0.1	0.0
12. Ferrous metals	10.6	-16.0	-4.6	-0.1	0.0
13. Non-ferrous metals	0.8	-10.7	-4.3	-0.1	0.1
14. Metal products	-2.8	-27.7	-14.7	0.1	0.0
15. Motor vehicles and parts	-2.3	-18.0	-9.5	0.0	0.0
16. Transport equipment nec	8.4	1.9	-12.0	-0.3	0.1
17. Electronic equipment	-2.2	0.3	-11.0	-0.3	0.1
18. Machinery and equipment nec	15.8	-10.3	-5.2	-0.1	0.1
19. Manufactures nec	-0.9	-13.5	-4.7	-0.1	0.1
20. Services	1.6	-2.3	-2.2	-0.0	0.0
Capital goods (CGDS)	4.9	6.9	9.5	0.0	-0.0

Source: Simulation results

Given the unilteral nature of the tariff liberalisation, the pattern of deindustrialisation is being provoked in part by the sharp increase in the imports of industrial and manufactured products from the EU (table 7), but also by the rise in the costs of intermediate inputs, as North African firms begin to switch sourcing from relatively inexpensive suppliers outside the Euro-Med area towards higher cost inputs from the EU (the trade diversion impact). Particularly worrying is the way in which the EMAs lock the North African manufacturing sectors even more firmly into their current pattern of specialisation, favouring a few labour-intensive sectors such as clothing and apparel, for which preferential access to the EU has been significant. While this may have been attractive in the past, it appears to be a far less satisfactory strategy today, with international trade barriers continuing to fall and the North African economies facing the inevitable erosion of their trade preferences with the EU. Such concerns are particularly relevant in the textile and apparel sectors, where the phasing out of quotas since January 2005 under the elimination of the Multi-Fibre Arrangement is sure to have a highly significant impact (Elbehri and Hertel, 2006; Soderling, 2005).[32]

Table 7 Increase in Imports from the EU (Millions US$ 2001)

	Egypt	Morocco	Tunisia
1. Agriculture	*-8.5*	*-4.8*	6.6
2. Processed agriculture	181.6	335.5	144.0
3. Fuel	113.2	22.6	27.2
4. Textiles	735.7	849.6	800.6
5. Wearing apparel	1935.9	301.0	126.8
6. Leather products	60.5	197.9	73.0
7. Wood products	118.2	152.8	71.8
8. Paper products, publishing	128.8	147.6	56.9
9. Petroleum, coal products	23.1	62.0	10.0
10. Chemical, rubber, plastic products	502.2	460.6	82.6
11. Mineral products, nec	169.7	174.2	44.7
12. Ferrous metals	177.7	20.6	7.5
13. Non-ferrous metals	125.3	22.1	23.2
14. Metal products	229.3	200.8	35.4
15. Motor vehicles and parts	359.1	161.4	63.2
16. Transport equipment nec	63.9	19.0	37.7
17. Electronic equipment	221.8	17.2	49.6
18. Machinery and equipment nec	757.0	362.2	269.3
19. Manufactures nec	108.6	53.8	59.4
20. Services	*-140.2*	*-9.8*	15.4

Source: Simulation results

What about the impact of the agreements on the trade balance (annex table 5)? Given the unilateral nature of the liberalisation on the part of the North African countries one would initially expect a sharp increase in the bilateral trade deficit. In fact, only Egypt suffers a significant increase in the trade deficit with the EU (figure 2). In the case of Morocco and Tunisia, exports expand sufficiently to compensate for the increase in imports. In this context, it is important to bear in mind that Egypt's trade pattern is in fact entirely different from Morocco's and Tunisia's (Soderling, 2005: 18). Overall, Egypt's current export composition appears less susceptible to trade creation with the EU than that of Morocco and Tunisia. Although Egypt is a slight net oil importer, hydrocarbons still represent a major share of exports. Egypt's textiles exports to the EU have fallen dramatically since the mid-1990s, and manufactured goods are in relatively low value-added sectors, such as metal goods. Moreover, it is necessary to take into account the extent to which the Egyptian economy is not tied in with the EU economy, but rather that of the US.[33]

Figure 2 EU – North African Trade Balance (Millions US$ 2001)

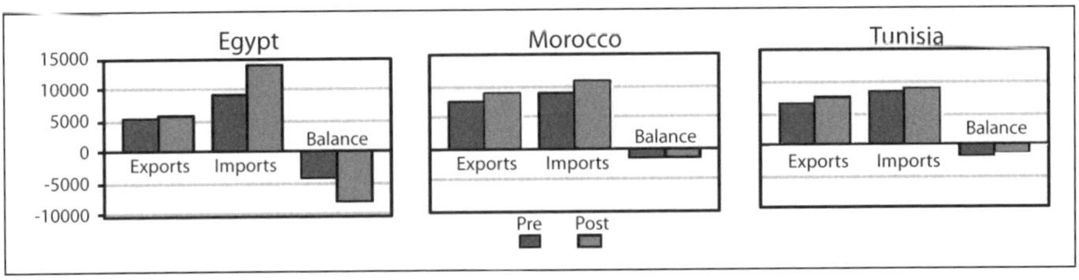

Source: Simulation results

In summary, these simulations cannot satisfactorily answer all the pertinent questions raised by the EMAs. In particular, it would be prudent to further investigate the welfare impacts associated with a deeper liberalisation of agricultural trade. However a much greater disaggregation than the GTAP database would be required to analyse that impact with precision. Ideally, such an analysis would distinguish between Mediterranean and temperate-zone crops, and if possible also distinguish between rain-fed and irrigated production to account for constrained water availability. It would also be important to distinguish between Northern and Southern EU countries, as the North African exports would expect to come into direct competition with producers on the other side of the Mediterranean (Kruiper, 2004: 18). Nevertheless, it is possible to hypothesise some additional impacts of agricultural trade liberalisation. By increasing international trade in food products and increasing the incentives for commercial food production, for example, the EMAs might increase the vulnerability of both rural and urban households to fluctuations in EU and world market prices. Effects would be insignificant for households whose expenditure on basic foods is a small proportion of their incomes, but may be important for poorer households. Such effects may be particularly significant in countries such as Egypt which are already highly dependent on food imports (SIA, 2006: 38).

6. Conclusions and Recommendations

It should by this stage be fairly clear that, in their present form at least, the potential advantages of the EMAs from the point of view of the SEM countries are limited, and some of the potential costs, in terms of lost manufacturing and industrial capacity, quite large. Our simulation results suggest that it is reciprocity itself, rather than the exclusion of certain sectors (particularly agriculture) from the agreements, which is responsible for the potential welfare losses.

None of this is to deny that the North African economies are clearly in need of reform. Given their natural resources and achievements in terms of human development, their economies are clearly underperforming. Thus there is little doubt that some of the reform agenda which the EMAs hope to catalyse is merited. But even a fairly neutral impact of the Euro-Med agreements is condemnation enough – it would mean that the Euro-Med agreements were not achieving their goals. That is exactly what the simulation exercise in this chapter, and in other similar recent studies (e.g., Elbehri and Hertel, 2006) show – negligible, or possibly even negative, impacts.

That being the case, the benefits of the EMA seem to hinge on the rather weak argument that these countries need to be locked into the discipline of a free trade agreement, so as to make the reform process 'credible'.[34] This provokes the question 'credible to whom?' Outside investors? The International Monetary Fund? The EU? What about the respective electorates of these countries? Certainly, the experience with the countries that have acceded to EU membership suggests that accession is a uniquely powerful tool to leverage reform and convergence. But as accession is not on offer either in the Barcelona Process or the European Neighbourhood Policy, it is natural to question whether the sort of rapid transformation of economies and strong productivity growth achieved in Eastern and Southern European accession countries can be replicated in the Mediterranean region (Nsouli, 2006). As Tovias (2001: 159) has observed,

> The Euro-Mediterranean Partnership in its economic basket has all the ingredients of the relatively outdated North-South approach. The EU allocates massive development aid to Arab Mediterranean and non-Mediterranean countries ... In exchange, the EU wants market access to MENA countries for its industrial products, and that is all.

From a European perspective, the EMAs have generally been presented as a successfully negotiated package of agreements. Seen from the SEM countries, the perspective is quite different. It was very much a negotiation between unequal partners. To a substantial extent, the problems identified in this study stem from the lack of bargaining power of the SEM countries vis-à-vis the EU. For instance, the so-called Singapore issues became a key bone of contention during the Doha round of multilateral trade negotiations. However, after considerable pressure from developing countries, the EU was forced to abandon pursuing these issues. The suspicion is that the EU is now using bilateral trade deals like those embodied in the Euro-Mediterranean agreements to advance the same agenda on issues such as intellectual property rights and protection for EU investments, above and beyond the disciplines implied by the multilateral system.

The basic point is, therefore, that the SEM countries need greater room to manoeuvre, something that the EMAs do not currently offer them. On the contrary, the current agreements simply reinforce *the principal of reciprocity* embodied in WTO arrangements. In this paper, we have tried to argue that this is both unnecessary and, in the long run, counter to the interests of SEM countries and Europe itself. In their present format, there is a very real danger that the EMAs degenerate into a NAFTA type arrangement, bereft of all social and developmental content. Thus a shift in emphasis in European policy towards the SEM countries is clearly needed.

All this also gives rise to some important strategic questions for the SEM countries themselves. SEM exports are already highly concentrated in Europe, a market that is growing more slowly than the rest of the world (UN, 2001: 15). Given the reluctance of European firms to invest in the region, direct investment from Asia should also be encouraged. This would complement the increase in Asian trade that has been taking place since 1980 and that is bound to continue, if only because Asia has been the fastest growing region in the world. In strategic terms, therefore, 'the Arab world should take renewed advantage of its geographical position as an "open" trading region between European and the rest of Asia – something that it did with remarkable success in pre-modern times' (Bolbol, 1999: 15).

Similarly, within the SEM countries, there is a keen awareness of the need to promote regional integration among themselves. To this end, the Agadir Agreement, concluded in March 2004 and signed by Morocco, Tunisia, Jordan, and Egypt, marks an important step toward building a Euro-Mediterranean free trade zone, creating an integrated market of more than 100 million people in the four signatory countries. It is true that intra-regional economic links are currently limited. But there is plenty of scope for deepening those links. Local markets are too small to be attractive to foreign investors, and the regulatory and administrative norms are excessively diverse. There is also need for greater coordination in a context of increasing concern over 'competitive bidding between countries', where countries become locked in a 'race to the bottom' in terms of salaries, environmental legislation, workers' rights, etc. Yet despite the importance of the issue, it remains the case that there is no mechanism under either the EMA or the Neighbourhood Policy to encourage such regional agreements.[35]

Finally, there is the thorny question of financial aid. While MEDA funds have been complemented by additional investments through the European Investment Bank (EIB) (Nsouli, 2006), the financial help provided to assist with the structural adjustments required in the SEM countries' economies has proved inadequate.[36] According to the European Commission's own external evaluation of the programme (EC, 2005: 15), 'MEDA resources can be considered as low relative to the ambition levels for the three pillars in the Barcelona Declaration and given the increasing political relevance of MEDA countries development for the European Union. The average amounts per year available for programming in MEDA II are not higher than under MEDA I.'[37] Moreover, because of bureaucratic and administrative errors and delays, a high percentage of assigned resources are not currently distributed. In the first five years of the EMAs, only 26 percent of the amount committed to aid under the MEDA programme was actually disbursed (Yaboubian, 2004). With its multi-year budget cycles and volumes of paperwork, the MEDA programme is exceptionally cumbersome bureaucratically. The EU needs to resolve these problems of disbursements and make financial commitments that correspond with the scale of the social and economic problems faced by the region.

Notes

1 The views expressed herein are those of the author and do not necessarily reflect the views of the United Nations. The author is grateful to Mohammed Chemingui for useful comments on an earlier draft of this chapter. Any remaining errors are of course the responsibility of the author.

2 Some critics argue that these and other terrorist attacks led to the regrettable situation whereby security considerations have taken precedence over those of economic and social development. Although clearly a resolution of the Arab-Israeli dispute is at the heart of problem, a more enlightened view would also stress that these objectives are closely intertwined, and that without progress in the social, economic, and political spheres, and an improvement in the well-being of the disaffected populations of North Africa, progress on security will inevitably be limited.

3 Negotiations for agreements already concluded include those with Tunisia (1995), Israel (1995), Morocco (1996), Jordan (1997), Egypt (2001), Algeria (2002), Lebanon (2002), Syria (2004), and the Palestinian Authority. Those with Tunisia (1998), Morocco (2000), Israel (2000), Jordan (2002), and Egypt (2004) have been ratified and are in force.

4 European Commission, External Relations, available at http://europa.eu.int/comm/external_relations/euromed/

5 Tunisia was the first country in the region to sign an association agreement with the EU in 1995 and began dismantling tariffs in 1996, even before the agreement came into force in 1998. Tariffs have been totally dismantled for capital goods since 1996 and for raw materials and intermediate goods since 2000. Import duties on consumer goods had been cut by about a half by the end of 2001, and 60 percent of EU industrial products had duty-free access by 2003. By 2004, tariff rates on imports competing with local production had been cut to 44 percent of their level in 1995, and 55 percent of the tariff reductions scheduled under the association agreement were in place (SIA, 2006: 21).

6 It has been estimated, for example, that around 15 percent of Morocco's population now lives in Europe (Yacoubian, 2004).

7 Such a statement does not preclude acknowledging the existence of dynamic competitive sectors in the SEM countries, such as the electronics industry in Tunisia. Prior to the phasing out of the Multi-Fibre Arrangement, Egypt and Syria had succeeded in building up their textile industries, and Tunisia and Morocco their clothing industries.

8 These concessions deal more with quantitative restrictions than tariffs. Some significant increases in quotas have been granted to the North African economies on products like olive oil and cut flowers, these new quotas being calculated on a floating basis or granted in a seasonal manner. The increase in quotas is still being negotiated with most North African countries.

9 For example, between 1971 and 1980s European wine imports from the Maghreb and Cyprus dropped by 55 percent, while imports from Spain increased by 20 percent.

10 To the extent that high tariffs do not impede high levels of imports, this can be taken as indirect evidence of the lack of competitiveness of producers in the SEM countries. This reveals an important (but often neglected) truth about tariff protection – as part of a policy to promote or protect domestic industry a given tariff is only effective in so much as it impedes imports. It is thus misleading to talk about a particular ad valorem tariff between trading partners as 'high' or 'low', this depending on the relative productivities of the industries in the two countries. Thus whereas a 10 percent tariff might be considered as exceedingly high for an EU industry (with very high rates of productivity), except from the point of raising government revenue it might be meaningless for a developing country to impose such a tariff as it will have no protective effect for domestic industry and simply raises costs for consumers.

11 To cite just one example, between 1980 and 1994, the terms of trade with the rest of the world (i.e., the units of imports that one unit of exports can buy) for the MENA group of countries as a whole declined by more than 30 percent (Bolbol, 1999: 4). This forced these

countries to undertake harsh adjustment policies that adversely affected living standards for the vast majority of their populations.

12 See, for instance Auty (2001).

13 In Tunisia, for instance, the textile sector accounts for around 45 percent of total exports, and 48 percent of manufacturing employment. Approximately 95 percent of the exports are destined for the European market. In the case of Morocco, in 2002 there were 1,692 firms employing a total of 205,600 employees (Ben Hammouda et al., 2005: 18-19).

14 The principal problems with the analysis are the data limitations regarding relative endowments. Wood and Mayer use the average annual years of schooling as a proxy for human capital, and land area as a proxy for resource endowments. This second variable is particularly problematic for the MENA countries – in Egypt, for example, only 3 percent of the total land mass is under cultivation. On the other hand, the MENA countries are richly endowed with mineral resources, which compensates for the lack of cultivable land. As Wood and Mayer concede, these problems are fairly intractable in this kind of analysis, but the results are at least suggestive.

15 Historically, the Nile Valley and Delta were considered perhaps the richest and most productive agricultural land on earth. Similarly, during the time of the Roman Empire, Tunisia was known as the 'granary of Rome'.

16 As the SIA (2006) study notes, however, these effects would be countered by a shift of production out of products for which the North African countries open their markets to imports from the EU (notably cereals, meat and dairy products), implying that the net effect on value added and welfare might be smaller.

17 See 'Los precios del aceite de oliva se recuperan por la baja producción', *El País*, 26 November 2001.

18 Cited in 'Finding Jobs for the Masses' by Mark Husband, Egypt-Survey, 9 May 2001, *Financial Times Online*, available at http://ft.news.com.

19 In a CGE analysis of the liberalisation of the Tunisian agricultural sector, Chemingui and Desuss (2000) conclude that reform of Tunisian agriculture can be viable only if accompanied by greater access to the European market for the country's exports. Under such a scenario, not only would the EU itself benefit from greater export opportunities for both manufactured and agricultural goods, but the corresponding increase in rural household incomes in Tunisia would make the necessary reforms politically palatable.

20 For instance, if the whole process of policy change takes place over a period of 10 years, those gains represent at best an additional 0.2 percent of GDP, something which could be considered trivial in macroeconomic terms.

21 In this case, the common external tariff should be set at the highest level consistent with protecting the industry in the least 'efficient' country. As Andic et al. (1971: 41) point out, 'Trade creation and trade diversion are misleading terms in the context of less-developed countries, deriving as these terms do from conventional comparative cost theory. What a customs union of the style outlined here is maximising is development creation, not trade creation, and minimizing development diversion which means diverting development potential to an already developed country.'

22 Moreover, Tovais stresses that these losses would be far higher if EU exporters managed to form a cartel to raise export prices. Tovias also acknowledges that the losses calculated for Tunisia are also considerably lower than in an earlier partial equilibrium study by Boudhiaf (1997), *who predicted static losses of as much as 7 percent of Tunisian GDP.*

23 See, for instance Taylor and von Arnim (2006). For a less disparaging review, see Piermartini and Teh (2005).

24 Dessus and Suwa-Eisenmann (1999: 2) comment that if the pessimistic predictions of the static models were accurate, neither Egypt, Morocco, nor Tunisia would have signed the agreements. As we shall see later, however, this ignores the important political component in the negotiations. The basic argument here is that the motivation on the part of the SEM countries was not economic, but political.

25 For a definitions of each sector and how these correspond to the ISIC Rev. 3 system, see https://www.gtap.agecon.purdue.edu/databases/contribute/concordinfo.asp

26 Processed agricultural products pose somewhat of a problem for the simulation, in the sense that tariffs are not reduced for the raw materials. Here we follow the procedure adopted by Elbehri and Hertel (2006) – tariffs for processed food products were proportionately adjusted for the content of primary agricultural inputs, since only the non-agricultural components of processed products are imported duty-free into the EU (and the same has been supposed of North African imports of processed agricultural products from the EU). It is worth noting that because primary agricultural inputs suppose a relatively smaller share of total value added for the EU processed agricultural products (around 25 percent of value added, vis-à-vis approximately 50 percent for the North African economies), the corresponding tariff reduction is relatively higher for EU exports to North Africa compared to North African exports to the EU market.

27 There is, in fact, some evidence to suggest that such a process is already underway – Tunisia, for instance, has been replacing tariffs on imports from the EU with domestic taxes to substitute for the lost tariff revenue, thereby leaving the overall tax take more or less unchanged.

28 It might also be considered that tariffs are low on EU imports of agricultural products from Egypt, Tunisia, and Morocco, especially compared with the very high tariffs that Tunisia and Morocco impose on their own agricultural imports from the EU. But this is perhaps misleading, for two reasons. GTAP generates trade-weighted tariffs and exports from the North African economies are concentrated in a few products. That does not mean that prohibitively high tariffs do not exist in other product lines. Secondly, the GTAP database does not adequately capture restrictions to trade caused by quotas and seasonal restrictions, one of the major bones of contention within the context of the agreements.

29 It is important of course to analyse what is driving these results. Annex table 4 shows the breakdown for the welfare results. One important factor here are the terms of trade losses, which more than offset the gains through the better allocation of resources derived from the trade liberalisation. An important part of the welfare losses also derive from the assumption built into the model regarding fixed wages. The reliability of the results therefore hinge on the realism of this closure.

30 The irony of this all is that, according to some CGE studies (e.g., Mold and Fosu, 2005), the North Africa region is the one with the most to gain from multilateral liberalisation. The logic behind this might, to the uninitiated to this kind of model, seem rather contradictory, but it is precisely because the North African economies have retained very distorted trade structures (whereas in other regions tariffs have come down quite sharply due to the Uruguay Round and bilateral pressures). Thus they subsequently have the most to gain from multilateral (or indeed unilateral) liberalisation.

31 Soderling (2005: 18) notes that Egypt's textile exports to the EU are predominately intermediate inputs, in addition to raw cotton. Although the data do not permit the exact tracing of commodities, about ¾of the textile exports to the EU are directed to Italy, France, Germany, and the United Kingdom, the very same countries that export intermediate

textile inputs to Tunisia. It is plausible, therefore, that we are witnessing a 'hub-and-spoke' type effect, whereby a European firm which imports intermediate inputs from Egypt, provides a design, and subsequently outsources the final stages of assembly to Moroccan and Tunisian firms.

32 Note also that the simulation does not take into account the MFA phase-out. Potential losses are thus likely to be far larger than those indicated here.

33 Drysdale (2000: 83-84) notes how, between 1974 and 1995, Egypt received approximately $20 billion in economic assistance from the United States, and an additional $21 billion in military aid, to such an extent that 'Egypt is indisputably hooked on foreign finances'. The aid has been heavily tied to the purchase of US goods, especially agricultural products. In 1994, for example, more than 85 percent of funds made available for economic assistance were spent in the US for goods and services.

34 For instance, the former Moroccan minister of industry, Hasan Abouyoub, claimed that trade liberalisation in his country "would have been infeasible without first entering into a free trade arrangement with the EU. These arguments apply both for initial tariff cuts, and for the commitment not to reverse policy" (World Bank, 2001: 27).

35 This is not to deny that there have been some steps in the right direction. For example, by an October 2005 decision of the European Council, the system of cumulation of origin was extended to Mediterranean countries, permitting goods processed in one or more countries to benefit from the same preferential access to the EU market as goods exported directly from the country of origin, provided that the countries involved have a free trade agreement in place (Nsouli, 2006).

36 MEDA I (1995-1999) was budgeted for a total amount of €3,435 million. For MEDA II this was stepped up to €5,350 million. European Investment Bank (BEI) funds made available to the EuroMed countries were also stepped up, from €4,808 million for 1995-99 to €6,400 million for 2000-2007.

37 The total resources made available under MEDA II (2000-2006) are in fact only equivalent to half the aid provided to Eastern Europe under the PHARE programme. It is also less than the aid received by Egypt and Israel annually from the United States.

References

Alessandri, Piergiorgio (2000), 'European and Euro-Mediterranean Agreements: Some Simulation Analysis on the Effects of the EU Trade Policy', Centro Studi sui Processi di Internazionalizzazione, Milan, Working Paper no. 110, June.

Adams Jr, Richard H. and John Page (2003), 'Poverty, Inequality and Growth in Selected Middle East and North Africa Countries, 1980-2000', World Development, vol. 231, no. 12, pp. 2027-2048.

Andic, Fuat, Suphan Andic and Douglas Dosser (1971), A Theory of Economic Integration For Developing Countries, London: George Allen and Unwin Ltd.

Augier, Patricia, Michael Gasiorek and Charles Lai-Tong (2005), 'The Impact of Rules of Origin on Trade Flows', Economic Policy, July, pp. 567-624.

Auty, Richard (ed.) (2001), Resource Abundance and Economic Development, UNU/WIDER Studies in Development Economics, Abingdon: Routledge.

Bacaria, Jordi and Alfred Tovias (eds.) (2000), Librecambio euromediterráneo-Impacto del área de libro comercio en el horizonte 2010, Barcelona: Icaria Antrazyt.

Ben Hammouda, Hakim Karima Bounemra Ben-Soltane, Nassim Oulmane, Stephen Karingi, Mustapha Sadni-Jallab, Aissatou Gueye, and Abdelilah Ouaqouaq (2005), 'Comment sauver le textile maghrébin?', African Trade Policy Centre Working Paper, no. 17, United Nations Economic Commission for Africa, Addis Ababa.

Bolbol, Ali A. (1999), 'Arab Trade and Free Trade: A Preliminary Analysis', International Journal of Middle East Studies, 31, pp. 3-17.

Boudhiaf M. (1997), 'Impact de la Xonde de Libre-Échange Tunis-Union européen sur le revenu national tunisien', cited in Alfred Tovias (with Jordi Bacaria) (2000), Librecambio Euromediterraneo, Barcelona: Icaria.

Brown, Drusilla K., Alan V. Deardorff and Robert M. Stern (1997), 'Some Economic Effects of the Free Trade Agreement between Tunisia and the European Union', in Ahmed Galal and Bernard Hoekman, Regional Partners in Global Markets: The Limits and Possibilities of Euro-Med Agreements, London and Cairo: The Egyptian Center for Economic Studies (ECES) and the Centre for Economic Policy Research (CEPR), pp. 71- 97.

Chahberli, Nabil and Moataz El-Said (2000), 'Impact of the WTO Agreement on MENA Agriculture', Economic Research Forum Working Paper 2007, Cairo.

Chemingui, M. A. and S. Dessus (2000), 'The Liberalization of Tunisian Agriculture and the European Union: A Prospective Analysis', in S. Dessus, J. Devlin and R. Safadi (eds.), The Dynamics of New Regionalism in MENA Region, OECD Development Centre and World Bank.

Cooper C. and Massell B.F. (1965), 'Toward a General Theory of Customs Unions for Developing Countries', Journal of Political Economy, vol. 73, October, pp. 461-477.

Deraniyagala, Sonali and Ben Fine (2001), 'New Trade Theory versus Old Trade Policy: A Continuing Enigma', Cambridge Journal of Economics, 25, pp. 809-825.

Dombey, Daniel and Roula Khalaf (2005), 'Euro-Med leaders look to build on Barcelona process', The Financial Times online, 26 November.

Dunkley, Graham (2004), Free Trade – Myth, Reality and Alternatives, Zed Books, London.

European Commission (2005), 'Mid-term evaluation of the MEDA II programme. Final report.' Report carried out by ECORYS-NEI at the request of European Commission, EuropeAid Co-operation Office. 18 July, available

at http://ec.europa.eu/europeaid/reports/meda-evaluation-midterm-report-2005_en.pdf
Elbehri, Aziz and Thomas Hertel (2006), 'A Comparative Analysis of the EU-Morocco FTA vs. Multilateral Liberalization (Revised Version)', Global Trade Analysis Project, Purdue University.
Fosu, Augustin and Andrew Mold (2005), 'The Gains from Trade for Africa: Implications for Labour Markets and Poverty Reduction', paper presented at UNU-WIDER Third Project Conference 'The Impact of Globalisation on the Poor in Africa', Johannesburg, South Africa, 1-2 December, 2005.
Galal, Ahmed and Bernard Hoekman (eds.) (1997), Regional Partners in Global Markets: Limits and Possibilities of the Euro-Med Agreements, Centre of Economic Policy Research, London, and the Egyptian Center for Economic Studies.
Ghesquiere H. (1998), 'Impact of European Union Association Agreements on Mediterranean Countries', IMF Working Paper WP/98/116, August.
Haddad, Mona (2000), 'Export Competitiveness: Where does the Middle East and North Africa Region Stand?', Economic Research Forum for the Arab Countries, Iran, and Turkey (ERF), Working Paper 2030, available at http://www.erf.org.eg/.
Hertel, Thomas W. (ed.) (1997), Global Trade Analysis – Modeling and Applications, Cambridge: Cambridge University Press.
Hoekman, Bernard and Simon Djankov (1996), 'The EU's Mediterranean Initiative', World Economy, vol. 19, no. 4, July, pp. 387-406.
Inama, Stefano and Lorenza Jachia Inama (2000), 'Assessing Market Access Preferences for Mediterranean Countries in the EU Market for Industrial Goods', Economic Research Forum for the Arab Countries, Iran and Turkey (ERF), Working Paper 2013, available at http://www.erf.org.eg/.
Karshenas, Massoud (2001), 'Structural Obstacles to Economic Adjustment in the MENA Region: The International Trade Aspects', in Hassan Hakimian and Ziba Moshaver (eds.), The State and Global Change: The Political Economy of Transition in the Middle East & North Africa London: Curzon Press, pp. 59-79.
Konan, Denise Eby and Keith E. Maskus (1997), 'A Computable General Equilibrium Analysis of Egyptian Trade Liberalization Scenarios', in Ahmed Galal and Bernard Hoekman (eds.), Regional Partners in Global Markets: Limits and Possibilities of the Euro-Med Agreements. London: CEPR.
Kuiper, Marijke (2004), 'Fifty Ways to Leave your Protection – Comparing Applied Models of the Euro-Mediterranean Association Agreements', European Network of Agricultural and Rural Policy Research Institutes (ENARPRI), Working Paper no. 6, April.

Kuiper, Marijke (2006), 'An Economy-wide Perspective on Euro-Mediterranean Trade Agreements with a Focus on Morocco and Tunisia', European Network of Agricultural and Rural Policy Research Institutes (ENARPRI) Conference Paper, May.

Kuiper, Marijke and Frank von Tongeren (2004), 'Mediterranean Association Agreements and European Security', European Network of Agricultural and Rural Policy Research Institutes, Policy Brief no. 9, October.

Krugman, Paul (1994), 'Competitiveness: A Dangerous Obsession', Foreign Affairs, March/April, pp. 28-44.

Lall, Sanjaya (2000), 'Turkish Performance in Exporting Manufactures: A Comparative Structural Analysis', QEH Working Paper Series no. 47, available at http://www2.qeh.ox.ac.uk/.

Maresceau, Marc and Erwan Lannon (eds.) (2001), The EU's Enlargement and Mediterranean Strategies: A Comparative Analysis, Basingstoke: Palgrave MacMillan.

Mold, Andrew (2002), 'Liberalización del comercio y acceso a los mercados: ¿Hacia una postura más coherente?' in José Antonio Alonso, Finanzas para el Desarrollo, Civitas, Madrid.

Mold, Andrew (2003), 'Regional Trading Blocks as a Response to Global Poverty? A Critique of the Euro-Mediterranean Agreements', Documentos de Trabajo Serie Desarrollo y Cooperación DT-DC-03-02, Julio, Instituto Complutense de Estudios Internacionales, Madrid.

Mold, Andrew and Augustin Fosu (2005), 'The Gains from Trade for Africa: Implications for Labour Markets and Poverty Reduction', paper presented at the UNU-WIDER Conference on 'The Impact of Globalization on the Poor in Africa', 1-2 December, 2005, Johannesburg.

Mubarak Jamil A. (1998), 'Middle East and North Africa: Development Policy in View of a Narrow Agricultural Natural Resource Base', World Development, vol. 26, no. 5, pp. 877-895.

Nsouli, Saleh M. (2006), 'The Euro-Mediterranean Partnership Ten Years On: Reassessing Readiness and Prospects', statement by Saleh M. Nsouli, Director, IMF Offices in Europe, at Crans-Montana Forum, Monaco, 23 June.

Oxfam (2005), 'Euro-Med: Ensuring a Fair Deal', Oxfam Briefing Note, 26 November.

Piermartini, Roberta and Robert The (2005), 'Demystifying Modelling Methods for Trade Policy', WTO Discussion Paper no. 10.

Rutherford, Thomas F., E.E. Rutström and David Tarr (1993), 'Morocco's Free Trade Agreement with the European Community – A Quantitative Assessment', Policy Research Working Papers WPS 1173, World Bank, September.

Soderling, Ludvig (2005), 'Is the Middle East and North Africa Region Achiev-

ing its Trade Potential?', International Monetary Fund, Working Paper WP/05/90.
Sustainability Impact Assessment (SIA) (2006), 'Sustainability Impacts of the Euro-Mediterranean Free Trade Area – Final Report on Phase 2 of the SIA-EMFTA Project', Institute for Development Policy and Management, University of Manchester.
Taylor, Lance and Rudiger von Arnim (2006), 'Modelling the Impact of Trade Liberalisation: A Critique of Computable General Equilibrium Models', Oxfam International Research Report, July.
Tovias, Alfred (2000), 'Impacto Comercial de las Futuras Zonas de Libre Comercio', in Bacaria and Tovias, op.cit. pp. 57-101.
Tovias, Alfred (2001), 'The Optimum Strategy for a Spoke: Linking with Other Spokes or Other Hubs?', in Maresceau and Lannon, op.cit., pp. 141-152.
United Nations Economic and Social Commission for Western Asia (1999), Euro-Mediterranean Partnership Agreements: A Critical Assessment, New York.
United Nations Development Programme (2004), Arab Human Development Report 2004, available at: www.undp.org.
White, Gordon (2001), A Comparative Political Economy of Tunisia and Morocco – On the Outside of Europe Looking In, New York: State University of New York Press.
Wood, Adrian and Richard Mayer (1999), 'Africa's Export Structure in Comparative Perspective', Institute of Development Studies, available at http://www.ids.ac.uk/ids/global/strat1.html.
World Bank (2000), Trade Blocs, World Bank, Washington.
World Bank (2001), Global Economic Prospects and the Developing Countries 2002, World Bank, Washington.
World Bank (2005) World Bank Development Indicators on CD ROM, Washington: World Bank.
Yacoubian, Mona (2004), 'Promoting Middle East Democracy: European Initiatives', United States Institute of Peace, Washington, Special Report, available at www.usip.org.

Statistical Annex

Annex Table 1 Summary Data on the Economies of Egypt, Morocco, and Tunisia (1995-2005)

	Egypt		*Morocco*		*Tunisia*	
	1995	2005	1995	2005	1995	2005
Inflation	9.4	11.4	10.3	0.3	6.2	2.0
Government balance	-1.3	-10.5	-5.5	-6.7	-4.2	-2.8
Agriculture, value added (% of GDP)	16.8	16.1	14.6	16.8	11.4	12.1
Industry, value added (% of GDP)	32.3	34.0	33.0	29.6	29.0	28.1
Services, etc., value added (% of GDP)	50.9	49.8	52.4	53.6	59.6	59.8
GDP per capita (constant 2000 US$)	1320	1622	1060	1278	1655	2215
GDP per capita, PPP (constant international 2000 US$)	3025	3732	3214	3783	5083	6765
Foreign direct investment, net inflows (% of GDP)	1.0	0.3	1.0	5.2	1.5	2.2
Rural population (% of total population)	56.9	57.2	48.0	42.6	38.1	32.6
Current account balance (% of GDP)	0.6	2.8	-3.6	0.9	-4.3	-1.3
Trade taxes (as % of total revenues)	12.9	5.5	17.9	11.9	15.8	3.7
Average tariff rates (% ad valorem)	24.3	18.9	20.6	19.3	28.5	29.6
External debt (as % of GDP)	47.1	38.6	67.6	42.9	51.5	61.0
Unemployment, total (% of total labour force)	11.3	9.0	22.9	11.6	na	15.6

Sources: Nsouli, 2006; World Bank Development Indicators 2005; EIU 2006

Annex Table 2 Pre-Simulation Destination of Exports

Source/ Destination	*Egypt*	*Morocco*	*Tunisia*	*EU25*	*US*	*ROW*	*Total*
Egypt	0.0%	0.5%	0.4%	35.8%	26.2%	37.2%	100.0%
Morocco	0.4%	0.0%	0.5%	60.3%	9.5%	29.3%	100.0%
Tunisia	0.5%	0.6%	0.0%	70.9%	6.3%	21.7%	100.0%
EU25	0.3%	0.3%	0.3%	58.7%	11.2%	29.1%	100.0%
US	0.6%	0.1%	0.1%	29.6%	0.0%	69.6%	100.0%
ROW	0.4%	0.1%	0.1%	23.5%	27.9%	48.0%	100.0%
Total	0.4%	0.2%	0.2%	37.8%	17.9%	43.5%	100.0%

Source: Simulation results

Annex Table 3 Pre-Simulation Source of Imports

Source/ Destination	*Egypt*	*Morocco*	*Tunisia*	*EU25*	*US*	*ROW*	*Total*
Egypt	0.0%	0.5%	0.4%	0.2%	0.3%	0.2%	0.2%
Morocco	0.2%	0.0%	0.5%	0.3%	0.1%	0.1%	0.2%
Tunisia	0.2%	0.4%	0.0%	0.2%	0.0%	0.1%	0.1%
EU25	33.1%	61.2%	71.3%	58.9%	23.7%	25.4%	37.9%
US	18.7%	6.0%	5.4%	10.0%	0.0%	20.4%	12.8%
ROW	47.8%	31.9%	22.4%	30.3%	75.9%	53.8%	48.8%
Total	100.0%	100.0%	100.0%	100.0%	100.0%	100.0%	100.0%

Source: Simulation results

Annex Table 4 Welfare Breakdown

	Allocative efficiency	*Fixed wages*	*Terms of trade effect*	*Investment/ Savings balance*	*Total*
1 Egypt	326.0	*-732.7*	*-500.2*	*-355.9*	*-1262.8*
2 Morocco	161.4	*-674.9*	*-326.0*	*-15.0*	*-854.4*
3 Tunisia	*-3.4*	*-165.1*	*-101.7*	1.9	*-268.3*
4 EU	272.4	0.0	1850.0	75.7	2198.2
5 ROW	*-353.0*	0.0	*-908.6*	295.1	*-966.5*
Total	403.4	*-1572.6*	13.6	1.9	*-1153.8*

Source: Simulation results

Annex Table 5 Change in Trade Balance (millions US$ 2001)

	Egypt	*Morocco*	*Tunisia*	*EU*	*ROW*
1. Agriculture	105.0	*-26.3*	*-48.3*	*-151.4*	126.8
2. Processed agriculture	56.7	*-153.6*	71.9	64.2	*-66.3*
3. Fuel	6.1	93.1	*-17.1*	*-57.9*	-45.2
4. Textiles	*-327.1*	*-160.5*	*-647.2*	1574.5	*-585.9*
5. Wearing apparel	*-1593.4*	1243.1	1059.0	705.5	*-1565.2*
6. Leather products	1.6	*-166.0*	*-36.7*	143.0	44.7
7. Wood products	*-30.5*	*-107.4*	*-61.1*	174.4	*-10.4*
8. Paper products, publishing	*-15.4*	*-124.9*	*-43.1*	151.4	13.2
9. Petroleum, coal products	9.7	*-28.6*	3.6	66.4	*-54.6*
10. Chemical, rubber, plastic products	185.7	*-236.7*	*-66.8*	*-63.0*	149.4
11. Mineral products, nec	*-81.0*	*-138.9*	*-26.4*	244.6	*-27.0*
12. Ferrous metals	125.4	14.7	6.9	*-48.6*	*-103.3*
13. Non-ferrous metals	17.5	4.6	*-16.4*	*-47.1*	37.1
14. Metal products	*-96.6*	*-175.3*	*-11.5*	249.9	13.9
15. Motor vehicles and parts	*-84.8*	*-99.8*	*-49.0*	123.2	103.2
16. Transport equipment nec	-3.4	*-1.1*	*-22.7*	*-293.4*	318.6
17. Electronic equipment	*-45.5*	*-15.4*	*-37.4*	*-699.1*	788.5
18. Machinery and equipment nec	116.8	*-185.3*	*-179.9*	*-456.2*	696.7
19. Manufactures nec	*-18.5*	*-39.2*	*-16.2*	*-140.5*	201.9
20. Services	1188.6	*-74.7*	*-293.2*	*-1813.3*	1530.3
Total trade balance	***-483.3***	***-378.2***	***-431.5***	***-273.4***	**1566.4**

Source: Simulation results

Annex Table 6 Post-Simulation Change in Bilateral Exports (millions US$ 2001)

Exports/imports	*1 Egypt*	*2 Morocco*	*3 Tunisia*	*4 EU*	*5 ROW*	*Total*
1. Egypt	0.0	*-15.0*	*-4.1*	1101.1	1391.7	2473.8
2. Morocco	*-7.3*	0.0	*-11.0*	2388.6	189.7	2560.0
3. Tunisia	*-14.3*	*-18.5*	0.0	1533.2	*-161.2*	1339.2
4. EU	5862.8	3546.5	2004.7	*-3787.4*	*-5557.1*	2069.6
5. ROW	*-3453.5*	*-1088.7*	*-470.6*	3048.7	1970.6	6.6
Total	2387.8	2424.4	1519.0	4284.2	*-2166.2*	8449.1

Source: Simulation results

Annex Table 7 Structure of the Egyptian, Moroccan, and Tunisian Economies, 2001

Egypt	Value output	%	Morocco
Total	68750.90	100.0	Total
Processed agriculture	18539.58	27.0	Processed agriculture
Textiles	8122.41	11.8	Chemical, rubber, plastic products
Wearing apparel	8070.68	11.7	Wearing apparel
Fuel	5922.34	8.6	Mineral products, nec
Chemical, rubber, plastic products	4865.39	7.1	Fuel
Mineral products, nec	4119.63	6.0	Leather products
Petroleum, coal products	3852.57	5.6	Machinery and equipment nec
Motor vehicles and parts	2225.23	3.2	Petroleum, coal products
Electronic equipment	2063.17	3.0	Textiles
Metal products	2052.31	3.0	Paper products, publishing
Ferrous metals	1940.54	2.8	Electronic equipment
Wood products	1878.19	2.7	Metal products
Paper products, publishing	1589.94	2.3	Motor vehicles and parts
Non-ferrous metals	1517.7	2.2	Wood products
Manufactures nec	698.83	1.0	Ferrous metals
Leather products	497.47	0.7	Manufactures nec
Machinery and equipment nec	464.03	0.7	Non-ferrous metals
Transport equipment nec	330.89	0.5	Transport equipment nec

Source: Calculated from the GTAP 6.02 database

Value output	%	Tunisia	Value Output	%
27357.60	100.0	Total	15956.05	100.0
5368.18	19.6	Wearing apparel	2833.55	17.8
3577.45	13.1	Processed agriculture	2279.35	14.3
3190.95	11.7	Chemical, rubber, plastic products	2064.85	12.9
2106.71	7.7	Fuel	1958.35	12.3
1347.59	4.9	Textiles	1217.01	7.6
1313.4	4.8	Machinery and equipment nec	1103.2	6.9
1309.46	4.8	Wood products	715.47	4.5
1290.17	4.7	Leather products	706.25	4.4
1185.52	4.3	Non-ferrous metals	517.88	3.2
1153.82	4.2	Motor vehicles and parts	458.77	2.9
1090.61	4.0	Paper products, publishing	456.44	2.9
1016.61	3.7	Electronic equipment	337.01	2.1
956.69	3.5	Petroleum, coal products	313.16	2.0
851.27	3.1	Ferrous metals	309.65	1.9
645.88	2.4	Manufactures nec	219.19	1.4
487.59	1.8	Mineral products, nec	204.71	1.3
340.17	1.2	Metal products	166.86	1.0
125.6	0.5	Transport equipment nec	94.35	0.6

6 Challenges of Forging a Partnership Between the European Union and Latin America

Christian Freres[1]

1. Introduction: The EU's Enlargements and Ties with Latin America

The European Union's relations with developing regions have evolved considerably with successive enlargements since the early 1970s. In this regard, the first enlargement (United Kingdom, Ireland, and Denmark) is linked with the creation of the Lomé Convention and the emergence of the Africa, Caribbean, and Pacific (ACP) group of countries which formed the core of European Community (EC) development policy until recently.[2] However, as the United Kingdom was not able to incorporate its former Asian colonies in this scheme, these were placed in a residual category of 'non-associated' developing countries, together with Latin American nations. This latter group of countries increased its profile within the EC's scheme of external relations as a result of the second, 'Southern widening' (1981-1986: Greece, Spain, and Portugal), when the Community finally incorporated a member state interested in championing deeper ties with Latin America. This enlargement also led to a stronger, more visible policy towards the southern nations of the Mediterranean.

The third enlargement in the mid-1990s coincided with greater EU interest in strengthening links with Central and Eastern Europe, as a result of the post-Cold War political opening up of that zone. This also started a process of re-shaping the prevailing development policy focused largely on the ACP group. Its impact was compounded by the most recent – and largest in terms of the number of countries – EU enlargement in 2004, which contributed to the creation of the new Neighbourhood Policy. Although this is not a development policy instrument as such it does deal with relations with various developing countries in the Mediterranean basin.

From this quick overview it is clear that European Union relations with Latin America increased particularly as a result of Spain's accession in the 1980s, but it also seems that later EU enlargements may have diluted the progress achieved in those ties. In a sense, it is too early to tell how great an impact they have had, but some indirect effects are already evident. Overall, the enlargement from 15 to 27 members has increased the internal heterogeneity of the EU. As such, it is no longer the same partner that Latin America – or any other region – dealt with just five or ten years ago. To what extent are the Latin American countries, or the EU itself, aware of this and to what degree have they considered the implications?

In this regard, one of the conclusions of this chapter is that the changes brought about by the latest enlargement are part of a series of transformations in both regions that have contributed to a growing divide between the European Union and Latin America. This situation was particularly evident at the IV European Union – Latin American and Caribbean summit held in Vienna, Austria, in May, 2006. In this context, what does the future hold for bi-regional relations? Is there any possibility to convert the Euro-Latin American 'strategic partnership' rhetoric into reality, or will this relationship be yet another casualty of the EU's inability to forge a truly global development policy?[3]

This chapter is organised into two main parts. The first section looks at the efforts to date to build a bi-regional partnership. It begins by describing the context after the Vienna Summit, followed by a review of the three 'pillars' of Euro-Latin American relations. The partnership concept is then analysed in general and through the summits and the main policy documents. This section ends with reflections on changes that have taken place in both regions over the past decades and on whether the European Union has something special to offer Latin America. The second major part of this chapter analyses the extent to which it is possible to construct a partnership between the two regions. The chapter ends with brief conclusions that summarise the main points and reflect on prospects for the next EU-Latin America summit in 2008.

2. Building the 'Partnership': Progress to Date

Overview of bi-regional ties after the Vienna Summit

In the months and weeks leading up to the 2006 Vienna Summit, it became clear that no one expected much in terms of results from this Fourth Summit of Heads of State and Government of the European Union, Latin American and Caribbean. A significant outcome that could have proven false, these low expectations would have been an advance in negotiations for association agreements (AA), key tools for a true bi-regional partnership. Although the proposal of European Parliament member José Ignacio Salafranca for a 'European-Latin American free trade zone' to be in place by 2010 (European Parliament, 2006) was an unlikely outcome of the Vienna Summit, a 'network of association agreements' was seen as a possible result within a few years after the summit.

In any case, to date association agreements are only in effect with two countries in the region, Chile and Mexico. With regard to pending agreements, the key accord under consideration is that between the European Union and Mercosur. However, no progress was made on this in Vienna, nor were the parties able to set a deadline to complete negotiations. There are two main obstacles in achieving the goal of finalising talks. The first is that key decisions depend on the outcome of global trade negotiations and as long as the Doha Round does not advance, little progress may be made in these bi-regional deals. This factor is related to the EU's denial of greater market access to Mercosur agricultural goods. The second obstacle is the divisions within the Mercosur and the limited progress in its integration process (despite the incorporation of Venezuela in 2006). The only clear decision taken in Vienna was to start AA negotiations with Central American countries. Meanwhile negotiations with the Andean Community (CAN) were postponed mainly due to divisions in this sub-regional scheme.

Even if they were approved, the pending AAs face a fundamental limitation: they fail to take into account different Latin American realities. That is, there is a tendency to try to impose a 'one-size-fits-all' model, regardless of the developmental differences among Latin American partners. The agreement with the Mercosur could be similar in design to the AAs with Chile and Mexico, although in the Mercosur case it would be necessary to include clauses related to regional integration, with the possibility of developing sectoral dialogues with the sub-region. Meanwhile, in the cases of CAN and Central America, agreements would have to take into account the greater assymetries existing between these countries and the EU in order to avoid excessive negative effects. This means that these AAs should also include more ambitious co-operation chapters than the agreements currently in effect.

In the political realm, Vienna did produce two interesting achievements. First, it established the basis for advancing focused sector dialogues, which may contribbute to reviving this component of EU-Latin American relations.[4] Secondly, the leaders of both regions decided to support the proposal to create a Euro-Latin

American Assembly. In early August 2006, members of the European Parliament and of several Latin American regional parliaments constituted this assembly in a ceremony in Cartagena, Colombia.

Finally, this summit did not result in any advance in the field of development co-operation, the third pillar of bi-regional relations. This may not be surprising as the lack of agreement on the main policy areas makes it difficult to move forward on what is often seen as a secondary aspect of EU-Latin American ties. In addition, this instrument's potential may have been adversely affected by the EU's interest in pushing a social cohesion agenda over the past few years which met with considerable resistance from a number of Latin American countries who see it as a form of interventionism. Although some analysts may regard the Vienna meeting as an outright failure, it should not be seen as such. The summit demonstrated how far relations have advanced (considerably since the early 1980s), but also how much further they need to progress before these ties can considered a true partnership. In that sense, Vienna was but a small step in a long, and not necessarily continuous, process.

Brief review of EU-Latin American relations

To have a better idea of just how far EU-Latin American ties have advanced since the early 1980s until now this section provides a brief overview of economic relations, co-operation, and political dialogue, the 'three pillars' of EU-Latin American relations, to determine the nature of these ties and the trends in relations over recent years. Economic relations between the two regions are stagnant today after a period of relative dynamism in the second half of the 1990s.[5] Although the EU is currently Latin America's second largest trading partner, total commerce between the two regions is just over half of trade between Latin America and the United States. In addition, Asia – particularly China – is rising rapidly as a destination and source of trade in goods. Since the 1990s the European Union has dropped from representing 20 percent of total Latin American trade to just over 15 percent in 2004 (see figure 1). New trends are beginning to emerge for some Latin American countries that have traditionally had the EU as its main trading partner. The case of Uruguay is worth noting, where the US has surpassed the EU as its major foreign partner, explaining Uruguay's interest in exploring the possibilities of a bilateral free trade agreement (FTA) with the US. There is a positive note in this panorama: the current EU-Latin American balance of trade favours Latin American countries, probably a result of the strength of the euro and higher prices for many Latin commodities.

Figure 1 **European Union Trade with Latin America**

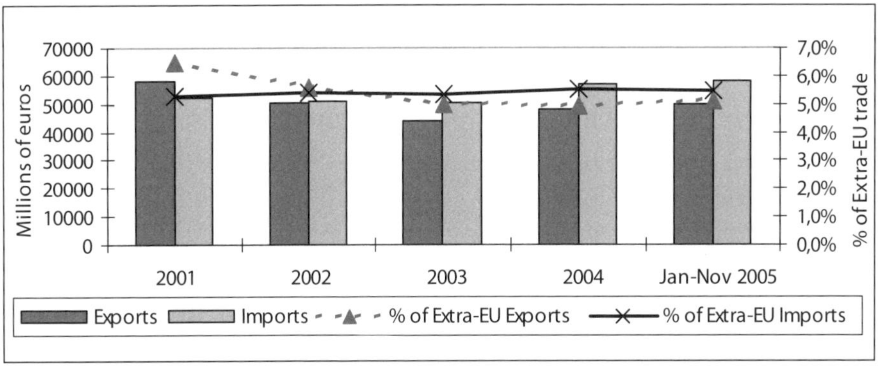

Source: Eurostat

For the EU, Latin America has never been a very significant trading partner, but its relative importance has decreased slightly in recent years (from 6 percent of extra-EU trade in 1994 to less than 5 percent in 2003). Thus, while European imports from Latin America grew by 180 percent from 1991 to 2000, EU purchases from Southeast Asian and Mediterranean countries grew by 807 percent and 354 percent, respectively. A similar trend can be seen with respect to foreign direct investments (FDI). Since 2000 there has been a significant drop in FDI going to Latin America from the EU, with flows going from more than US$40 billion in 2000 to less than US$5 billion in 2003. There has also been a process of disinvestment during this period in which the total FDI stock has also dropped. At any rate, even at its highest point, investment in Latin America was less than 15 percent of extra-EU FDI (Eurostat, 2005: 60-65). Furthermore, there has been a clear tendency to concentrate flows in a few Latin American countries via both investment and trade. Indeed, 75 percent of EU-Latin America trade involves the four Mercosur countries, Chile, and Mexico. The concentration of investments is even greater, with more than 80 percent of European FDI going to Argentina, Brazil, Chile, and Mexico.

When describing relations with Latin America, European representatives tend to emphasise the fact that the EU is the region's largest donor. Indeed, as can be seen in figure 2, official development assistance (ODA) provided jointly by EU member states and the European Commission accounts for more than half of the resources Latin America receives from Development Assistance Committee (DAC) members. This fact is undoubtedly important for demonstrating the relative generosity of the EU, but does it say anything about the nature of the partnership existing between the two regions? Obviously not, for at least two reasons.

Figure 2 **Net Flows of ODA to Latin America and the Caribbean, 1990-2003**

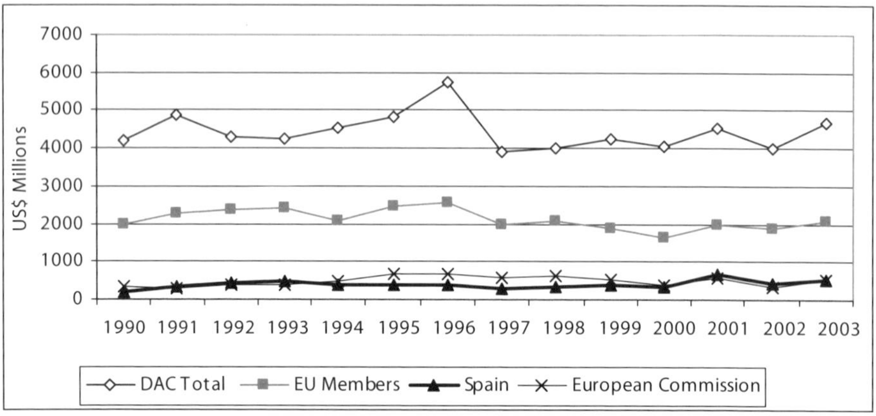

Source: OECD

First of all, because ODA flows for this region are of limited relevance. International aid represents a significant part of the GDP or the national budget in only two or three Latin American countries. For several countries other foreign inflows, such as remittances from emigrants, are much higher than aid.[6] In addition, in the current context of the Millennium Declaration (and the Millennium Development Goals), which is clearly skewed in favour of the poorest countries (most of which are outside of Latin America), development aid levels will probably prevail for many more years. Even if the EU maintains its relative share, it is likely that development co-operation aid will decline in absolute terms. Secondly, European development co-operation aid for Latin America is the sum of close to 20 bilateral programs and that of the European Community (European Commission and the European Investment Bank/EIB). That is, the EU is not a single donor, and in practice each agency operates with its own goals, interests, and focus.[7] It is not easy to see how the EU can work as a unified actor in this situation.

On the other hand, European co-operation is also seen – and is an important factor – in the differentiated approach dominating EU policy towards Latin America since the mid-1990s: the division between partners and 'co-operation countries'. The first group consists of countries with relatively high levels of development; the second is made up of the CAN, Central American countries (where three quarters of EU ODA is concentrated), and Paraguay. In essence, in this way – together with the concentration of economic ties pointed out earlier – the EU is fostering a two-speed partnership (or three, if the differentiated approach for the Caribbean countries in the African, Caribbean, and Pacific group is taken into account[8]).

The third pillar, political dialogue, is where the summits come in (taken up in the next section), as well as diverse mechanisms for relations such as the so-called San José Dialogue between the EU and Central American countries (since 1984), the political dialogue between the EU and the Río Group (since 1990), the political dialogues with the Mercosur, Chile, Mexico, and the Andean Community (since the 1990s), and specialised dialogue, such as on drugs (since 1996). Added to these official dialogues are EU-Latin American inter-parliamentary conferences, held since 1973, and various dialogues among civil and social stakeholders that have taken place since the 1990s.

This is a complex set of relations that has included some highly active periods, such as during the Central American crisis of the 1980s. Since the end of the 1990s, however, it has shown signs of slowing down (Freres and Sanahuja, 2006). Indications of this include the lack of high-level representatives at ministerial and presidential meetings (especially as regards to representatives from Europe), limited efforts to follow up on agreements, meagre resources assigned for joint activities, and the lack of a truly bi-regional effort to increase the institutional level of dialogue (see Freres, et al., 2006). In sum, the three pillars of EU-Latin America relations do not appear to sustain a very sturdy building, in spite of the huge steps made from the early 1980s to the present.

The strategic partnership through the summits and key documents[9]

The concept of 'strategic partnership' in bi-regional relations was originally introduced at the First Latin American, Caribbean, and European Union (LAC-EU) Summit in Rio de Janeiro in June 1999. However the term was not precisely defined at the time. On the contrary, the Rio Declaration refers very generally to the concept, which is based on shared cultural heritage, the principles of international law, the multilateral system, the common goals of democracy and human rights, a shared vision of the importance of regional integration, etc. The Declaration was accompanied by a document of 'action priorities' (55 priorities, which later had to be cut to a more manageable 11 priorities), which was more a list of good intentions than a plan of action.

In a sense, the Rio Summit was a high point for the strategic partnership, because the growing gap between the two parties was already evident at the following summit meeting in Madrid in May 2002. This was mainly a result of the inability of the EU to offer an ambitious response (or even a strong gesture) to the acute economic crisis in several Southern Cone countries. Another key factor was the host country's efforts to impose security issues on the bi-regional agenda, in contrast to the other side's desire to emphasise topics more closely linked to their development challenges. This tension was somewhat eased at the Guadalajara Summit in 2004, but no progress was made on a definition of the partnership. The concentration on multilateralism, integration, and social cohesion appeared to reflect a desire to advance towards a definition, but the final statement once again did not reach that goal.

In its Communication of December 2005 the European Commission (2005) does not fully acknowledge this situation or truly admit the generalised danger of stagnating Euro-Latin American relations (Freres and Sanahuja, 2006). Instead, it affirms that relations have developed considerably and it set about to reverse the erroneous perception that the EU does not have much interest in Latin America (European Commission, 2005: 4). The Communication established the goal of providing a fresh impetus to the partnership which currently faces a number of challenges. The Commission goes on to reaffirm that the association with Latin America is not merely a matter of fact but is also vital for the interests of both regions, for both the present and the future (European Commission, 2005: 5). The objectives of the Communication are to contribute to:

- The establishment of an enhanced strategic partnership through a network of AAs;
- Achieving more effective political dialogues in order to increase the influence of both regions on the international scene;
- Developing effective sectoral dialogues with a view to sustainable reduction of inequalities and promoting sustainable development;
- Contributing to a stable framework to attract more European investment which will ultimately contribute to the economic development of Latin America;
- Tailoring aid and co-operation more to the needs of the countries concerned; and
- Increasing mutual understanding through education and culture (European Commission, 2005: 6).

The member states of the EU, through the Council, gave their approval to this Communication in their Conclusions of February 27, 2006, without adding any new ideas (Council, 2006: 12-14). Undoubtedly, reaffirming the relevance of the relations for the EU is important, especially since some time had passed since the EU's last strategic document on Latin America (1994). However, the Communication in itself does not seem sufficient to provide the desired impetus. In fact, it merely reflects the European vision and illustrates the unarguable fact that Latin America has not articulated its own vision.[10] Indeed, a call is made in the Communication for this region to provide a firm commitment in return (European Commission, 2005: 5).

The problem is that Latin America as such has no institutional mechanism for this purpose. Even the sub-regional schemes with a limited organisational structure have not been able to fulfil this function (Fanzio, 2006). This limitation is aggravated in the context of the summits, because the Caribbean countries are also included, thus considerably increasing the heterogeneity of interests (Alemany, 2006). The Vienna Summit was a clear example of the increasingly fragmented Latin American position on many issues (Maihold, 2006). On the other hand, even though it includes some new, fairly concrete proposals, it is not clear if the Communication is ambitious enough in aspects such as resources and follow-up mechanisms. In effect, it does not propose a fundamentally new model of relations. Although it includes some improvements, such as the introduction of sectoral dialogues, they do not constitute a different framework.

Changes in the two regions and the world

The lack of a truly new approach could be a problem to the extent that the reality for both regions has changed notably since the 'golden decade' of relations – the mid-1980s to the Rio Summit in 1999 – and there have also been many changes in the world in general. The EU has expanded twice in this period so that there are twice as many member states in 2006 as there were in 1985; in the last expansion 10 countries joined the EU with per capita incomes well below that of the Community average and with little interest or history of relations with Latin America. Aside from enlargement, the EU has undergone several internal changes and since 2005 has been involved in an ongoing process of reflection to define a more adequate institutional structure. In addition, various differences have arisen on what direction EU external relations should take (especially as a result of the military intervention in Iraq).

For its part, Latin America has gone through a new economic crisis and a series of predominantly leftist governments have come to power in South America. In the realm of foreign relations, integration schemes have entered a period of crisis due to a lack of progress in reaching established goals and internal conflicts among Latin American countries. The fact that the Free Trade Area of the Americas (FTAA) has given way to bilateral free trade agreements with Central American countries and the Dominican Republic (CAFTA-DR) and some Andean countries has also contributed to a growing division in the entire region[11] in terms of positions with respect to the US, reflected in open conflict at the hemispheric summit in Mar de Plata in 2005. The emergence of Venezuela as a regional actor, with its leadership of the so-called Bolivarian Alternative for the Americas (ALBA) as an alternative to the FTAA and its entry into the Mercosur, has had profound repercussions – still undefined– in the area. Although it remains largely a political project, the South American Community of Nations also has enormous potential for transforming the region. Finally, the armed conflict in Colombia continues, and there is no regional initiative to deal with it. In economic terms, relatively low growth rates have been the norm and the region's share of world trade has fallen to very low levels over the past few decades.

On an overall level two issues should be emphasised. One is the intensification of globalisation, which has facilitated transnational interconnections, but at the same time has led to a series of social (such as dislocation or emigration) and economic problems (financial shocks), with serious political implications. The second issue is the predominance of the security doctrine, which since 9/11 has radically transformed the international agenda. Global governance structures, especially the United Nations system, have demonstrated a clear inability to find sustainable solutions for these twin challenges. One example of this is the lack of progress in global trade negotiations at the World Trade Organization (WTO). The main reason for this failure is the head-on clash between wealthy countries wishing to extend trade regulations to new areas and the leading countries of the South fighting to improve access to prosperous markets. Both parties are unwilling to cede ground to the other, and at the same time criticism and doubts over trade liberalisation are growing among not only non-governmental organisations (NGOs) and 'alter-globalists' but also an increasing number of independent analysts who question the existence of a direct link between globalisation and reduced poverty. This debate adds an extra layer of complexity to EU-Latin American relations, which have been dominated by trade concerns since the 1990s.

3. Does the EU Offer Something Different for Latin America?

In sum, EU-Latin America relations face a complex panorama of challenges. The world is not the same as it was 20 or even ten years ago and neither are the two regions. If a decade or more ago the European Union appeared to provide an alternative or counterweight to the hegemonic power of the United States, today it is not so clear what its 'comparative advantage' in political (or moral) terms is. There are legitimate doubts about whether the European approach is so different from that of the United States. Indeed, despite reference to the association agreements going 'beyond trade' – an 'FTAA with a soul', as one European politician put it – the fact is they continue to be free trade agreements in essence. In theory, they are not the same as the FTAs with the US because the EU has a less domineering negotiating style, but EU interests are not so different from those of Washington. Although in its rhetoric the EU has defended the importance of regional integration promoted through the AAs, the truth is that it has only signed accords with two countries who do not participate in any sub-regional schemes and have no intention of doing so (Mexico and Chile). In contrast, despite the fact that it has negotiated country-by-country, the United States was the first to sign an FTA (CAFTA) with a group of Latin American countries, in effect beating out the EU, which has been talking with the Mercosur for seven years with still no agreement in sight.

With respect to development assistance, the EU appears to lead, but only in terms of combined volume of Community and member state aid. In addition, the vision governing the Community's co-operation policy has not lead to a differentiated strategy for this region of middle-income countries. Instruments requiring less management such as budget support receive increasing interest, although a clear understanding of their advantages and disadvantages seems to be lacking in Commission services. The biggest problem is that no progress has been made towards the goal of achieving greater complementary between the Commission and member states, which would be especially desirable given the reduced presence of several European donors in the region.

One topic that came out of the Guadalajara Summit which indicated somewhat of a difference between the EU-Latin America process and other systems is that of social cohesion. However, in both the Hemispheric and the Ibero-American summits, issues such as employment and education, both closely linked to social cohesion, have been emphasised. It is also not so clear that the so-called 'European social model' is as promising for Latin America as it seemed at the time, partly because its viability is being questioned in Europe itself and partly because in reality there are various models coexisting in the EU. In addition, EU-level social cohesion mechanisms, such as cohesion funds, would be hard to apply in Latin America given their high cost. Even so, inspired by the European experience, the Andean Community promoted the Integrated Plan of Social Development (PIDS), which has received technical support from the European Commission.

Another difficulty with this concept is the growing perception among official Latin American representatives that social cohesion is a European imposition, or even a new way to avoid addressing the need to open the European market to Latin American goods.

With regards to political dialogue between the EU and Latin America, this does not appear to offer any special advantages over other schemes in which Latin American countries participate (Freres, 2006). The Ibero-American Summits are more institutionalised, with inter-government and quasi-community implementation and follow-up structures for Ibero-American programs. Even the hemispheric system, with all its core problems, is much more developed, with mechanisms such as the Summit Implementation Review Group providing it with the greatest degree of transparency of the three systems.

In addition, the participation of non-official stakeholders in the Euro-Latin American political dialogue is not as visible as in the other schemes (Freres, 2006). The involvement of civil society organisations (CSOs) has increased in recent years with respect to association agreements or sub-regional relations (EU-CAN, EU-Mercosur, EU-Central America) and bilateral relations (EU-Mexico and EU-Chile). The same can be seen in the support for civil society forums prior to the summits. All these examples show a desire to give CSOs a certain role in the different processes, but it is also true that CSOs do not actively participate in these processes. Instead, the EU has promoted a sort of 'parallel participation' whereby CSOs marginally influence without directly affecting official processes. In addition, participation depends greatly on the will of officials in both regions, and even though there has been a tendency to favour some participation in the EU, many Latin American governments resist it (which explains why hardly any of the meetings initiated in the EU have been continued in Latin America).

In response to these criticisms, the EU notes that it is a global actor seeking to foment a rules-based international system and that Latin America could be a key partner in this venture. The EU also repeatedly states that the two regions are the only two that truly 'believe in' regional integration models that go beyond mere free trade agreements, as a phenomenon intrinsic to their identities. These are undoubtedly powerful intellectual arguments, but is the European Union able to convert these common values into something real and convincing, so that Latin American countries choose this extra-regional alternative – not as a substitute to others, but as a complement to them?

4. Is Another Bi-regional Partnership Possible?

Given the situation described above, is it possible to envision a new model of relations that would contribute to a true partnership (or something that comes closer to this concept than that which now exists) between Latin America and the European Union? To answer this, it is first necessary to ask whether there is a true alternative to AAs with FTAs. That is, is it possible to think of an AA without the FTA?

In fact, this 'alternative' already exists: the situation that the Andean Community and Central American countries currently have through their Political Dialogue and Co-operation Agreements signed in 2003, together with the new Generalized System of Preferences (GSP) that went into effect in January 2006. However, as they are aware that the GSP does not offer a very attractive medium- or long-term outlook for their economies,[12] both groups of countries have demanded an AA which includes an FTA. The European Union took a long time to respond clearly to these demands. At the Guadalajara Summit in 2004 both sides agreed to start a joint evaluation of the state of preparation of the two schemes in terms of regional integration, a condition the EU imposed for signing FTAs with the groups. The evaluation was completed in late 2005. Finally, at the Vienna Summit, the EU agreed to start negotiations for an AA with an FTA with Central America, but it was not possible to do the same with the Andean Community at that point. Negotiations between the EU and the Mercosur, however, did not progress at Vienna.

Andean and Central American countries are somewhat anxious not be left out of the FTAs signed by the main global powers with developing nations. For this reason they responded positively to the CAFTA-DR and the bilateral agreements Peru and Colombia each signed with the United States. What would their alternatives be? The basic problem is that the Doha Round is still uncertain, so some market access problems that could be better resolved within the global framework have to be dealt with using less favourable options such as bilateral agreements or a GSP (which responds to a fully unilateral design and implementation).

This leads to the question of whether those same AAs with FTAs could be improved to take into account the large imbalances between European and Latin American economies. In the Economic Partnership Agreements (EPAs) the EU hopes to sign with the ACP group, there is a possibility of incorporating some sort of 'variable geometry' that would take into account the different development levels within the sub-regional groups (and with respect to the EU itself) (Jessop,

2006). This reflects the surprising fact that detailed evaluations of the possible effects of AAs, especially for relatively less developed countries such as several Andean and Central American states have not been carried out – or at least they have not been made public.[13] There is also a lack of in-depth analysis of the different alternatives that could exist for AAs with FTAs.[14]

In any event, it is worth remembering that AAs are not limited to the economic dimension. These agreements should lead to more in-depth political dialogue and improved development co-operation. The agreement in effect between the EU and Chile shows that if the Latin American party is interested and able to articulate interests forcefully, it can substantially expand the scope of political dialogue. Chile has been able to open sectoral dialogues with departments in the European Commission and member states that were not used to dealing with third party countries. This achievement is due to the fact that the Chilean government interpreted its AA partnership in the broadest manner possible.

The Chilean experience shows that AAs can lead to many additional benefits as long as Latin American countries and groups know how to take advantage of them. The December 2005 Communication of the Commission, based on this positive precedent, includes the strengthening of sectoral dialogues at the regional level. AAs offer the possibility of maintaining much more highly-focused, specialised dialogues based on goals determined by Latin American countries. However, if this channel is expanded too much, a problem might arise in terms of the capacity of the Commission's services to respond to new demands, and appropriate measures would have to be created to deal with this contingency.

Another topic is the introduction of conditions linked to development goals (including but not limited to the Millennium Development Goals) in the AAs. The GSP+ that went into effect in 2006 forces countries that wish to benefit from the regime to sign a series of international agreements on labour and social rights. This is a unilateral instrument that has not excluded any Andean or Central American country and could stimulate progress in these areas. However, the Commission does not appear to have made an in-depth evaluation of the issues. Instead, it limits itself to determining if the agreements have been signed and ratified. The problem is that international instruments in these areas have deficient mechanisms for determining the level of compliance with the commitments undertaken by signatories, so if the EU is serious about promoting social and labour rights through this market access regime, it ought to develop better monitoring tools.

Latin American countries may resist applying this type of conditionality within AAs since, unlike the GSP+, the AA is an international treaty and non-compliance could be sanctioned (in theory). A precedent exists in the North American Free Trade Agreement (NAFTA), although in this case the labour and environmental clauses were imposed unilaterally by the US on Mexico. If such clauses were decided jointly it could become a truly differentiating element of the AAs, and would relate extremely well to the social cohesion priority that the EU would like to put at the forefront of EU-Latin American relations.

This last topic of social cohesion is an important action area for CSOs in this bi-regional partnership. In addition to providing critical follow-up on the Euro-SociAL programme, which has been slow in getting underway and seems to follow an excessively technocratic approach, civil society organisations could more actively participate in the initiatve. They could also contribute ideas on how to better incorporate the social cohesion goal into the association agreements. Since there are many entities in civil society with extensive experience in carrying out development and co-operation programmes, their voice will be important for ensuring that changes proposed for greater budgetary support have clearly positive effects on human development. Their watchdog task is essential and must be reinforced now as aid flows into Latin America are being reduced. To this effect it would be a good idea to reexamine some strategies for the fight against poverty. For Latin America this is not a medium-term objective, since it is the end goal of all action in the region; it must be considered together with other goals of institutional strengthening (including market institutions), reduction of horizontal inequality (among groups and territories), and measures aimed at improving the region's international integration (see Alonso, 2006).

5. Final Reflections: Looking Towards the Lima Summit

What kind of partnership is possible in the medium- and long-term? As stated above, it should be possible to have a network of AAs that covers all the countries in the region. However, achieving this will depend on how Latin America develops, as well as on international system factors (i.e., the WTO), and on the EU itself. The December 2005 Communication of the European Commission appears to show Europe's political will to achieve this objective. Over the past decade, AAs have definitely become an essential element – not optional – for a bi-regional partnership.

Nevertheless, these agreements do not have to be the same as those that have been signed to date. In the case of Mexico they barely go beyond an FTA, largely due to a lack of Mexican initiative, but also because the EU does not have many resources available for other purposes. The EU's agreement with Chile is more advanced in many economic matters, but perhaps the most interesting aspect is the possibilities that have opened up by establishing specialised dialogues responding to concrete Chilean demands. This shows that AAs hold much more potential than simply expanding trade, investments, or even aid, in the case of relatively less-developed countries. A partnership implies opening up new fields of co-operation, which in turn provides possibilities for new stakeholders on both sides to get involved. Future AAs should base themselves on this principle.

To this end, civil organisations can play a pivotal role. They have the interest and ability to influence Latin American states, particularly so that they increasingly aim their agreements at solving their development challenges. The main contribution of CSOs to a bi-regional partnership will definitely be along this line. Another essential role is to ensure that negotiators take into account imbalances between the parties and seek measures to cushion any adverse effects on the weaker party, the Latin American countries. CSOs also have to insist that Latin American countries entering into these negotiations come prepared with policies for addressing the needs of those groups and sectors adversely affected by trade liberalisation that come with AAs.

Finally, CSOs should insist on improving channels for participation in the Euro-Latin American political dialogue. While this dialogue is kept at a low institutional level with little transparency, other stakeholders will find it difficult to participate. CSOs, therefore, will have to insist on greater institutionalisation, implying greater transparency and more integrated participation of CSOs. As many expected, the Vienna Summit did not bring about major changes in Euro-Latin American ties. However, the small advances that did take place should not be underestimated. If the association agreement with Central America moves forward and is able to establish a different model of relations, it could prove that the European Union truly has something special to offer to Latin America. The agreement with the Andean Community will be more challenging, mostly because the CAN needs to define its goals and its membership more clearly before undertaking such a serious commitment.

The next bi-regional summit in Lima, Peru, in 2008 will provide a chance to see whether the modest advances in Vienna are converted into real progress in relations between Latin America and the EU. The initiative by the regional parliaments in Cartagena to create the Euro-Latin American Assembly ought to provide renewed political drive, needed to mobilise states in both regions that fail to see the opportunities that a strategic partnership has to offer. Finally, the election of Alan Garcia as president of Peru – and, therefore, host of the Lima Summit – is a positive factor in that he is solidly in favour of regional integration, he is a defender of close ties with the EU, and he is a firm member of moderating forces in Latin America. It remains to be seen, however, whether on the European side there will be sufficient leadership actively engaged in this process. If not, Lima will be another failed opportunity.

Notes

1 Associate Researcher, Instituto Complutense de Estudios Internacionales (ICEI), Madrid, Spain. The opinions expressed in this text are the exclusive responsibility of the author and do not reflect the position of ICEI or of any other organisation to which he is connected.

2 Indeed, the ACP group was considered to be at the top of what came to be known as the 'pyramid of privilege' which the Community had implicitly established as a way of hierarchically organising its relations with the Third World.

3 Over a decade ago, Enzo Grilli (1993: 331) disputed the claim by Eurocrats that EC development policy had become global in scope. He noted the regional focus on Africa was never fundamentally altered. In his opinion, the weight of colonial ties (and the predominant role of more 'regionalist' member states such as France) came at the expense of relations with other developing areas, especially Latin America. The situation may have changed somewhat but his analysis remains useful today.

4 For an in-depth analysis of political dialogue, see Freres, et al., 2006.

5 Data used in this subsection on economic ties is mainly from the Directorate General for Trade of the European Commission. See http://ec.europa.eu/comm/trade/issues/bilateral/data.htm.

6 A recent report by the Latin American Economic System (SELA, 2005) provides ample evidence on how private flows are outdistancing official flows, and within these latter flows, how aid is declining in relevance.

7 The variety of perspectives can be seen in a simple comparison of two extreme cases: Spain and the United Kingdom. While the Spanish government is committed to spending around two fifths of its aid in Latin America, in the UK, the bilateral programme with Latin America has been practically dismantled and Latin America was hardly even mentioned in it's the government's latest White Paper on development policy (DFID, 2006).

8 This chapter focuses on EU-Latin America relations, so it will not go into depth on the specifics of relations between the EU and the Caribbean which, as stated, are clearly different. However, the dominant framework in the summits is that of the EU-Latin America, and in fact the Caribbean's role here has not been satisfactorily resolved.

9 These documents can be found on the website of the External Relations Directorate General: http://ec.europa.eu/comm/external_relations/la/index.htm.

10 This is a common argument in much recent analysis of bi-regional relations. See, for instance, Freres and Sanahuja, 2006 and Fanzio, 2006.

11 See analysis of Shifter and Jawahar (2006) on different divisions in the Americas.
12 See the analysis of Freres and Mold (2004) on the previous GSP and its impact on the fight against poverty. They argue its benefits for poverty reduction are, at best, unclear, and most probably, marginal. In addition, as the new regime introduced in 2006 includes a number of conditionalities related to social and labour policies, some Latin American countries may not be able to continue enjoying its benefits once the present transition period expires.
13 In this light, the EU did recently carry out an impact assessment on the EU-Mercosur agreement, focusing on environmental factors.
14 See Bilar and Rampa (2006) for an exercise carried out with respect to the ACP countries and their EPA with the EU.

References

Alemany, Cecilia (2006), 'Balance de los distintos mecanismos de diálogo', paper for the seminar '¿Para qué sirve el diálogo político entre la Unión Europea y América Latina?,' ICEI/FRIDE/Fundación Carolina, Casa de América, Madrid, 9-10 March (mimeo).

Alonso, Jose Antonio (2006), 'América Latina Las trampas del progreso' in C. Freres and J.A. Sanahuja (eds.) *América Latina y la Unión Europea. Estrategies para una asociación necesaria*. Barcelona: Icaria, pp. 321-341.

Bilal, Sanoussi and Francesco Rampa (2006), '*Alternative (to) EPAs: Possible Scenarios for Future ACP Trade Relations with the EU*', ECDPM Policy Management Report 11, February, Maastricht: European Centre for Development Policy Management, available at www.ecdpm.org/pmr11.

Council of the European Union (2006), *EU-Latin America Relations – Council Conclusion*, General Affairs and External Relations, 2711th Council Meeting, 27 February.

Department for International Development/DFID (2006), *Eliminating World Poverty: Making Governance Work for the Poor*, London: Her Majesties Stationary Office, available at www.dfid.org.uk.

European Commission (2005), Communication of the Commission to the Council and the European Parliament: Una Asociación reforzada entre la Unión Europea y América Latina. Estrategia para una Asociación reforzada entre la Unión Europea y América Latina: presentación detallada, COM (2005) 636 final, available at: http://europa.eu.int/comm/external_relations/la/doc/com05_636_es.pdf

European Parliament (2006), 'Informe sobre una Asociación reforzada entre la Unión Europea y América Latina', speaker: José Ignacio Salafranca, Brussels, available at: http://www.europarl.eu.int/meetdocs/2004_2009/documents/pr/598/598579/598579es.pdf.

EUROSTAT (2005), *European Union Foreign Direct Investment Yearbook 2005. Data 1998-2003*, Luxembourg: Office of Official Publications of the European Communities, available at http://epp.eurostat.ec.europa.eu/cache/ITY_OFFPUB/KS-BK-05-001/EN/KS-BK-05-001-EN.PDF.

Fanzio, Hugo (2006), 'Unión Europea y América Latina: ¿Interacciones en lugar de relaciones?' Bogotá, Colombia, OBREAL/EULARO Specialist Paper.

Freres, Christian (2006). '¿Hay Lecciones para el Dialogo Euro-Latinoamericano de otros Foros Internacionales de Participacion Latinoamericana? Un Analisis Comparativo Preliminar', paper for the seminar '¿Para qué sirve el diálogo político entre la Unión Europea y América Latina?,' ICEI/FRIDE/Fundación Carolina, Casa de América, Madrid, 9-10 March (mimeo).

Freres, Christian and Andrew Mold (2004), 'European Union Trade Policy and the Poor: Towards Improving the Poverty Impact of the GSP in Latin America', Working Paper WP 02/04, ICEI, Madrid, available at: http://www.ucm.es/info/icei/pdf/WP%2002-04.pdf.

Freres, Christian and Jose Antonio Sanahuja (2006), 'Hacia una nueva estrategia en las relaciones Unión Europea-América Latina,' in C. Freres and J.A. Sanahuja (eds) *América Latina y la Unión Europea. Estrategies para una asociación necesaria*, Barcelona: Icaria, pp. 23-104.

Freres, Christian, Gratius, Susanne, Mallo, Tomas, Sanahuja, Jose Antonio and Ana Pellicer (2006), 'What Purpose does the Political Dialogue between the European Union and Latin America Serve? Recommendations for the Euro-Latin American Summit in Vienna', Madrid, ICEI/Fundación Carolina/FRIDE/Casa de América, available at: www.fride.org.

Grilli, Enzo (1993), *The European Community and the Developing Countries*, Cambridge: Cambridge University Press.

Inter-American Development Bank/IADB (2006), *Inclusive Integration for Global Competitiveness. Strengthening the EU-LAC Partnership*, Washington, DC, IADB.

Jessop, David (2006), 'The Week in Europe,' 17 February, Caribbean Council.

Maihold, Gunter (2006), 'La Cumbre de Viena entre América Latina/Caribe y la UE: El éxito relativo de un encuentro de bajas expectativas', *ARI* N° 59/2006, Madrid, Real Instituto Elcano.

Sanahuja, Jose Antonio (2004), 'La Cumbre de Guadalajara (México, 2004) y el Interregionalismo en las Relaciones Unión Europea-América Latina y el Caribe,' *Circunstancia*, Año II, Número 5,Septiembre, available at: http://www.ortegaygasset.edu/circunstancia/numero5/art3.htm#2.

– (2006a). '*Regiones en construccion, interregionalismo en revision. Las relaciones Union Europea-America Latina y el cambiante mapa de la integracion en America Latina*', for the seminar '¿Para qué sirve el diálogo político entre la Unión Euro-

pea y América Latina?,' ICEI/FRIDE/Fundación Carolina, Casa de América, Madrid, 9-10 March (mimeo).
– (2006b). '*Hacia el Logro de un Verdadero Multilateralismo en las Relaciones entre la Unión Europea y América Latina*', Working Paper for the European Parliament, Brussels (mimeo).
Shifter, Michael and Vinay Jawahar (2006), '*The Divided States of the Americas*', *Current History*, vol. 105, no. 688, pp. 51-57.
Sistema Económico Latinoamericano/SELA (2005). *La Ayuda Oficial para el Desarrollo en América Latina y el Caribe: Contexto y perspectivas, XXXI* Reunión Ordinaria del Consejo Latinoamericano, Caracas, Venezuela, 21-23 November (SP/CL/XXXI.O/Di Nº 10 – 05), available at www.sela.org.

7 The EU and Democracy Promotion in Africa: High on Rhetoric, Low on Delivery?

Gordon Crawford

1. Introduction

This chapter contrasts EU democracy promotion policy in Africa with the reality of its efforts in Ghana. It focuses on sub-Saharan Africa in the context of EU relations with the African, Caribbean and Pacific (ACP) nations; North Africa is not covered. The chapter argues that the policy is high on rhetoric but remains low on delivery. Although it is not possible to generalise from the one example, Ghana provides a particularly favourable context for external actors to support democratisation efforts. Therefore, if policy performance is poor here, it is argued that it is unlikely to be better elsewhere in Africa where the political environment is less conducive to external democracy promotion.

This chapter locates itself in the tradition of critical accounts of aid policy that contrast the principled rhetoric of bilateral and multilateral aid 'donors' with the reality of their practices.[1] Such critiques frequently focus on hidden agendas in aid policy and this piece aims to look beneath the surface at the less idealistic motives that alternatively may underpin or undermine EU democracy promotion policies.[2]

The chapter is divided into six main parts. After this brief introduction, the second part outlines the rhetorical vigour of EU democracy promotion policy in Africa, examining the evolution and operationalisation of policy at different institutional levels, including in the recent development policy statement, the European Consensus, and in the new EU Strategy for Africa. The third part then looks at democracy promotion in practice through an investigation into EU democracy assistance in Ghana, inclusive of both European Community (EC) and member states' programmes. Findings are of remarkably little attention to this area by EU actors, despite the strong policy statements and the favourable political context that Ghana provides. The rhetoric-reality gap is most evident within the European Community's own aid programme, but levels of member states' democracy assistance also remain low, with the possible exception of Denmark. Fourth, in seeking to explain this rhetoric-reality gap, two propositions are outlined. These suggest: (1) that democracy promotion policies will be at a low level where the EU has few economic or security interests[3] and (2) that the EU is promoting a limited form of democracy, one that is compatible with neo-liberalism. Fifth, these two propositions are considered in relation to evidence from Ghana, suggesting that both have significant explanatory value. The low *volume* of assistance tends to confirm the first proposition, while the *content* of (limited) democracy assistance provides support for the second. Finally, conclusions are two-fold. One is that the EU's motivation in promoting democracy in Africa is more instrumentally than normatively driven. The other is that democracy is narrowly conceived by the EU, more concerned with limiting state power than extending popular control, consistent with hegemonic neo-liberalism.

2. EU Democracy Promotion Policy: High on Rhetoric[4]

The promotion of democracy and human rights has been a stated priority objective of EU development policy for more than 15 years. This section explores this rhetoric, initially within external relations policy generally and then specific to sub-Saharan Africa. It looks at the most recent pronouncements first, then briefly traces policy emergence and its operationalisation.

Democracy promotion in EU development policy

Democracy promotion continues to be prominent in the most recent statement of EU development policy, the European Consensus on Development, adopted in November 2005 by the Council, the European Parliament, and the Commission.[5] It is claimed that this document provides 'for the first time ever, a common framework of objectives, values and principles' for the EU, inclusive of the 25 member states, the Commission, and the European Parliament, as a global player in international development (European Commission, 2005a: 18). The document is divided in two main parts. The first outlines the 'EU vision for development', inclusive of the promotion of common values of 'human rights, fundamental freedoms, peace and democracy' (Council, 2005: 6). This 'vision' is applicable to development co-operation programmes of both member states and the Commission. The second part is specific to Community development policy (i.e., Commission programmes), with the primary objective of EC programmes stated as 'the eradication of poverty ..., including pursuit of the MDGs, as well as the promotion of democracy, good governance and respect for human rights' (Council, 2005: 15). It is further stated that such 'objectives will be pursued in *all* developing countries and applied to the development assistance component of *all* community co-operation strategies with third countries' and that 'progress in the protection of human rights, good governance and democratisation is fundamental for poverty reduction and sustainable development' (Council, 2005: 25, citing the 2003 Commission Communication on 'Governance and Development').

Such statements are the latest in a long line that stretches back to the landmark Council Resolution of November 1991 on 'Human Rights, Democracy and Development', which introduced the promotion of human rights and democracy as an objective and a condition of development co-operation, applying uniquely at the time to both Community programmes and those of the member states. This resolution emerged in the immediate post-Cold War context of a shift in relations with African governments, signalled in particular by the French and British governments. In June 1990, almost simultaneously, important speeches had been made by French and British politicians that indicated the introduction of this 'new policy agenda' (Robinson, 1994). At the French-African Summit at La Baule, President Mitterand stated that France 'will link its financial efforts to the efforts made towards liberty' and would be less generous towards 'those regimes that conduct themselves in an authoritarian manner without accepting evolution towards democracy' (cited in Crawford, 1994: 3). In the same month, the British foreign secretary, Douglas Hurd, speaking at an international conference on Africa, introduced the concept of 'good government' and stated the intent to base aid allocation on the criteria of 'pluralism, public accountability, respect for the rule of law, human rights and market principles' (cited in Crawford, 1994: 6). A second key landmark for EU policy was the Treaty on European Union (the 'Maastricht Treaty'), entering into force in November 1993, with far-reaching implications. Regarding the external policies of the EU, efforts to 'develop and consolidate democracy and the rule of law, and respect for human rights and fundamental freedoms' (article 11) were stated as objectives of the Common Foreign and Security Policy (CFSP), while article 177 provided a legal basis for Community development co-operation and included the promotion of democracy and human rights as a priority aim.

Since the Maastricht Treaty, the promotion of democracy and human rights within development policy has been operationalised on a number of different fronts. First, democracy promotion has been incorporated into the EU's regional co-operation agreements, purportedly as a shared value and objective, for example, in the Cotonou Agreement with ACP nations. A human rights and democracy clause has also been inserted into agreements with individual countries, standardised since May 1995, where the breach of such 'essential elements' can trigger punitive measures (Crawford, 1998).

Second, increased importance has been attached to the notion of 'political dialogue' in external relations, especially with regard to addressing human rights and democracy issues (Council, 2003: 31). Indeed, EU agreements with other regions and countries are now commonly seen as having 'three pillars', with political dialogue a relatively new addition to the traditional elements of trade and development co-operation.

Third, attempts have been made to ensure the coherence and consistency of democracy promotion policy between different EU actors. This was most evident in the Commission's Communication of May 2001 on 'The EU's Role in Promoting Human Rights and Democratisation in Third Countries', which attempted both to increase the profile of democracy and human rights promotion and to provide for a more coherent approach. It aimed at 'placing a higher priority on' and developing a 'more strategic approach to' human rights and democratisation in relations with third countries (European Commission, 2001: 5). Measures to achieve such aims included the mainstreaming of democracy promotion activities into regional development co-operation programmes, as well as a more focused approach to the European Initiative on Democracy and Human Rights (EIDHR), the Commission's own democracy-assistance fund (see below). Democracy and human rights issues were to be integrated into all regional and country strategy papers, and indeed to 'permeate all Community policies, programmes and projects' (European Commission, 2001: 3).

Fourth, funds for positive support for democratisation have been made available from two main sources. A legal basis for democracy and human rights expenditure from mainstream regional aid programmes was provided by two Council regulations in 1999.[6] Additionally, Commission-managed thematic budget lines are available to all regions, of which the EIDHR is clearly the most significant in this area. The EIDHR was created by the European Parliament in 1994, bringing together a number of Commission budget headings (Crawford, 2000). Since 2000, the EIDHR budget has been approximately €100 million per annum, rising in 2004 to €125 million (Youngs, 2006: 62). Distinctly, EIDHR funds can be provided without the agreement of the host country government and are disbursed mainly to NGOs and international organisations (Council, 2003: 44).

Other budget lines available to non-state actors, notably 'co-financing operations with EU NGOs', could in principle support human rights and democracy-related projects. Budget-line funds are complementary to the main regional instruments of development co-operation.

These four elements of EU democracy promotion policy are examined further below with regard to EU-Africa relations.

3. Democracy Promotion in EU-Africa Policy

There have been many explicit references to the promotion of democracy in Africa, particularly in the context of EU-ACP relations, a number of which are outlined below. However, in the recent EU Strategy for Africa, adopted by the European Council in December 2005, a shift in language was discernible. Although the emphasis on democracy effectively remained, it was expressed more implicitly through the language of security and governance. Claimed as the first practical implementation of the European Consensus on Development, the principal objective is the achievement of the UN Millennium Development Goals (MDGs) in Africa, in line with the Consensus document's emphasis on poverty eradication. In order to achieve such objectives, however, prerequisites are perceived as, first, 'peace and security' and, second, 'good and effective governance' (European Commission, 2005a: 3-4). Clearly issues of democracy are intrinsic to both, and the first priority (of three) of the new EU Strategy for Africa is to strengthen its support, from both the European Community and the member states, in these prerequisite areas (European Commission, 2005a: 21). There are also direct references to democracy, notably in the context of promoting good governance. It is noted that 'there is a strong linkage between the promotion of development and the promotion of democracy', while recognising that 'the path towards sustainable democracy in Africa is difficult, long and rarely straight' (European Commission, 2005a: 24). It is also acknowledged that democracy cannot be imposed from outside and that 'the appropriate role of external actors is to support and encourage domestic efforts to build, strengthen and sustain democratic norms, procedures and institutions' (European Commission, 2005a: 24).

While the EU Strategy for Africa represents the most recent policy document, the emphasis on democracy and human rights promotion in Africa has a significant recent history. This is examined briefly below, using the same four-fold structure as above.

Regional agreements and democracy clauses

First, for sub-Saharan Africa the most significant agreement has been the Lomé Convention (1975-2000), succeeded by the Cotonou Agreement (2000-2020). This agreement between the EU and the ACP nations now includes all 48 countries of sub-Saharan Africa as signatory states.[7] Originally an aid and trade agreement, the political dimension of the Lomé Convention, and now the Cotonou Agreement, has become increasingly prominent over the past 15 years. A political element was first introduced in Lomé IV in 1989, preceding the general policy statements that came in the post-Cold War period, making 'respect for human rights' a fundamental clause of the agreement (article 5). Subsequently, in accordance with the Maastricht Treaty, this political dimension was extended and strengthened in the mid-term review of Lomé IV in 1995. Respect for democratic principles, the rule of law, and good governance were added to human rights, with all but good governance becoming 'essential elements' of the convention, backed up by a non-execution or suspension clause in the event of a serious violation (Crawford, 1996: 506-7). Similarly, the Cotonou Agreement affirms 'respect for human rights, democratic principles and the rule of law' as essential elements of the Agreement (article 9), while 'good governance' becomes a 'fundamental and positive element' (Salama and Dearden, 2001: 7).[8] A new consultation procedure (article 96) was introduced to deal with violations of essential elements, including the taking of 'appropriate measures' where an acceptable solution is not forthcoming, while stressing that 'suspension would be a measure of last resort'.

Political dialogue

The political dimension of development co-operation has been emphasised as a separate 'pillar' within the Cotonou Agreement. It has been enhanced in particular by the introduction of regular political dialogue between the EU and the ACP, described as a 'key element in the new partnership' (David, 2000: 14). The intention is stated to undertake dialogue at regional, sub-regional, and national levels (article 8(6)), including 'a regular assessment of the developments concerning the respect for human rights, democratic principles, the rule of law and good governance' (article 8(6)), presumably focusing on individual country performance. It is intended that dialogue will involve regional and sub-regional organisations as well as representatives of civil society (article 8(7)), the general inclusion of whom is a further innovation of the Cotonou Agreement. The first five-yearly revision of the Cotonou Agreement, signed in June 2005, has enhanced processes of political dialogue through establishing a more systematic and formal dialogue on the three essential elements of the agreement (human rights, democratic principles, and the rule of law). It is claimed that these revisions make political dialogue 'more structured, more permanent and potentially more effective' (European Commission, 2005c). A related amendment makes formal political dialogue a requisite step before the consultation procedure provided for by article 96 can be launched. This amendment emphasises the Commission approach that essential element clauses covering democracy and human rights, integrated here into the overall Cotonou Agreement instead of into individual country agreements, should serve a 'positive' purpose to prevent violations rather than a 'punitive' purpose (Youngs, 2006: 54).

Coherence and consistency

Prior to the Commission Communication of 2001, the internal coherence of member states' democracy promotion policies in Africa was addressed through the adoption of a 'common position' by the Council on 25 May, 1998 concerning 'human rights, democratic principles, the rule of law and good governance in Africa' (Council, 1998). A common position is one of the main legal instruments of the CFSP, defining the position of the EU on a particular issue. Its significance is that all member states must subsequently ensure that their national policies conform to the declared position. The intention is that the various EU actors should speak with one voice and act in a consistent manner.[9] The stated aim of the common position of May 1998 was to enhance the coherence of EU activities and policy responses to political trends in individual African countries. The common position also reaffirmed that positive support for democratic political change in Africa is a priority objective of the EU. Significantly, it stated that 'democratisation is a process which can be assisted by appropriate support from the international community' (article 1) and commits the Union 'to encourage and support the on-going democratisation process in Africa' (article 2), working with both government and civil society (article 3). Additionally, the intent is stated to consider *increased support* 'for African countries in which positive changes have taken place' (article 3), with Ghana falling into such a category.

Funding sources

The most substantial Community resource for sub-Saharan African countries is the European Development Fund (EDF), the financial instrument of the Cotonou Agreement. A country strategy and national indicative programme is negotiated by the government of each ACP state with the European Commission, determining the focal sectors for assistance and potentially including 'democracy and governance'. Additionally, other Commission-managed thematic budget lines are available to all regions, with clearly the EIDHR as the most significant.

As regards funding from EU member states, each has its own bilateral aid programme within which democracy and governance assistance has become an increasingly prominent element. Most member states have made their own aid policy declarations in support of democracy, human rights, and good governance, but even if not, they remain committed to support democratisation efforts through their EU obligations, for example, the 'common position' of May 1998 on democratisation issues in Africa (Council, 1998).

4. EU Democracy Assistance in Africa: Low on Delivery?

It is evident that democracy promotion has repeatedly been asserted as a priority objective of EU development policy, including in the recent European Consensus policy statement and its Strategy for Africa. But what has been the reality of democracy assistance in Africa? To what extent has the EU translated its policy rhetoric into support for democratisation on the ground? This is a difficult question to answer from the available statistical information on EC aid, given that sectoral classifications of EC assistance do not include a democracy and human rights category.[10] Therefore a case-study approach is adopted here, assessing EU democracy assistance to Africa through a study of Ghana. This also has the advantage of examining EU assistance as a whole, in other words from both the EC and member states. The information presented here was gathered through fieldwork interviews and document reviews. In this section, background information on Ghana is provided first, including the reasons for its selection as an appropriate case study, followed by the presentation of EU democracy assistance in Ghana in tabular form.

Ghana: democratisation and democracy assistance

Like many other African countries, Ghana embarked on political reform in the early 1990s, with constitutional and democratic government restored in 1992 after 11 years of (quasi-)military rule under the Provisional National Defence Council (PNDC) led by Jerry Rawlings. Subsequently, while democratisation has stalled or reversed in many countries of sub-Saharan Africa, it is generally recognised that democratic processes in Ghana have qualitatively improved with regard to, for instance, electoral processes (Lyons, 1999; Gyimah-Boadi, 2001), human rights protection (Map Consult, 2002) and civil-military relations (Agyeman-Duah, 2002).[11] Post-transition, four sets of multiparty elections have been held since 1992 on a four-year cycle. While the first two rounds of presidential and parliamentary elections in 1992 and 1996 were won by Rawlings and his National

Democratic Congress (NDC), the unprecedented peaceful transfer of power between political parties following the elections in December 2000 represented a very significant moment in Ghana's political history, claimed as 'mark(ing) a real step toward democratic consolidation' (Gyimah-Boadi, 2001: 104). The closely-contested presidential and parliamentary elections were won by John Kufuor and his National Patriotic Party (NPP), with the new government taking office in January 2001. The Afrobarometer survey of public opinion reports widespread public support for democracy in Ghana.[12] The strengthening of democratic values was again confirmed by the virtually trouble-free elections of December 2004, with President Kufuor and the NPP re-elected for a second term.

Nevertheless, despite this significant democratic progress, it is uncontroversial to state that much remains to be done in difficult circumstances if democratisation is to be sustained. Ghana is a low-income country with a per capita national income of US$ 320 per annum (World Bank, 2004, table 1), where public expenditure remains severely constrained after more than two decades of structural adjustment. Yet a democratic political system is expensive to construct, entailing not only the cost of elections but also the considerable expenditure involved in strengthening the range of democratic institutions and processes required at national and local levels. A number of commentators, mainly Ghanaians, have highlighted various shortcomings and weaknesses in key institutions of democratic governance, ones where external financial assistance could play an important role. Some examples are given here.

Regarding the electoral system, key problems for the Electoral Commission to address include the bloated Voters' Register and the malapportionment of parliamentary seats (Smith, 2002: 623-8), with failure to do so potentially threatening the legitimacy of future elections. Another source describes voter registration as the 'Achilles' heel of election administration in Ghana' (Map Consult, 2002: 18). Yet the Electoral Commission's ability to implement such reforms depends largely on its capacity, with its funding from government described as 'well below the requirements and subject to unpredictable timing' (Map Consult, 2002: 6). Since independence, Parliament has suffered greatly at the hands of military intervention, with Oquaye (2001: 12) observing that parliament's dissolution 'on the occasion of every military coup (1966, 1972, 1979, 1981) has checked the systematic and sustained development of the institution'. Assessments of parliament's performance in the Fourth Republic since 1992 have noted improvements while simultaneously emphasising continued weaknesses, especially in its legislative and oversight functions (Center for Democratic Development-Ghana / Friedrich Naumann Stiftung, 2000a: 4); (Oquaye, 2001: 12).[13] Parliamentary capacity is regarded as weak in both material and human terms, largely perceived as a resource issue stemming from Parliament's 'low priority in the governmental budget' (Oquaye, 2001: 16). Similarly the judiciary is weakened by its 'lack of the basic tools of the trade', including a lack of a complete set of Ghana Law Reports and law journals (Center for Democratic Development – Ghana / Friedrich Naumann Stiftung, 2000b: 36). More thorough judicial reform is also required to renew and strengthen the judicial system, yet a workshop on this subject noted that 'the lack of resources was a common theme running through all discussions' (Center for Democratic Development – Ghana / Friedrich Naumann Stiftung, 2000b: 40). Indeed this 'common theme' of financial constraint can be applied to all institutions of democratic governance examined here. Regarding the protection and promotion of human rights, the Commission for Human Rights and Administrative Justice (CHRAJ) is described as 'woefully under-resourced' (Center for Democratic Development – Ghana, 2002: 7), while the effectiveness of the National Media Commission has been constrained by 'a lack of human and material resources to fulfil its mandate' (Oquaye, 2001: 44). A comment by Oquaye concerning the plight of the National Media Commission, but one that could be generalised to all the above areas, is that 'this [issue] should be addressed by those who seek the deepening of democracy in Ghana' (2001: 44).

Within sub-Saharan Africa, Ghana was perceived as a suitable case-study for examining the EU's democracy promotion policies for two main reasons. First, Ghana is a major recipient of EU development assistance. In 2004, Ghana was the fifth largest recipient of EU aid in sub-Saharan Africa and the eighth largest globally (European Commission, 2006: 26), despite being a relatively small country. Disbursements from the EU, both member states and the EC, totalled US $706 million in 2004 (European Commission, 2006: 21). Given the nature of the policy pledges outlined above regarding democracy promotion in all third countries, it is anticipated that such commitments would certainly be implemented in Ghana as a major recipient of EU aid.

Second, Ghana's political context offers a favourable situation for the provision of democracy support. Not only is the context positive for ongoing democratisation efforts, but also there is a significant demand for external democracy assistance, entailing a clear (and potentially legitimate) role for external actors. The Ghanaian case resonates well with the EU's acknowledgement in its Strategy for Africa that 'the path towards sustainable democracy in Africa is difficult, long and rarely straight' and that 'the appropriate role of external actors is to support and encourage domestic efforts' (European Commission, 2005a: 24). Democratic progress has been achieved in Ghana, led by domestic actors, but external support could help to maintain a positive engagement with democratisation. Further, the EU's acknowledgement of Ghana's regional role as 'an example of what can be achieved in a favourable political climate' (European Commission, 2005a: 10) would imply a particular concern to ensure that democratisation is sustained and further consolidated.

For these reasons, therefore, the study of Ghana provides a good test for EU democracy assistance in Africa, involving what might be considered a best-case scenario.[14] The implication, however, is that if the reality does not live up to the rhetoric in Ghana, then it is unlikely to do so elsewhere in Africa.

EU Democracy Assistance to Ghana

Financial and technical support provided to Ghana in the areas of democracy, human rights, and good governance is investigated here, described in shorthand as 'democracy assistance'. Such support is provided as part of the development co-operation programmes of the European Community and of the member states, four of whom are major aid donors in Ghana, namely Denmark, Germany, the Netherlands, and the United Kingdom.[15] What activities have they undertaken in the democracy and governance field? The democracy assistance programmes of these five EU actors are outlined here, with information presented in table 1.

Table 1 EU Democracy and Governance Assistance to Ghana

European Community	Under the Cotonou Agreement, the National Indicative Programme (€311 million over 2002-07) contains virtually no political aid. The promotion of good governance is not a focal area, but identified as a non-focal area 'for a series of possible interventions' (Republic of Ghana – European Community, 2002: 22), though none had been undertaken under this heading to date.[16] Governance projects *within* focal areas are limited to support to the Ghana Audit Service (1999-2004, € 3.6 million, second phase commenced 2005) and training to local government personnel (1997-2003, € 3.8 million, with € 3 million earmarked for further decentralisation support). Electoral support was provided for the 2000 and 2004 presidential and parliamentary elections. No democracy and human rights projects have been funded in Ghana from Commission thematic budget lines.[17]
Denmark	Human rights and democracy support has been relatively significant, with 60 projects from 1990-99 involving expenditure of 225 million Danish crowns (DKK), three-quarters (76 percent) of which was focused on civil society, including support for pro-market think tanks like the Institute of Economic Affairs (Ministry of Foreign Affairs / Danida, 2000: 37). It was acknowledged, however, that assistance was 'mainly on an ad hoc basis'

Denmark (continued)	(Ministry of Foreign Affairs / Danida, 2003: vii). Consequently, a thematic programme in 'good governance and human rights' was introduced as a focal area in Danida's current Country Assistance Strategy (2004-08). This governance programme has four components: 1. multi-donor budget support (MDBS) (70 million DKK), i.e., financial assistance for the Ghana Poverty Reduction Strategy (GPRS); 2. decentralisation (58 million DKK); 3. key governance institutions (59 million DKK), e.g., Parliament, the judiciary, Commission on Human Rights and Administrative Justice; 4. civil society (19 million DKK) (Ministry of Foreign Affairs / Danida, 2003: viii – xi).[18] The civil society component has two elements. One strengthens community-based organisations involved in governance and human rights activities, especially advocacy work in relation to district assemblies. The other contributes to a multi-donor programme, the Ghana Research and Advocacy Programme (discussed below)
Germany	'Democracy, civil society and public administration' is stated as one of three priorities of GTZ's programme in Ghana, though implementation only seriously commenced in 2004. The two activities, the 'Good Governance Programme' (GGP) and the 'Local Governance and Poverty Reduction Support Programme' (LG-PRSP), are largely focused on government at central and local levels respectively. GGP has four components, with a clear emphasis on public administration. These are: legal pluralism, land management and administration, support to the Serious Fraud Office and to the Inland Revenue Service. LG-PRSP aims to strengthen the capacity of district assemblies to plan and implement local poverty reduction programmes, with the statement that it 'does not focus much on democracy *per se*, but more on poverty reduction at the local level'.[19]
The Netherlands	'Good governance' plays a paradoxical role in Dutch development co-operation in Ghana. It is a key selection criterion for focus countries, of which Ghana is one. Yet, until recently, a democracy and governance component has been virtually absent from the Dutch co-operation programme.[20] Support was negligible before 2004, limited to: electoral assistance in 2000; one-off sponsorship of Ghana Integrity Initiative workshops in 2001; core funding since 2002 for two market-oriented advocacy NGOs, the Institute of Economic Affairs and the Centre for Policy Analysis. From 2004, a governance component has been included in the aid programme, though only amounting to € 0.5 million per annum out of a total budget of € 28 million. Almost all of this is expended on the Ghana Research and Advocacy Programme (G-RAP), a multi-donor project. Commencing in 2005, 17 research and advocacy organisations are being funded,[21] all Accra-based, professionalised NGOs, including many of the most well-established Ghanaian NGOs.
United Kingdom	The Department for International Development's (DFID) governance activities are significant but limited in scope, largely focused on public sector reform. Three large programmes were supported during the 1990s. First, from 1995, a Civil Service Performance Improvement Programme (US$5 million) was funded (Map Consult, 2002: 40). Second, launched in

United Kingdom (continued)	1999, the Public Sector Management Reform Project, supported by both the World Bank and DFID, entailed overall funding of US$ 150 million over 11 years (Map Consult, 2002: 41-2). Third, the UK supported a Public Financial Management Reform Project, again co-ordinated by the World Bank, with DFID's contribution including a new government payroll system (Emerging Market Economics Ltd., 2002: 22-23). Two smaller projects were also in the area of public sector reform, focusing on financial management: the 'Value for Money' project was concerned with government procurement, while the 'Ghana Reintroduction of Revenue Project' supported the introduction of value-added tax (VAT). Decentralisation assistance was provided through the Brong-Ahafo District Support Project (2000-2004), a capacity-building project aimed at improving planning and financial management in five of Ghana's (then 110) districts. The current Country Assistance Plan (2003-06) shows a broadening of governance activities, with support extended to civil society organisations through two activities: a contribution to the multi-donor G-RAP programme; a 'Rights and Voice Initiative', aiming to support smaller NGOs in advocacy and empowerment work, which commenced in 2005.

Source: data collected by author

From the information in table 1, it is evident that EU democracy assistance in Ghana has not lived up to expectations created by its democracy promotion policy rhetoric. The reality is of limited support for democratisation processes in Ghana, despite the conducive political environment. This rhetoric-reality gap is most evident within the European Community's own aid programme. Astonishingly, there is no democracy promotion element in the National Indicative Programme (NIP), with the exception of one-off grants towards the cost of holding national elections in December 2000 and December 2004. Nor does Ghana receive any funding from thematic budget lines that encompass democracy and human rights projects, including EIDHR. Such minimal attention is quite remarkable given the policy rhetoric about supporting democratisation processes that has emanated from Brussels institutions for well over a decade, including the Commission (2001: 3) statement that democracy issues would 'permeate all Community policies, programmes and projects', reiterated in the recent European Consensus on Development (Council, 2005: 15).

The current EDF-funded NIP in Ghana, ongoing until 2007, shows little change from a traditional aid programme focusing on rural development, road transport, and macroeconomic support. Detailed examination of the NIP's focal areas was also undertaken in order to ensure that no concealed elements of democracy support were missed. Yet this only uncovered a decentralisation project involving human capacity building at local government level and support to the Ghana Audit Service, categorised under 'rural development' and 'macroeconomic support' respectively. Of the four member states, levels of democracy assistance remain generally low with relatively little emphasis on this area, though clearly there are variations between governments. Denmark is the one exception, having given significant attention to this area for over a decade, though, acknowledged as *ad hoc* support until fairly recently. Danida's current 'Good Governance and Human Rights' programme (2004-08) is more strategically-based, but with proportionately more assistance now provided to government institutions than to civil society.

Regarding the other three bilateral agencies, those of Germany, the Netherlands, and the UK, at best it can be said that they have begun to give more attention to democracy promotion activities, largely since 2004. Before this, despite the policy statements emanating from agencies' headquarters since the early 1990s, democracy assistance from these three countries was insignificant. GTZ in Ghana was not involved in this area prior to the adoption of its current strategy paper (GTZ, Ghana, 2003). Rather bizarrely, the Netherlands uses the criterion of good governance for selecting Ghana as a focal country, but, until fairly recently, disregarded democratisation and governance as key areas for ongoing support and assistance. The UK's preoccupation with public sector reform, in alliance with the World Bank, has a more tenuous link with democratisation issues, with such measures relating to bureaucratic effectiveness, whatever the political regime, and more directly connected to economic reform programmes.

As a proportion of overall overseas development assistance (ODA), democracy and governance support remains relatively small. One source from the late 1990s, covering all the major donors in Ghana, indicates that only US $23.3 million went to the generic 'governance' sector out of a total of $724.8 million disbursed to ten sectors in a 30-month period (December 1995 to May 1998) (CIDA, 1999: 27).[22] This is little over three percent of total ODA, with governance assistance ranked ninth out of ten sectors, with only the 'environment' receiving less. Although democracy and governance support has increased recently, it remains highly unlikely that it amounts to more than five percent of overall ODA. Regarding EC and Dutch democracy assistance, the figure seems to be in the region of two percent of overall aid. Governance projects currently allocated from the EC's NIP amount to approximately two percent of EDF funds for 2002-2007. Similarly, the new governance component in the Dutch aid programme amounts to just less than two percent of total aid.

5. Explaining the Rhetoric-Reality Gap: Two Propositions

The reality has not lived up to the rhetoric. Within sub-Saharan Africa, Ghana offers a best-case scenario where positive measures in support of democratisation could in principle be implemented effectively. Yet this has not happened. Why is this? Two general propositions are outlined that aim to explain the Ghana case, one relating the low level of democracy assistance to the EU's own lack of economic and security interests and the other pertaining to the EU's understanding of the concept of democracy and its relationship with economic liberalisation. These are outlined below, followed by an analysis of their explanatory value in the Ghana case.

The first proposition suggests that the implementation of democracy promotion policies is likely to be at a low level where the EU has few interests, either of an economic or security nature. This is based on an understanding that EU democracy promotion policy is not normatively oriented, as presented, but has instrumental underpinnings. Therefore declared policy will be pursued with more vigour where EU interests exist and are perceived as compatible with democracy promotion and less so where such interests are either largely absent or political stability is deemed more important than democratisation to protect EU interests.[23] Two related developments, one post-Cold War and the other post-9/11, contribute to generating this proposition. In the post-Cold War period, EU interests in sub-Saharan Africa have waned, while its interests in the 'near abroad' of Central and Eastern Europe and the southern Mediterranean countries of the Middle East and North Africa have increased. The EU Donor Atlas shows a notable shift in the regional allocations of EC aid in the 1990s in comparison with previous decades. Aid to sub-Saharan Africa declined from 62 percent of total EC aid in the decades 1973-82 and 1983-92 to 40 percent in 1993-02 (European Commission, 2004a: table 9).[24] In contrast, aid to the Middle East and North Africa doubled from eight and nine percent in 1973-82 and 1983-92 respectively to 17 percent in 1993-02 (European Commission, 2004a: table 9). Such trends in EC aid allocations may well continue as the European Neighbourhood Policy is progressively implemented. In the post-Cold War period in Africa, the EU is no longer concerned with providing support and maintaining close relations with ideological allies, while its economic interests are largely confined to trade in primary commodities, notably minerals and tropical agricultural products. Residual political interests in sub-Saharan Africa focus mainly on stability, especially conflict management, given that the instability arising from civil conflict can have adverse effects on the EU itself (Olsen, 2003: 10-12). Such concerns are expressed in particular through the EU's Common Foreign and Security Policy (CFSP), with a number of 'common positions' declared and 'joint actions' taken since the mid-1990s regarding civil wars in Africa.[25] Clearly the EU fears the burdens in military and financial terms of having to contribute to resolving conflicts and to providing humanitarian assistance, as well as the attendant consequences of increased migration and asylum applications to Europe. Thus, it is suggested that the EU places more emphasis on political stability in Africa than on democracy (Olsen, 2003: 10-12). The second development has come post-9/11, with the EU's democracy promotion policy increasingly interpreted as security policy, in contrast to democracy being promoted simply as a desirable goal in itself. The perceived compatibility between security interests and democracy promotion is most evident in the EU's European Security Strategy, with the statement that 'the best protection for our security is a world of well-governed democratic states' (European Council, 2003: 10).[26] One consequence is that, since September 2001, the Middle East has become a major focus for EU (and US) democracy promotion efforts, with the EU stating an intent to increase resources for Middle East political reform (Council and Commission, 2003).[27]

The second proposition suggests that EU actors are promoting a limited form of democracy, one that encompasses the political component of the neo-liberal development model. Again this questions the motives of EU democracy promotion policy and points to a perceived mutuality between economic and political liberalisation. This proposition is based on the argument that the EU is less interested in promoting democracy and good governance in Africa as an end in itself, but more as a means of sustaining economic liberalisation and of maintaining neo-liberal hegemony.[28] Whereas the first proposition is based on 'real world' events, this second proposition stems from an understanding that the actions of the EU, in common with other international actors, are largely driven by an acceptance of neo-liberal theoretical premises. Advocates and critics alike generally acknowledge the continued dominance of neo-liberalism in development policy, including within such initiatives as the New Partnership for African Development (NEPAD) (Owusu, 2003). Over the past two decades most attention in Africa has been placed on the economic aspects of neo-liberalism, notably structural adjustment programmes and their recent rebranding as 'poverty reduction strategies' (World Development Movement, 2001; Zack-Williams and Mohan, 2005: 501-03). But critics remind us that neo-liberalism is both an economic and political theory. Ronaldo Munck (1994: 35) notes that, 'the neo-liberal conception of freedom virtually equates political democracy and the "free" market', while Adrian Leftwich (1994: 368) comments that 'neo-liberalism is not only an economic theory but a political one as well'. The accuracy of such statements by critics is confirmed in the work of Milton Friedman, the guru of contemporary neo-liberals, who asserted in the early 1960s that:

> Historical evidence speaks with a single voice on the relation between political freedom and a free market. I know of no example in time or place of a society that has been marked by a large measure of political freedom, and that has not also used something comparable to a free market to organize the bulk of economic activity. (Friedman, 1962: 9)

Thus, as suggested by this proposition, the EU and other international organisations are influenced by a neo-liberal development model that emphasises 'democratic politics and a slim, efficient and accountable public bureaucracy (as) not simply desirable but *necessary* for a thriving free market economy, and vice versa' (Leftwich, 1994: 368-9). Such a form of democracy is oriented less towards strengthening popular control over public decision-making and removing an elite monopoly (Beetham et al., 2002: 13), but instead is more concerned with challenging the power of the state. By this interpretation, democratic politics is perceived as a means to:

a) *limit state power* and its sphere of decision-making, including its ability to intervene in the economy and regulate capital; and
b) *bring residual state power under formal democratic control*, through elections for instance, as a safeguard against any tendencies towards the arbitrary exercise of that power.

It is a conception of liberal democracy where the tension and struggle between its liberal and democratic components, either to limit or extend the spheres of democratic control (Beetham, 1993: 56-8), has resulted in the predominance of the liberal over the democratic element.

6. Propositions Explored: Learning from Ghana

Returning to the Ghana case, do these two propositions help to explain why the democracy promotion rhetoric expressed at EU policy-making levels has not been translated into democracy assistance in practice?

The Ghanaian case provides some support for the first proposition that EU democracy promotion policy is instrumentally driven by self-interests and that low-level implementation is likely where few direct interests (economic or security) exist. Evidence here relates to the *volume* of democracy assistance. If the EU was seriously committed to assisting democratisation in Africa as an intrinsic goal, then Ghana should receive substantial support given the favourable context and the excellent opportunity for contributing to the consolidation of relatively new and fragile democratic institutions. Yet low levels of actual democracy assistance suggest that the rhetoric cannot be taken at face value. It would appear that Ghana does not attract significant support for ongoing democratisation because the EU has few direct interests there. Ghana is politically stable, offers no threat to European security, and the sustained extraction of primary resources, notably cocoa and gold, is reasonably secure. Despite Ghana's important role within West Africa as a relative haven of democracy and political stability, and as a potential model for its neighbours, its security and economic interests for the EU are low. EU attention is focused elsewhere within Africa, notably on situations of conflict, where its own interests are more likely to be directly affected. In North Africa and the Middle East, perceived threats to EU security interests are more likely to generate greater attention to democratisation issues, despite the less conducive context. Thus, the lack of EU interests is at least a partial explanation of why Ghana attracts such a low volume of democracy assistance, contradicting the stated intentions by the Council in their 'common position' of May 1998 to provide significant support to countries making 'positive changes' and their more recent pledges in the Strategy for Africa to support domestic efforts in the 'difficult, long and rarely straight' road to sustainable democracy (European Commission, 2005a: 24).

Therefore can the multiple references to 'respect for human rights and democratic principles' made at various institutional levels of the EU, including in the Ghana country strategy, simply be understood as largely symbolic? Or do they fulfil other purposes? It is Olsen's view (2002: 145) that the policy declarations themselves serve to enhance the EU's international moral profile and hence contribute to its status in international affairs, while incurring limited financial commitments. Therefore the instrumentality of democracy promotion policy seems evident in two distinct respects. One is that the lack of EU interests partly explains low-level implementation in Ghana, while the policy declarations themselves serve the EU's own purposes by, ironically, promoting its international profile as a normatively-oriented actor (Olsen, 2003).

As regards the second proposition, to what extent are EU actors promoting a limited form of democracy in Ghana, one that is oriented at challenging state power rather than extending popular control over decision-making? This requires an examination of the *content* of the EU's democracy assistance. Although levels of assistance are low, two priorities are clearly discernible in table 1 from amongst the range of democracy and governance themes. These are decentralisation and public sector reform. Additionally, the limited assistance to civil society is concentrated on a narrow sub-set of civil society organisations. What does this thematic prioritisation tell us about the *form* of democracy being promoted?

Four of the five EU agencies examined here are involved in support for *decentralisation*. Two member states have a particular focus on decentralisation – Denmark and more recently Germany – while the European Commission and the UK's DFID have smaller capacity-building projects at district assembly level. At face value, the contributions of EU actors to the strengthening of decentralisation reforms would appear to have positive implications for democratisation in Ghana, given the claims that decentralisation enhances opportunities for political participation and that local government can be more responsive to local needs. Yet, why are international actors so universally keen on promoting decentralisation? A key reason appears to be the compatibility of decentralisation with the anti-statism of neo-liberalism. Decentralisation entails further pressure on the central state to relinquish and to fragment its power. The concern to also limit local state power is demonstrated in the facilitation of bottom-up demands on district assemblies in Ghana. For example, Danida's emphasis on 'popular participation' within the decentralisation process. Although this can be interpreted in pro-democratic terms, it also entails the intensification of demands on relatively fragile local government institutions, operating under severe financial and administrative constraints, ones which require prior, or at least simultaneous, strengthening.

The United Kingdom has concentrated its governance assistance on *public sector reform* for a considerable number of years, while GTZ's recent 'good governance' programme has a public sector reform focus. Valuable as such activities may be, the democratic component of such programmes is questionable in two respects. First, many measures aim to strengthen the efficiency and effectiveness of the public bureaucracy, irrespective of the type of government, democratic or otherwise. It can be contended that public sector reforms in Ghana have done little to enhance democratic oversight mechanisms such as strengthening checks and balances and holding the executive to account.

Second, DFID's public sector reform agenda, in collaboration with the World Bank, has been more aligned to structural adjustment and to economic liberalisation than to strengthening democratic institutions and processes. Measures have aimed at slimming down the state, for example civil service downsizing, and at reconceptualising it in a form that is deemed appropriate for a free market economy. Further, it can be argued that the particular interest of international agencies in improved public financial management is partly to ensure that expenditure of their own grants and loans can be adequately accounted for. In other words, this prioritisation reflects a concern by international agencies for upward accountability to themselves rather than downward accountability to Ghanaian society, as democratic processes would entail.

The nature of EU *civil society assistance* also indicates an underlying concept of the relationship between civil society and the state that is derived from neo-liberal thought, one where the primary role of civil society is perceived as a counterweight to state power. This is evident in two respects. Firstly, the direct support provided in recent years by the Dutch and Danish governments to Ghanaian pro-market reform think-tanks such as the Institute for Economic Affairs and the Centre for Policy Analysis, both based in Accra, themselves acting as advocates for the preferred donor policy option of sustained economic liberalisation. Ongoing financial support to these organisations has been reinforced recently through the provision of G-RAP core grants (2005-2007). Secondly, although encompassing a broader range of interests than market-orientation, the channelling of the bulk of civil society assistance through the multi-donor G-RAP programme entails a narrow focus on a particular *type* of civil society organisation, those professionalised, advocacy organisations that are based in the capital city. Such organisations are primarily oriented towards keeping a check on state activities and exerting influence on government policy-making, and it would seem that the main intent of EU civil society support is to strengthen the capacity of a core group of advocacy organisations in Accra to perform such functions. Although EU civil society assistance is relatively limited, a small amount of funds can have a significant impact when concentrated on this sub-set of civil society actors, with this elite group of NGOs in Accra having 'the possibility of exercising inordinate influence' (Carothers and Ottaway, 2000: 16), especially when strengthened by donor funding. Yet the representative nature of such 'trustee organisations', themselves deciding what is in 'the public interest' or in 'the interests of the poor', is questionable. In contrast, membership organisations such as trade unions and student associations have been relatively disregarded in EU civil society support, despite their credentials as more democratic and representative bodies. The pattern of inclusion and exclusion evident in EU civil society assistance suggests less of an interest in strengthening civil society as a means of democratic participation, and more of a concern to consolidate that segment of NGOs that can keep watch over a perceived arbitrary and capricious state.

In sum, through examining both the volume and the content of EU democracy assistance in Ghana, there is evidence to support both explanatory propositions. First, the limited volume of assistance confirms that democracy assistance is at a low level where there are few EU self-interests, despite favourable conditions in a particular country. This indicates the instrumentality behind the implementation of democracy promotion policy, despite its presentation as motivated by normative principles. Second, examination of the three priority elements of democracy assistance in Ghana (decentralisation, public sector reform, and civil society) supports the proposition of an intent to promote a limited form of democracy, one oriented at challenging state power and sustaining economic liberalisation rather than extending popular participation and control.

7. Conclusion

The European Commission's communication on human rights and democratisation stated that it 'wants to be judged on its performance in meeting the EU's policy goals' (2001: 3). Through a case study of Ghana, this chapter has sought a favourable test for the democracy promotion efforts of EU actors in Africa, one where conditions are particularly favourable. The high profile of democracy promotion policy was noted within the framework of EU-Africa relations. But the reality of democracy assistance in Ghana was rather different, with relatively low levels of support. In particular the EU delegation in Accra has given astonishingly little attention to democracy and governance issues. At best, the member states examined had begun to give more emphasis to this area, well over a decade after both their own policy statements in this field and the democratic transition in Ghana. Denmark was the only member state that had provided more consistent support and had moved from *ad hoc* assistance to programmatic support. Further, it was noted that the provision of democracy assistance has been concentrated on two main sectors, decentralisation and public sector reform, with a relative neglect of key national level institutions of democratic governance, such as Parliament and the judiciary, as well as political society (especially political parties) and civil society.[29] Thus, from the evidence in the Ghana case, the assessment of the EU in meeting its stated policy goals of promoting democratisation can only be one of weak implementation and poor performance. Although it is not possible to generalise from one case study, it is suggested that if policy performance is poor in Ghana, then it is unlikely to be better elsewhere in Africa where the political context resonates less well with the EU's purported democracy promotion objectives.

Subsequent to these empirical findings in Ghana, the EU has continued to articulate the same democracy promotion rhetoric, for example, in its influential development policy statement, the European Consensus (2005), and in the recent

Strategy for Africa (2005). While aware of the limitations of findings from a single study, the experience of Ghana suggests, nevertheless, not only that African countries cannot expect much support from the EU for domestic attempts to extend democratic practices, but also that the limited measures undertaken are oriented more to limiting state power than extending democratic control over decision-making. It is argued that this constitutes the political dimension of neo-liberalism and can be seen as part of wider efforts by the EU and other Western governments to re-constitute the state and state-society relations in Africa in a manner consistent with the maintenance of neo-liberal hegemony.

Notes

1 Teresa Hayter's classic *Aid as Imperialism* (1971) was probably the first of this genre, as well as her later *Aid: Rhetoric and Reality* (1985).

2 The critique of EU democracy promotion policies may be a contemporary example of espoused principles being compromised in practice. But again the longer history should be recalled where 'European ideals' expressed through aid policy have been perceived as tarnished, for example, the critique that EC assistance during the Ethiopian famine of 1984-1985 was used to support the Derg, the ruling military junta, itself largely responsible for the full effects of the famine.

3 A related proposition, though not one that is relevant to the case of Ghana, is that democracy promotion policies will be downplayed where there are significant economic and security interests, with 'political stability' taking precedence over democratisation. This may appear converse to the proposition considered here, but in fact there is consistency in the argument that economic and/or security goals regularly trump democracy promotion in the hierarchy of competing foreign and development policy objectives. In other words, democracy will be promoted where it is perceived as compatible with economic and security interests and downplayed or ignored when it is not.

4 This section examines the democracy promotion policies emanating from EU institutions, many of which apply to both Commission programmes and those of member states. Additionally member states often have their own similar policies, but these are not examined here.

5 This revised and replaced the European Community's Development Policy Statement of November 2000, jointly issued by the Council and Commission.

6 Regulation 975 covered developing countries and Regulation 976 other third countries.

7 Four North African countries – Morocco, Tunisia, Algeria, and Egypt – belong to the Euro-Mediterranean Partnership concluded in Barcelona in 1995. Within the African continent, only Libya has not entered into a formal agreement with the EU.

8 Discussion concerning the inclusion of good governance in the Cotonou Agreement was one of the most controversial aspects of the negotiations between the ACP states and the EU. The ACP resisted the introduction of good governance as an 'essential element', subject to a non-execution or suspension clause. The compromise of good governance as a 'fundamental and positive element' entails linguistic contortions, with good governance becoming a theme for regular dialogue and an area for positive support. The main differ-

ence is that good governance is not subject to a non-execution clause, with the exception of 'serious cases of corruption' where significant funds provided by the Community are involved (article 97).

9 It can also be argued that a 'common position' is often illusory. This was evident, for example, in the differing reactions by EU member states to the post-election crisis in Ethiopia in 2005. Whereas the EU itself took a very critical position, the UK government (especially Prime Minister Blair) took a 'softly-softly' approach, tacitly supporting the election results, while mildly criticising the 'over-reaction' of Ethiopian authorities to the demonstrations.

10 In the statistical tables in its Annual Reports on Development Policy, the European Commission uses the purpose codes of the OECD DAC for its sectoral breakdown. This includes the category of 'government and civil society', as an element of 'social infrastructure and services', but there is no specific 'democracy' category. 'Government and civil society' is clearly broader than democracy assistance, presumably encompassing all assistance to governments, including budget support, and all assistance to NGOs, including service provision activities. Rather confusingly, in the breakdown of EU aid by sector in the EU's Donor Atlas, 'democracy' is included in the catch-all 'multi-sector' category, along with environment and others (European Commission, 2006: 50). In 1995-2004, such multi-sector assistance amounted to eight per cent of EU aid, including both EC and member states (ibid.). Therefore, even though accurate figures are not available, one can confidently state that democracy assistance as a proportion of overall EU aid has been no more than five per cent over the past decade. A more exact figure is that EIDHR funds amount to just under two per cent of total Commission aid annually (Youngs, 2006: 62).

11 Of the approximately 30 countries in Africa that were involved in attempted democratic transitions in the early 1990s, Thomas Carothers (2002: 9) cited Ghana as the *only* African country that had made significant democratic progress and remained positively engaged in democratisation.

12 The second Afrobarometer survey, undertaken in 2002, indicates strong support for democracy among Ghanaians, with 82 percent of respondents agreeing that democracy is always preferable to any other kind of government (Gyimah-Boadi and Mensah, 2003: 27).

13 Financial constraints translate into a lack of support staff, research assistants, library facilities, access to independent data, and so forth.

14 It could be argued that EU support should be concentrated on those countries where the political situation is worst and the need greatest, for example, countries in conflict or with serious governance problems. It is acknowledged that one priority of donors' democracy assistance to Africa should be post-conflict societies, such as Liberia or the Congo (DRC). However, it should also be noted that democracy promotion in such societies is both complex and potentially hazardous. Important pre-conditions are security and stability, notably the (re-)establishment of the state's monopoly of power and the political inclusion of warring factions, and that the premature introduction of political competition and democratic processes could heighten social and political divisions. In contrast, a country like Ghana offers a favourable context where the usual criteria for the successful utilisation of limited aid resources – effectiveness, efficiency, relevance, and sustainability – can be met more easily.

15 Globally these four member states, plus Sweden, appear to be main providers of democracy assistance, contributing 76 percent of EU aid for 'government and civil society' (European Commission, 2004a: 41).

16 Fieldwork research, including interviews, was undertaken in 2004.
17 European Commission official, Brussels, personal correspondence, 6 January, 2004; EuropeAid Co-operation Office official, Brussels, personal correspondence, 6 January 2004.
18 The categorisation of MDBS as good governance support appears to entail some mislabelling. Although good governance is one of five priority areas in the GPRS, it is the one that receives least emphasis and therefore MDBS is far from exclusively good governance support.
19 Interview with GTZ official, Accra, Ghana, 22 March, 2004.
20 The paradoxical argument runs as follows: because Ghana is perceived as already 'having good governance', then support for governance and democracy is not a priority. However, this contradicts the idea of improving the quality of governance as an ongoing process, similar to that of democratisation, one that is never complete.
21 Ghana Research and Advocacy Programme (G-RAP) Newsletter No.2, 15 April, 2005.
22 Additionally, of the US$ 23.3 million, a Japanese programme of US$ 9.2 million is categorised dubiously as governance assistance, despite being described as 'promotion of the economy'.
23 See footnote 3.
24 In 2001 and 2002 (averaged), sub-Saharan Africa only received 36 percent of total EC ODA (European Commission, 2004a: table 12). The regional allocation to sub-Saharan Africa of all EU aid (member states plus EC) has declined less dramatically over the same time period, averaging 43 percent in 1973-1982, increasing to 50 percent in 1983-1992, and then decreasing back to 43 percent in 1993-2002 (ibid.: table 8). Additionally, the aid policy decisions taken at the G8 Summit at Gleneagles in July 2005 should lead to an increase in overall EU aid allocations to sub-Saharan Africa.
25 For example, the EU deployed troops outside of Europe for the first time in the Democratic Republic of the Congo (DRC) in June 2003 (Olsen, 2003: 11).
26 Similarly BMZ has also stated that, 'Since functioning democratic states are a key factor for the security interests of the people in the North and South, we must make developing and strengthening them a focus of international policy' (BMZ, 2004: 7).
27 Thomas Carothers (2004: 227) states that the US government 'now ranks a democratic transformation of the Middle East as one of its top foreign policy goals'.
28 See, for example: Abrahamsen (2000); Barya (1993).
29 Again, Denmark is the exception to whom this criticism of neglect does not apply.

References

Abrahamsen, Rita (2000), *Disciplining Democracy: Development Discourse and Good Governance in Africa*, London: Zed.

Agyeman-Duah, Baffour (2002), 'Civil-Military Relations in Ghana's Fourth Republic', *Critical Perspectives*, no. 9, Accra: CDD-Ghana.

Barya, John-Jean B. (1993), 'The New Conditionalities of Aid: An Independent View from Africa', *IDS Bulletin*, vol. 24, no. 1, pp. 16-23.

Beetham, David (1993), 'Liberal Democracy and the Limits of Democratisation', in D. Held (ed.) *Prospects for Democracy*, Cambridge: Polity Press, pp.55-73.

Beetham, David, S. Bracking, I. Kearton, and S. Weir (2002), *International IDEA Handbook on Democracy Assessment*, The Hague: Kluwer Law International.
BMZ (German Federal Ministry for Economic Co-operation and Development) (2004), 'On development-based and military responses to new security challenges', BMZ Discourse No.002, Bonn: BMZ.
Canadian International Development Agency (CIDA) (1999), 'Ghana: Programming Framework 1999/00 to 2004/05', Hull, Quebec: CIDA.
Carothers, Thomas (2002), 'The End of the Transition Paradigm', *Journal of Democracy*, vol. 13, no. 1.
Carothers, Thomas (2004), *Critical Mission: Essays on Democracy Promotion*, Washington DC: Carnegie Endowment for International Peace.
Carothers, Thomas and Marina Ottaway (2000), 'The Burgeoning World of Civil Society Aid', in Marina Ottaway and Thomas. Carothers (eds.), *Funding Virtue: Civil Society Aid and Democracy Promotion*, Washington DC: Carnegie Endowment for International Peace.
Center for Democratic Development – Ghana (2002), *Human Rights and Administrative Justice in Ghana*, Accra: CDD-Ghana.
Center for Democratic Development – Ghana / Friedrich Naumann Stiftung (2000a), *Parliament and Democratic Governance in Ghana's Fourth Republic*, Accra: Friedrich Naumann Stiftung.
Center for Democratic Development – Ghana / Friedrich Naumann Stiftung (2000b), *The Judiciary and Democratic Governance in Ghana's Fourth Republic*, Accra: Friedrich Naumann Stiftung.
Council of Ministers (1991), 'Resolution of the Council and the Member States meeting in the Council on Human Rights, Democracy and Development,' 28 November, 1991 [Doc. No. 10107/91], Brussels: European Commission.
Council of the European Union (1998), 'Common Position of 25 May, 1998 concerning human rights, democratic principles, the rule of law and good governance in Africa' (98/350/CFSP), Official Journal of the European Communities, L 158/1, 2 June.
Council of the European Union and the European Commission (2000), 'The European Community's Development Policy – Statement by the Council and the Commission', Brussels: European Commission.
Council of the European Union (2003), 'EU Annual Human Rights Report for 2003', 10 October, Brussels: Council of the European Union.
Council of the European Union and the European Commission (2003), 'Strengthening the EU's Relations with the Arab World', 4 December, available at: http://www.medea.be/files/UE_monde_arabe_12_2003_EN.pdf
Council of the European Union (2005), 'The European Consensus on Development,' joint statement by the Council and the Representatives of the Governments of

the member states meeting within the Council, the European Parliament and the Commission: November, Brussels: Council of the European Union.

Crawford, Gordon (1994), 'Promoting Democracy, Human Rights and Good Governance through Development Aid: A Comparative Study of the Policies of Four Northern Donors', Working Papers on Democratisation, no. 1, Leeds: Centre for Democratisation Studies, University of Leeds.

Crawford, Gordon, (1996), 'Whither Lomé? The Mid-Term Review and the Decline of Partnership', *Journal of Modern African Studies*, vol. 34, no. 3, pp. 503-518.

Crawford, Gordon (1998), 'Human Rights and Democracy in EU Development Co-operation: Towards Fair and Equal Treatment', in M.R. Lister (ed.), *European Development Policy*, Basingstoke: Macmillan, pp. 131-78.

Crawford, Gordon (2000), 'European Union Development Co-operation and the Promotion of Democracy', in P. Burnell (ed.), *Democracy Assistance: International Co-operation for Democratization*, London: Frank Cass, pp. 90-127.

Danish Ministry of Foreign Affairs / Danida (2000), 'Evaluation of Danish Support to Promotion of Human Rights and Democratisation 1990-1998: Vol. 6 Ghana', Copenhagen: Danish Ministry of Foreign Affairs.

Danish Ministry of Foreign Affairs / Danida (2003), 'Ghana: Thematic Programme Support Document – Programme for Good Governance and Human Rights', Accra: Royal Danish Embassy.

David, Dominique (2000), 'Forty Years of Europe-ACP Relationship', *The Courier*, special issue on the Cotonou Agreement, September, Brussels: European Commission.

Emerging Market Economics Ltd. (2002), 'Ghana Country Strategy Paper 1998-2001: End of Cycle Review – "Recognising Reality"', January 2, Accra: UK Department for International Development.

European Commission (2001), 'The European Union's Role in Promoting Human Rights and Democratization in Third Countries', Communication from the Commission to the Council, COM(2001) 252 final, 8 May, Brussels: European Commission.

European Commission (2003), 'Governance and Development', Communication from the Commission to the Council, the European Parliament and the European Economic and Social Committee, COM(2003) 615 final, 20 October, Brussels: European Commission.

European Commission (2003), 'EU relations with Ghana', updated 17 November, available at http://europa.eu.int/comm/development/body/country

European Commission (2004a), 'EU Donor Atlas, Mapping Official Development Assistance', May, Brussels: European Commission.

European Commission (2004b), 'European Neighbourhood Policy – Strategy Paper', Communication from the Commission to the Council, COM(2004) 373 final, 12 May, Brussels: European Commission.
European Commission (2005a), 'EU Strategy for Africa: Towards a Euro-African pact to accelerate Africa's development', Communication from the Commission to the Council, the European Parliament and the European Economic and Social Committee, COM(2005) 489 final, 12 October, Brussels: European Commission.
European Commission (2005b), 'Implementing and Promoting the European Neighbourhood Policy', Communication to the Commission:, 22 November, SEC(2005) 1521, Brussels: European Commission.
European Commission (2005c), 'Information Note on the Revision of the Cotonou Agreement', available at http://ec.europa.eu/comm/development/body/cotonou/pdf/negociation_20050407_en.pdf.
European Commission (2006), 'EU Donor Atlas 2006, Volume I, Mapping Official Development Assistance', February, Brussels: European Commission.
European Council (2003), 'European Security Strategy: A Secure Europe in a Better World' adopted by European Council meeting in Brussels on 12 December.
European Union, Delegation of the European Commission (2004), 'Cooperation between the Republic of Ghana and the European Union: Annual Report 2003', Accra: Delegation of the European Commission.
Friedman, Milton (1962), *Capitalism and Freedom*, Chicago: University of Chicago Press.
German Technical Co-operation (GTZ) (2003), 'Ghana: Priority Area Strategy Paper – Democracy, Civil Society and Public Administration', draft, November, mimeo.
German Technical Co-operation (GTZ) (2004), untitled document on 'Local Governance and Poverty Reduction Support Programme', mimeo.
German Technical Co-operation (GTZ) website: http://www.gtz.de/themen/political-reforms/english.
German Technical Co-operation (GTZ) Ghana website: http://www.gtz.de/laender/ebene3.asp?ProjectId=55&spr=2&Thema=8.
Gyimah-Boadi, E. (2001), 'A Peaceful Turnover in Ghana', *Journal of Democracy*, vol.12, no.2, pp.103-17.
Gyimah-Boadi, E. and Kwabena Amoah Awuah Mensah (2003), 'The Growth of Democracy in Ghana Despite Economic Dissatisfaction: A Power Alternation Bonus?', Afrobarometer Working Paper No.28, available at http//www.afrobarometer.org.
Leftwich, Adrian (1994), 'Governance, the State and the Politics of Development', *Development and Change*, vol.25, pp.363-86.

Lyons, Terrence (1999), 'Ghana's Elections: A Major Step Forward', in Larry Diamond and Marc F. Plattner (eds.), *Democratization in Africa*, Baltimore: John Hopkins University Press, pp.157-69.

Map Consult Ltd. (2002), 'Good Governance in Ghana: Lessons Learnt from Donor Support to Governance in Ghana 1992-2002', Accra: Royal Danish Embassy.

Munck, Ronaldo (1994), 'Democracy and Development: Deconstruction and Debates', in L. Sklair (ed.), *Capitalism and Development*, London: Routledge, pp.21-39.

Olsen, Gorm Rye (2002), 'The European Union: An Ad Hoc Policy with a Low Priority', in P.J. Schraeder (ed.), *Exporting Democracy: Rhetoric vs. Reality*, Boulder, CO: Lynne Rienner, pp. 131-45.

Olsen, Gorm Rye (2003), 'The Africa Policy of the European Union: Challenges to Traditional Policy Options, Opportunities for New Choices', paper delivered at the European Consortium for Political Research (ECPR) conference, Marburg, Germany, 18-21 September.

Oquaye, Mike (2001), 'Government and Politics in Contemporary Ghana (1992-1999) – A Study', Accra: Africa Governance Institute.

Owusu, Francis (2003), 'Pragmatism and the Gradual Shift from Dependency to Neo-liberalism: The World Bank, African Leaders and Development Policy in Africa', *World Development*, vol.31, no.10, pp.1655-72.

Republic of Ghana – European Community (2002), 'Country Strategy Paper and Indicative Programme for the Period 2003-2007', Accra: European Commission.

Robinson, Mark (1994), 'Governance, Democracy and Conditionality: NGOs and the New Policy Agenda', in A. Clayton (ed.) *Governance, Democracy and Conditionality: What Role for NGOs?* Oxford: INTRAC.

Salama Clara Mira and Stephen Dearden (2001), 'The Cotonou Agreement', European Development Policy Study Group Discussion Paper No. 20, February, available at http://www.edpsg.org/Documents/Dp20.doc.

Smith, Daniel A. (2002), 'Consolidating Democracy? The structural underpinnings of Ghana's 2000 elections', in: *Journal of Modern African Studies*, vol. 40, no. 4, pp. 621-50.

UK Department for International Development Ghana (2002) Country Assistance Plan', draft, November, mimeo, Accra: DFID Ghana.

World Bank (2004), *World Development Report 2005: A Better Investment Climate for Everyone*, Washington DC: World Bank.

World Development Movement (2001), 'Policies to Roll-Back the State and Privatise: Poverty Reduction Strategy Papers Investigated', available at http://www.wdm.org.uk/cambriefs/debt/rollback.pdf.

Youngs, Richard (ed.) (2006), *Survey of European Democracy Promotion Policies 2000-2006*, Madrid: FRIDE.
Zack-Williams, Tunde and Giles Mohan (2005), 'Africa from SAPs to PRSP: Plus Ca Change, Plus C'est La Meme Chose', in: *Review of African Political Economy* 106, pp. 501-03.

8 A Critical Assessment of Proposed EU-ACP Economic Partnership Agreements

Oliver Morrissey, Chris Milner and Andrew McKay

1. Introduction

The European Union (EU) has a long history of providing trade preferences to selected developing countries – the African, Caribbean, and Pacific (ACP) former colonies – under the Lomé conventions. Irrespective of the question of how beneficial these preferences actually were (they are viewed by many commentators to be of limited value, e.g., Langhammer, 1992), a core feature was that they were granted to selected countries that were not required to grant trade concessions to the EU in return. Such non-reciprocated preferential access to the EU for ACP countries was challenged under the rules of the World Trade Organization (WTO). Preferences granted to specific developing countries can only be maintained in a General Agreement on Tariffs and Trade (GATT)- or WTO-consistent manner if there is reciprocity. In order to continue preferences, the EU has proposed introducing reciprocity through the establishment of a series of economic partnership agreements (EPAs), under which the EU and regional groupings of ACP countries offer reciprocal trade preferences to each other. The principle of EPAs is included in the Cotonou Agreement for future EU-ACP relations. Negotiations between the EU and ACP regional groups formally started in 2003 and enter what is intended to be the final stage in March 2007, with a view to agreements being implemented from 2008. Therefore it is timely to consider the potential impact of EPAs on regional groupings of ACP countries as, if agreed, they are due to be phased in after 2007.

Three features of the Cotonou Agreement are of particular relevance. First, the EU argued from the outset of the negotiations that groups of ACP countries form regional integration arrangements among themselves and these regional groups negotiate with the EU. The EU did not want to negotiate an EPA with the ACP as a whole nor with individual ACP countries. Second, the EPA is reciprocal so the regional ACP groups ultimately have to remove tariffs and barriers to imports from the EU. Third, EU aid programmes will be linked, in an as yet unspecified way, with the EPAs (there is also a promise of a development agenda and that investment from the EU will be attached). The analysis in this chapter concentrates on the first two of these features.

At face value, EPAs offer little to ACP countries. Least-developed ACP countries already qualify for preferential access under the EU's Everything But Arms (EBA) initiative. These least developed would be granting tariff-free access to the EU in return for preferences to which they are already entitled, although the conditions of access may be less restrictive and more assured under an EPA (the EBA, for example, could be unilaterally revoked by the EU). Developing ACP countries, however, are not entitled to preferences and are, to the extent that they compete in the same products, at a disadvantage relative to least-developed countries. For such countries, preferential access to the EU plus any net benefit from regional integration would have to be weighed against the cost of giving the EU preferential access to their own regional market. The approach outlined in section three is designed to evaluate these effects.

The ACP countries appear fully aware that EPAs offer questionable benefits to them and were reluctant at the outset to begin active negotiations, originally scheduled to start in September 2003. The Pacific islands argued that they would not be ready to begin negotiations until November 2004 and the Commission accepted that they face particular capacity constraints. The Caribbean probably made the most initial progress of any ACP region by at least putting in place some regional negotiating machinery. The Economic and Monetary Union of West Africa, (UEMOA) and the Economic Commission of West African States (ECOWAS) actually walked out of the initial negotiations in late 2003, and demanded an EU aid commitment up-front before re-entering negotiations. A specific problem for most African countries is that they do not yet know which countries will come together to negotiate as a region with the EU. Most existing regional trade agreements in Africa are, at best, weak. Thus, in addition to the administrative costs of negotiating with the EU, African countries face additional costs (economic and political) of forming effective regional trade agreements. A further complication has been that some African countries are members of more than one regional grouping that is negotiating with the EU, e.g, Tanzania and Zambia are potentially members of the East and Southern Africa Region (ESA) and the Southern African Development Community (SADC).

The EU has acknowledged that ACP countries needed to assess the potential impact of an EPA in order to be prepared for negotiations. The European Commission financed and commissioned studies of the impact of EPAs on ACP regions. As completed studies are not publicly available, there are few assessments in the literature of the impact of EPAs. Karingi et al., (2005) use a combination of general and partial equilibrium modelling and find that the potential impacts, especially in terms of revenue foregone and adjustment costs, will be costly for African countries. This paper draws on the work of a much earlier study, also commissioned by the European Commission for a sub-set of the negotiating regions (see McKay et al., 2000), to provide a relatively simple and tractable partial equilibrium method to identify the trade, revenue, and welfare impacts for individual countries. A more detailed version of the empirical evidence discussed here can be found in McKay et al., (2005).

The aim of this chapter is to consider the trade and welfare implications of the EPA proposal for ACP countries, both from first principles (i.e. in theory) and empirically. For the former we extend the analytical framework used by Panagariya (1998) to investigate the effects on the ACP members of a regional integration agreement (RIA) of moving from non-preferential to preferential treatment of EU imports. For the empirical analysis, we apply the analytical framework to estimate the trade and welfare effects on the East African Co-operation (EAC) comprising Kenya, Tanzania, and Uganda. The EAC countries signed a treaty to establish a Customs Union in November 1999 and agreed to negotiate as a block (within the WTO and with the EU) in April 2002, although subsequently Tanzania, at least, has indicated its intention to negotiate with other Southern African countries. The EAC captures a feature common to most potential RIAs amongst ACP countries in that most members are least-developed whilst at least one member is classed as a developing country (Kenya in this case). Thus, our results can be considered as illustrative of a more general case.

The remainder of the chapter is organised as follows. In section 2 we further explore the origins and institutional context of the EPA proposal. Section 3 presents a simple partial equilibrium method to analyse the potential trade and welfare effects of introducing an EPA between a large (EU) and a small (ACP) RIA. This is followed in section 4 by an application of the model, with estimates of the (hypothetical) impact of an EPA on the EAC. The estimates are indicative of the direction and order of magnitude of effects for any grouping of ACP countries. Finally, section 5 sets out the implications of the analysis and summary conclusions.

2. The Nature of EPAs

A partnership agreement between the EU and 71 ACP partners states was concluded in February 2000 (the Cotonou Agreement), covering various dimensions including economic relations, aid programmes, and trade co-operation. On the latter, the general principle of a WTO-compatible EPA arrangement for the future was agreed. The EU applied to the WTO for an eight-year waiver to provide a transition period for the arrangement and this was granted at the Doha Ministerial. Over this period the EU and ACP states are to negotiate and agree a new WTO-compliant trade agreement, which would then be implemented over a transitional period starting by 2008 at the latest. Such an arrangement could allow asymmetry, in other words more gradual liberalisation by ACP countries (the EU proposed a further 10-15 year transition period before the EU could export duty free to ACP countries in an EPA).

The EU's long-term aim to establish free trade areas with the ACP regions as a replacement for the Lomé agreements was to be approached in several stages. A key stage was the negotiation of EPAs with groups of ACP countries already engaged in a regional integration process. The Cotonou Agreement formed the basis for negotiation over the period 2000-2005 to set up the different regional partnership agreements. As regards the long-term aim of EPAs, GATT's article XXIV does allow for the negotiation of customs unions or free trade areas that offer preferential treatment to member countries, subject to certain conditions. The most important of these is that the free trade area should 'eliminate duties and other restrictive regulations of commerce ... on substantially all the trade between constituent territories in products originating in such territories' (GATT article XXIV, paragraph 8(b)).

There appeared to be no agreed definition of what 'substantially all the trade' means in practice. Qualitative and quantitative aspects are important. On the former, exclusion of whole sectors such as agriculture or textiles was unlikely to be acceptable. On the latter, full liberalisation of 80-90 percent of trade between the partners was likely to be required (although it may be acceptable for ACP countries to liberalise as little as 70 percent of trade, at least initially), but this raises a number of measurement questions. For example, should the quantitative target refer to the number of tariffs or value of trade before or after liberalisation?

Any interim arrangements leading up to the full establishment of the free trade areas 'shall include a plan and schedule for the formation of such a customs union or such a free trade area within a reasonable length of time' (GATT article XXIV, paragraph 5(c)). In this context, 'a reasonable length of time' is likely to mean not more than ten years. This implies that if an EPA is to begin in 2007 full liberalisation of 'substantially all the trade' should be achieved by 2017. Within this time period there do not appear to be any symmetry requirements; the ACP partner countries can liberalise much more slowly than the EU, subject to them meeting the 'reasonable length of time' criterion. Given the present non-reciprocity of trade relations between the EU and ACP countries, some asymmetry is likely to be desirable (and has been accepted in principle by the EU).

However, before they begin these negotiations with the EU, the ACP countries have, in effect, to form themselves into regional integration arrangements (RIAs). While there are theoretical arguments that integration can contribute to growth and development, notably by increasing the size of the market and attracting foreign direct investment (FDI), most of the evidence for beneficial effects of RIAs relate to integration among developed or middle-income countries (Schiff and Winters, 2003). The experience of low-income countries with integration is not very encouraging, with few cases of sustained deep integration, especially in Africa (Lyakurwa et al., 1997). East Africa is a good example of the problems even where the political will exists: Kenya is relatively more industrialised and exports manufactures to Tanzania and Uganda, whereas the letter two export little to Kenya or each other. This reflects the general problem that most of the benefits accrue to the largest and richest member, while few economic benefits accrue to the poorest members. This explains why deep integration has been difficult to achieve or sustain.

West Africa provides an example of where the difficulties are even greater. The EU is negotiating with the Economic Commission of West African States (ECOWAS). However, the level of integration within ECOWAS is minimal, especially among the Anglophone countries (the Francophone countries have fairly deep integration among themselves). Furthermore, Nigeria is a dominant economy while Liberia and Sierra Leone are unstable. The EU proposals for an EPA with the region therefore are imposing a burden on the countries. Not only are they under pressure to negotiate an RIA they may have little commitment to, but also they have to devote the limited time of their few trade officials to negotiations on three fronts – regional, EU, and WTO. This is a high cost given the limited institutional capacity.

Even if all the ACP regions manage to form RIAs, there will be many negotiating difficulties. Specifically, the requirement to liberalise 'substantially all trade' refers to the RIA, but individual members may disagree on which sensitive products should be excluded. The larger countries in the RIA have an interest in protecting their markets for manufactures in the smaller countries. In contrast, the smaller countries wish to protect whatever viable domestic manufacturing they have. The domestic political considerations that cause strain in agreeing an RIA are exacerbated in negotiations of an EPA with the EU.

The EU may counter that these problems can be addressed in the long time period allowed for the ACP countries to liberalise imports from the EU, during which period increased aid and FDI from the EU can benefit the ACP countries. However, it is worth noting that ten years is not really a long time for complex negotiations. For example, negotiations of a customs union for the EAC have progressed very slowly over the past five years (and progress in ECOWAS has been even slower). We will return to this in the final section. In the next section we turn to quantifying the possible welfare effect of trade integration between particular ACP groupings and the EU.

3. Modelling Framework

The theoretical framework for analysing the economic (welfare) effect of regional integration is well established (e.g., Balassa, 1974; Lyakurwa et al., 1997). In the standard approach, members remove barriers to trade between themselves and impose a common tariff on imports from outside the RIA. Two effects are of particular importance. The first is trade creation as inefficient production by domestic firms in a member country is displaced by tariff-free imports by more efficient producers in another member country. This is an economic benefit, as welfare is increased through a more efficient allocation of production within the RIA. The second effect is trade diversion; this imposes a welfare loss as the common external tariff diverts trade from more efficient extra-regional suppliers to less efficient intra-regional suppliers. In general, integration increases welfare provided that trade creation is greater than trade diversion. As domestic producers in low-income countries tend to be less efficient than producers in the rest of the world, an RIA rarely increases welfare because 'RIAs between small economies are likely to be trade diverting' (Schiff and Winters, 2003: 263). Thus, in general, integration amongst ACP countries would not give rise to static (welfare) gains. There may be dynamic gains if the increased size of the regional market encourages competition and efficiency gains and attracts FDI.

The situation is complicated in analysing EPAs as the RIA of the ACP countries then integrates with the (larger) EU. To analyse this situation we extend the model of Panagariya (1998) and examine the welfare effects of an EPA from the perspective of a small home country member (denoted H) of the RIA. Assume the larger partner country (R) in the RIA has an upward sloping supply curve and there are two extra-regional suppliers, the EU and the rest of the world (ROW), both with infinitely elastic supply curves. The analysis is partial equilibrium in nature, markets are assumed to be perfectly competitive, and there is perfect substitutability between imported and domestically produced import substitutes (allowing for imperfect substitutability would probably require a general equilibrium framework). The assumptions of perfect competition and homogeneity are reasonably appropriate in the case of agriculture and primary products. Although less appropriate in the case of manufacturers, for ACP countries fairly standardised and undifferentiated products are common.

Assume that H and R have already formed an RIA and that it is small relative to the EU and ROW. The possible situation is illustrated in figure 1 (for a given product): D_H represents the home country's demand for imports, S_R the partner's (upward sloping) supply of exports (to H), and S_{EU} and S_W are the respective extra-regional export supply functions. As the EU and ROW have infinitely elastic supply they can supply at constant cost (prices P_{EU} and P_W respectively). In the case of figure 1 we assume for expositional convenience that $P_{EU} > P_W$, therefore subsequent discriminatory trade policies by the RIA towards the outside countries can have both trade-creating and diverting effects. We also assume, for convenience, that the EU can meet all demand at P_{EU} (i.e., S_{EU} is below S_R). Other possibilities will be considered later.

Figure 1 **Effect of an EU-ACP EPA**

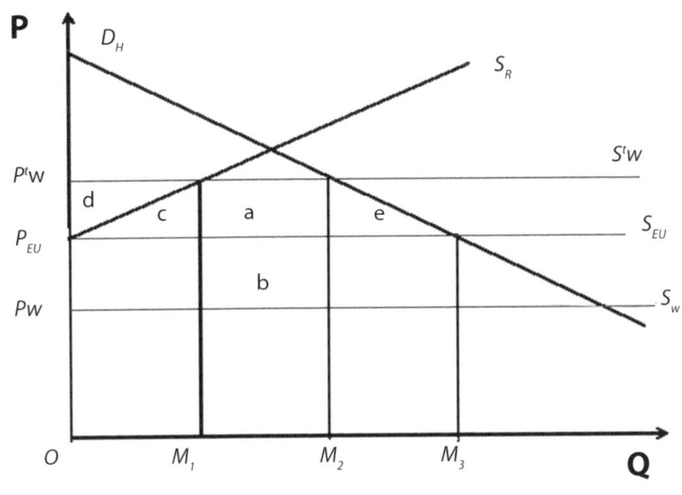

Initially, the RIA has a non-discriminatory (ad valorem) tariff (t) on extra-regional imports, where $P^t_W = P_W (1 + t)$ and P^t_{EU} is not shown as the EU is assumed for the present to be the higher cost supplier prior to the EPA. Initially, H imports OM_2 in total, with OM_1 coming from R and M_1M_2 from ROW. For convenience we assume no domestic production capability and can define welfare (W and change in welfare denoted ΔW) by reference to consumer surplus with respect to the import demand function, D_H. Thus W_{RIA} for H is given by the consumer surplus triangle (the area below D_H and above S^t_W) plus the tariff revenue on extra-regional imports (area $a + b$).

When the EPA with the EU is formed, the RIA continues to impose tariff t on imports from ROW but allows duty free imports from the EU. The relevant supply price is now P_{EU} with the total quantity of imports expanding from OM_2 to OM_3 and imports coming now wholly from the EU. There are strictly three components of this trade-welfare effect of the EPA: a consumption expansion effect M_2M_3, a trade diversion effect M_1M_2, and a trade creation effect OM_1. The first of these is straightforward as the lower price ($P_{EU} < P^t_W$) allows increased consumption (with consumer surplus gain, due to this increase, of triangle e). The last two effects deserve explanation.

In standard RIA analysis trade diversion relates to efficient extra-regional suppliers being displaced by less efficient intra-regional suppliers. The EPA, however, diverts between extra-regional suppliers; M_1M_2 is imported from the less efficient EU rather than the ROW. The resource cost of this is represented by the area b, with total tariff revenue lost by the home country being area ($a + b$). However, as imports M_1M_2 are cheaper ($P_{EU} < P^t_W$) there is a consumer surplus gain of area a to add to the consumption gain of area e. The less inefficient the EU relative to ROW, the smaller the costs of trade diversion (area b is smaller as P_{EU} is 'lowered' towards P_W). This increases the probability of a welfare-improving EPA, if $(a + b)<(a + e)$, or $b < e$. If $S_{EU} = S_W$ (prices converge), or if the EU is more efficient than the rest of the world, then the EPA tends toward the 'free trade' outcome. In this case there is no resource loss b and the consumption gain e is much larger (although the tariff revenue loss is still $a + b$).

Trade creation, in standard RIA analysis, usually describes inefficient home production being replaced by more efficient intra-regional production. In the case illustrated, however, the EPA involves the replacement of imports from regional member R by more efficient imports from the EU. The resource saving on this trade creation (or import source substitution) effect is shown by area c in figure 1. This and the loss in producer surplus for exporters in R (area d) allows consumer surplus on this component of the trade effect of the EPA to increase by area (c + d). This benefit (area c) is increased the less inefficient the EU is relative to ROW, and is maximised if $P_{EU} = P_W$.

In the case illustrated in figure 1 we assumed the EU was less efficient than ROW but more efficient than R. If we assume $P_{EU} < P_W$ the situation would be different, as initially all extra-regional imports would be from the EU. As indicated above, there would be no trade diversion resource loss (there would be a tariff revenue loss). The trade creation effect would depend on the position of S_{EU} relative to S_R. Figure 1 depicts the extreme where the EU replaces all imports from R. Another extreme would be where R is the globally efficient producer. In this case H derives all the welfare gains in forming the RIA, importing wholly from R (standard trade creation gains). An intermediate position is possible – after the EPA, R may be able to meet part of H's import demand, with the EU meeting the rest – but would be difficult to identify empirically.

As is often the case with theory, the welfare implications for H of shifting from the RIA to the EPA are ambiguous: the consumption and trade creation effects increase welfare whereas the trade diversion effect reduces welfare, i.e., $W = (c + d + e) - b$. The more efficient the EU is relative to other suppliers (ROW and R) the more likely is the net effect to be positive. There will always be a tariff revenue loss ($a + b$) but if the EU is the globally efficient producer the net welfare gain may exceed even this loss. However, welfare is not cash and ACP governments may expect compensation for the revenue loss. It will be convenient to assume that the EPA includes a net addition of aid at least sufficient to cover the revenue loss (and this loss is a useful guide to the additional aid that may be requested in negotiations). Consequently, in the next section we focus on estimating the welfare (trade) effects.

So far we only considered the welfare effect from the perspective of H, which can be interpreted as the perspective of all 'small' ACP members of the RIA. However, there will also be a large member (R) that is likely to lose some of its intra-regional market share and some of its domestic market to imports from the EU. In figure 1, replace D_H with D_R and treat S_R as domestic supply to illustrate one such case. The trade diversion and consumption expansion effects are basically the same, but the source substitution is standard trade creation as imports from the EU (OM_1) replace less efficient domestic production so that d is a welfare loss. Ignoring the revenue loss, $W = (d + c + a + e) - (b + d)$ and there is also a loss of intra-regional exports. The net effect could well be a welfare loss, but there is a potential benefit of preferential access to the EU (H-countries do not get this benefit as we assume they are least developed and already entitled to preferential access). Thus, ACP countries that are not least developed will have to evaluate the benefit of preferential access to the EU and consumer surplus gains against the costs of increased imports (loss of producer surplus and tariff revenue) and loss of regional market share under an EPA.

4. Illustrating the Welfare Effects: An EU-EAC EPA

We use the methodology set out above to estimate trade and welfare effects of an EU-EAC EPA on members of the EAC. This is a convenient example as it is a 'small' RIA, we only have to consider three countries, but has a pattern of intra-regional and EU trade typical of many ACP regions. In 1995, the year for which our estimates are based, the EU was their major trading partner. For Kenya, 30 percent of imports were from the EU, but less than one per cent from other EAC countries; just over 30 percent of exports were to the EU, but almost 10% were to the EAC. In Tanzania, 52 percent of imports were from the EU and almost five per cent from the EAC (mostly Kenya); 40 percent of exports were to the EU and about five per cent to EAC. The EU accounted for 30 percent and the EAC (again mostly Kenya) for 22 percent of Ugandan imports, but the EU absorbed 36 percent of exports and the EAC four per cent.

In volume terms, Kenyan exports to the EAC were more than twice the level of Tanzanian and Ugandan intra-regional exports combined. Kenyan exports to the EU, however, were about equal to combined Tanzanian and Ugandan exports to the EU. Intra-regional exports are clearly important to Kenya, while the EU market is very important to all countries. The pattern is different for imports. In volume terms, Tanzania imports as much from the EU as Kenya and Uganda combined. The volume of Kenyan imports from the EAC is negligible compared to that of Tanzania, and especially Uganda. We have the typical pattern: the regional market is important to the exports of the 'big' country and the imports of the small countries; the EU is the major trade partner of all countries. Results for the EAC should therefore be illustrative of the impact of EPAs with other ACP groups.

For convenience we assume full liberalisation of trade flows in both directions, and as such we represent a 'long-run' maximum welfare impact (sensitive sectors are discussed below). The analytical framework in the previous section could be conceived of as the aggregate picture for a homogenous single sector economy, where all three trade effects associated with a move from an RIA to an EPA occur simultaneously. In practice there is both product and tariff rate heterogeneity to accommodate in any application. As a result, in specific sectors there may only be one of the trade effects illustrated in the previous sector. Given data constraints, in particular about production and export supply conditions and elasticities within the EAC region, we adopt a framework that distinguishes between those sectors where the ROW is the dominant supplier and those where the EU is the dominant supplier prior to EPA formation. We estimate three particular cases (see the appendix for the formulae used, and McKay et al., 2000 for details).

Consumption effects only: In those sectors where the EU is globally efficient and therefore the dominant supplier (accounts for more than half of imports) to a particular EAC market prior to the formation of the EPA, we assume that only consumption effects would follow from the EPA. In terms of figure 1 this is equivalent to assuming that S_W lies above S_{EU} and that there is no competitive regional supply capability (i.e., no S_R). Let $P^t_{EU} = P^t_W$ so that after the EPA $P_{EU} = P_W$ prevails and we estimate area *e* and the revenue loss relative to the existing EU import levels.

Trade diversion with consumption effects: For those trade sectors in EAC imports where the ROW is the dominant supplier, we are constrained by data limitations to make further assumptions about the competitiveness of EU supply to the EAC market. If we assume $P_{EU} < P^t_W$ then, given a constant cost technology over the relevant range, the EPA will divert all imports for the ROW to the EU. This gives the upper limit of the value of trade diversion. For these sectors there will also be consumption effects. The same general approach is used here as above. As we do not have information about where the price of EU imports may lie between P_W and P^t_W, we assume that on average P_{EU} lies halfway between the two. It is this case that is depicted in figure 1.

Trade creation with consumption effects: For those sectors where other EAC countries are not relatively minor suppliers (i.e., provide greater than 25 percent of imports) we estimate the effects of trade creation (i.e., source substitution) with consumption effects in analogous fashion to the trade diversion case. We assume now that the EU is a more efficient supplier than the rest of the world (if it is not, we would have a variant of the trade diversion case). If the duty-free supply price from the EAC lies over the relevant range between P_W and P_{EU} then all of the current imports from the EAC to the home country will be replaced by more efficient production from the EU. This gives the maximum value of the trade created for the EU by this deflection from EAC sources. In order to estimate consumption effects in these sectors, we assume that the price from the EAC is as high as the tariff-inclusive price from the EU. In this case the pre-EPA tariff rate against EU imports provides an (upper) estimate of the extent to which the import price can fall as a result of the EPA.

Implementation

Our EPA scenario is a relatively simple one. We use 1995 values to establish the baseline and assume the EAC forms an RIA with zero internal tariffs (the revenue loss on intra-regional imports from doing this is included under the trade creation case). Then, we assume imports from the EU are allowed tariff-free. Using prevailing trade patterns, we identify products in each of the three cases to derive estimates of the value of trade effects due to consumption, trade diversion, and trade creation. The corresponding revenue and welfare effects are then aggregated.

Given data availability, detailed analysis is only possible for Tanzania and Uganda (see McKay et al., 2000). The import data is obtained from locally published trade statistics aggregated to obtain EAC-EU and EAC-ROW trade at the two-digit HS (harmonised system) level. Tariff data are obtained from two sources. Figures relating to Tanzania are calculated directly from customs records as the ratio of duty collected to total imports. For Uganda (and Kenya) we used data from the scheduled tariff. In this sense, the Tanzanian estimates are somewhat more reliable.

It is evident from the trade data that Kenya is the dominant intra-regional supplier. For example, Kenya supplies all products where intra-regional imports by Tanzania account for over 25 percent of the market. A similar pattern emerges with regard to Ugandan imports from the EAC. Kenya is the source of over 80 percent of imports to Tanzania and Uganda in several commodities. It follows that the 'source substitution' effects of an EPA could be considerable. This is realistic for Tanzania and Uganda as their exports within EAC are not generally of products that compete with imports from the EU. Both countries would, in principle, benefit from the EPA by being able to avail of cheaper imports of intermediate and raw material inputs from the EU. The situation is different for Kenya. In general, allowing for differences in product quality, imports from the EU could displace Kenyan exports to other EAC members (and indeed displace Kenyan local production).

Table 1 summarises the estimation results. In those sectors where the EU is already the dominant supplier, we allow only for the possibility of trade creation via consumption expansion (the first set of results). There may also be trade diversion

Table 1 **Summary of Trade, Revenue, and Welfare Effects (Percent change relative to 1995 values)**

		Tanzania	Uganda
a)	*Consumption effects only*		
	Imports from EU	11.1	10.3
	Tariff revenue	- 41.1	- 16.4
	Welfare (% base imports)	0.81	0.84
b)	*Trade diversion and consumption effects*		
	Imports from EU	65.5	122.3
	Tariff revenue	- 31.7	- 44.2
	Welfare (% base imports)	- 2.7	- 8.7
c)	*Trade creation and consumption effects*		
	Imports from EU	1.2	55.5
	Tariff revenue	- 0.04	- 8.5
	Welfare (% base imports)	--	3.2
d)	*Overall effect*		
	Value of imports	77.6	188.6
	Tariff revenue	- 73.2	- 69.1
	Net welfare effect (%1995 GDP)	- 0.5	-0.3

Notes: Values are given as percentage change relative to the base (1995) value of imports from the EU or tariff revenue, as indicated, and of GDP in the case of the net welfare effect. Individual values may not add up exactly to the overall totals due to rounding.

effects in these sectors. Given that maximum possible levels of trade diversion are identified in other sectors, this will be an offsetting source of measurement error. The EPA is estimated to increase imports from the EU in these sectors over base levels by about 11 percent in the case of Tanzania and 10 percent in the case of Uganda. This would benefit local consumers considerably (a positive welfare effect), but the direct loss of tariff revenue on imports (base and additional) from the EU is considerable. The base volume of imports from the EU for Tanzania is about twice the level for Uganda, so this could reduce Tanzanian tariff revenue by over 40 percent. There would only be limited scope to recoup this revenue by shifting to non-trade taxation (even if the latter were more efficient). Thus, although welfare is increased for both countries (area *e* in figure 1), the revenue loss will more than offset this.

The second set of results show that the largest effects are associated with diverting to the EU trade in products for which the ROW was initially the dominant supplier. Although the initial value of ROW imports of these products was similar for the two countries, Tanzania had base imports from the EU almost twice the level of Uganda. EU exports to Uganda more than double while those to Tanzania increase by almost two-thirds. Our approach allows for the welfare gains from consumption effects, but this welfare-raising trade expansion is swamped by the potential welfare cost of trade diversion. The potential loss of tariff revenue is again very high.

The approach estimates the maximum potential for trade diversion in these sectors. This potential will not be reached if the EU does not have an export capability, or if EU suppliers experience increasing costs or a cost disadvantage relative to the ROW that exceeds the non-preferential external tariff of the EAC. On the other hand, if the EU is almost as efficient as the ROW, the welfare cost (area *b*) may be over-stated. Note, however, that the scope for trade diversion might also increase prior to the establishment of an EPA if the external tariff is lowered in the process of creating an EAC customs union, and some intra-EAC trade is deflected to the ROW. Thus although the estimated value of trade diversion in table 1 is likely to be upwardly biased, the results certainly identify the potential for a net trade-diverting EPA, which is welfare and tariff-revenue lowering.

The third set of results identifies the scope for trade creation involving source substitution from less efficient EAC (Kenya in all cases) to more efficient EU suppliers as a result of an EPA. For those sectors where there is significant intra-EAC trade only we identify the maximum potential for trade deflection; again a potential that will not be reached if EU suppliers experience increasing costs or are not competitive with EAC suppliers. If the effect of the creation of an EAC custom union – full liberalisation of intra-regional trade and changes in the external tariff – is to increase intra-regional trade, then the scope for trade deflection may be increased. The potential for trade deflection is particularly significant for Uganda, given its current heavy dependence on Kenya for imports in some sectors. Consumers would gain substantially if under an EPA there was scope to shift to lower-cost EU suppliers. Indeed, despite a significant potential loss of tariff revenue (almost 10 percent), the net positive welfare effect from this source is potentially much greater than from consumption effects of tariff reduction against EU imports. The effects are negligible for Tanzania as it does not import significantly from other EAC countries.

The final set of results reports the overall effect. Increased imports from the EU are predicted for both Tanzania (a 78 percent increase) and Uganda (189 percent), but this is associated with large potential tariff revenue losses (roughly 70 percent in both cases). Although consumer and national welfare increases as a result of trade creation and consumption effects, the potentially large costs of trade diverted from efficient non-EU sources means that net welfare in both countries is likely to fall as a result of the static trade effects of an EU-EAC EPA.

In line with other evidence from empirical trade policy analysis the net welfare effects are small relative to GDP – no more than 0.5 percent in either case, less for Uganda because it benefits from trade creation. We exclude from the estimation procedure those sectors where EU exports to Africa are relatively small. This reduces the trade and welfare effects, but not markedly so. One would anticipate similar welfare effects relative to GDP in Kenya, although in the case of Kenya there are export losses to the other EAC members without any consumption gains as Kenya does not import large amounts from other EAC countries.

The net effects, of course, tend to obscure larger potential distribution effects within countries. Consumers gain significantly as a result of trade creation and consumption effects but at the expense of local producers and in particular government tax revenue. As table 1 shows, the base estimates of potential tariff revenue losses associated with the EPA are non-negligible. Although this is a potential, not necessarily actual, revenue loss (in the case of Uganda, we are identifying what could have been collected, given scheduled tariff rates on imports from the EU rather than actual collection values), it has important budgetary implications.

Identifying Sensitive Sectors

In order to identify potential adjustment implications of an EPA, we set out the sectors where major potential trade effects are indicated in table 2. The two 'consumption effects' columns identify, respectively, those sectors in Tanzania and Uganda where local producers can anticipate greater import competition from EU suppliers – these will be sensitive sectors in the countries. The two 'trade creation' columns identify those markets in which Kenyan producers might anticipate greater competition from EU suppliers; this increased competition being particularly important in the Ugandan market. These will be sensitive sectors for Kenya. The middle two columns identify the sectors where there are the greatest market opportunities for EU suppliers to displace ROW suppliers.

As the requirement is to liberalise 'substantially all trade' this allows for particularly sensitive products in EAC countries to be excluded. The pattern suggests that EAC countries would differ somewhat in the sectors they consider sensitive.

Table 2 Sectors Subject to Potential Major Trade Effects

	Consumption effects		*Trade diversion*		*Trade creation*	
Sector	Tanzania	Uganda	Tanzania	Uganda	Tanzania	Uganda
Food products			✓	✓		✓
Animal products				✓		
Forestry products		✓				✓
Mining					✓	✓
Sugar *		✓	✓	✓		
Manufactured food			✓	✓	✓	✓
Beverages & tobacco	✓		✓			
Textiles, clothing & footwear		✓	✓	✓		✓
Chemicals	✓	✓	✓	✓		✓
Metal products & machinery	✓	✓	✓	✓		✓
Other manufacturing	✓	✓	✓	✓	✓	✓
Transport equipment	✓	✓	✓			

Notes: A tick indicates the presence of one or more products in the sector that experience significant trade effects.
* Sugar includes coffee and cotton, but these products are unlikely to be affected.

All may have sensitive products, although not the same ones within the manufacturing sectors (chemicals, metal products, machinery, transport equipment, and other manufacturers) and Kenya and Uganda may have specific textiles, clothing, and footwear products of concern. Only Kenya is likely to have sensitive products in mining and food manufacturing (where it exports to the others), only Tanzania appears to have concerns for local producers in beverages and tobacco, whilst only Uganda appears to have concerns in sugar and forestry products. Obviously, trade patterns have changed since our 1995 base (e.g., Uganda recently exports food to Kenya), but this is sufficient to demonstrate that members of the EAC will each have different views on which products should be excluded from the EPA.

Assessing the Effects on Kenya

Comparable trade data were not available to apply the empirical method for Kenya. The results for Tanzania and Uganda provide a basis for qualitative comparison with Kenya. For instance, the pattern of Kenya's imports from the EU and the ROW is very similar to that of the other EAC countries. One would anticipate similar magnitudes for the expansion of Kenya's imports from the EU following an EPA arising from consumption and trade diversion (from the ROW) effects, with corresponding net welfare losses given the potential dominance of trade diversion over positive consumption effects. By contrast, with Tanzania and Uganda there is minimal scope for 'trade creation' displacement of EAC imports by EU imports because there is limited existing penetration of the Kenyan market by Tanzanian and Uganda suppliers, especially for products where displacement by EU suppliers is likely. Therefore, there is no scope for consumer welfare gains in Kenya from this source.

In addition to the import effect, in the case of Kenya there is a need to consider export effects. The earlier analysis of import effects in Uganda and Tanzania has established the scope for considerable displacement of Kenyan imports by EU imports, with corresponding scope for producer losses in Kenya. To the extent, however, that the EPA protects Kenya's preferential access to the EU market, these producer losses would need to be weighted against the export and producer losses avoided by the retention of this preferential access to the EU. If the EAC did not achieve an EPA, Kenya would only enjoy access to European markets on GSP terms from 2005 onwards. The costs of non-participation in an EPA would then be borne disproportionately by Kenya. Kenya has the strongest incentive to make the EAC work so it can participate in an EPA, even if the gains from the EPA are quite limited.

5. Conclusions

This paper has considered the static welfare or impact effects on EAC countries of forming an EPA with the EU. Whether the net welfare effects are positive or negative varies from sector to sector, depending on the relative production costs of imports from the EU compared to the rest of the world and local production. However, the approach allows one to estimate the direction of effects by distinguishing the relative importance of three cases. First, products for which the EU is the dominant supplier (hence globally efficient); in these cases there is a clear welfare (consumption) gain. Second, cases where intra-regional supply is displaced by the EU; the importing countries gain but the exporter loses. Third, cases where the EU displaces more efficient ROW suppliers. In this case the welfare effect is clearly negative, and the more so the less efficient the EU relative to the ROW. In all three cases there will be a loss of tariff revenue, probably quite significant.

Although no more than illustrative, our estimates suggest that the effect on the EAC is likely to be adverse – a net welfare loss of up to 0.5 percent of GDP and a loss of up to 70 percent of tariff revenue. There is no reason to consider this unrepresentative of RIAs amongst ACP countries. In principle, the EU could offer a net increase in aid to ACP countries to compensate for losses and adjustment costs. The net welfare effect may still be negative, as the trade diversion effect (from ROW to EU) is likely to be much greater than the consumption- and trade-creation effect. Note, furthermore, that the trade-creation gain is at the expense of another ACP country, while the consumption gains may be at the expense of local producers (increasing market dominance by the EU). It remains unlikely that the static welfare effect for the ACP countries will be positive. Many of the benefits of an EPA may be dynamic. Formation of an EPA may have beneficial impacts by making trade-liberalisation measures undertaken by ACP countries irreversible and therefore credible (Collier and Gunning, 1995). This in turn may bring benefits in terms of increased domestic and foreign investment. While there may be dynamic effects, these are only potential effects and there is no evidence of such effects being significant in RIAs among low-income countries in the past.

One should not understate the cost of the negotiating burden imposed on ACP countries, few of which have more than a handful of trade officials experienced in the issues and in negotiating. The most protracted and contentious part of negotiations will be over sensitive products – those not fully liberalised in the RIA and those excluded from the EPA. The selection of excluded products will probably reduce the potential welfare gains from an EPA. All members will want to protect local producers (where consumption gains are possible), and the large member will wish to protect its regional market (where trade creation gains are possible). It is worth remarking that in almost any RIA amongst ACP countries there will be a 'Kenya type' (large) economy that will lose import share in the region to EU competition, but may (more than) offset this with increased exports to the EU if given preferences. This will also complicate negotiations, even if it does increase the incentive for the large country to participate. These considerations imply that ACP countries should be allowed to liberalise vis-à-vis the EU only gradually over the ten-year permitted period. This appears to have been recognised by the EU in its discussions with ACP countries. However, it implies that potential welfare gains from an EPA will be reduced.

The rest of the world is unlikely to stay still; ROW exporters to the ACP are likely to want to set up similar partnership arrangements, and this could change the welfare implications of a partnership agreement with the EU. We have aimed to provide a tractable method, if adequate trade data are available, to estimate the welfare effects on ACP countries of forming an EPA with the EU. The core conclusion is that one cannot assume that the welfare effects on ACP countries will be positive; it is more likely that the static effects will be negative. This should be taken into account in negotiating an EPA. Of greater importance, least-developed ACP countries are unlikely to gain at all from an EPA, as they are entitled to preferential access anyway. Such countries can legitimately question the motives of the EU in requiring them to enter into an arrangement that requires them to make greater concessions than they are required to make under the WTO.

References

Balassa, Bela (1974), 'Trade creation and trade diversion in the European Common Market: An appraisal of the evidence', *Manchester School*, vol. 42, no. 1: 93-135

Collier, Paul and Jan Willem Gunning (1995), 'Trade Policy and Regional Integration: Implications for the Relations between Europe and Africa', *World Economy*, vol. 18, no. 3: 387-410.

Karingi, Stephen, Remi Lang, Nassim Oulmane, Romain Perez, Mustapha Sadni and Hakim Ben Hammouda (2005), *Economic and Welfare Impacts of the EU-Africa Economic Partnership Agreements*, Addis Ababa: UNECA, available at www.uneca.org/trid.

Langhammer, Rolf (1992), 'The developing countries and regionalism', *Journal of Common Market Studies*, vol. 30, no. 2: 211-231.

Lyakurwa, William, Andrew McKay, Nehemiah Ng'eno and Walter Kennes (1997), 'Regional Integration in Sub-Saharan Africa: A Review of Experiences and Issues', in Ademola Oyejide, Ibrahim Elbadawi and Paul Collier (eds), *Regional Integration and Trade Liberalisation in Sub-Saharan Africa* (vol. 1), London: Macmillan, pp. 159-209.

McKay, Andrew, Chris Milner and Oliver Morrissey (2000), 'The Trade and Welfare Effects of a Regional Economic Partnership Agreement', *CREDIT Research Paper 00/8*, available at www.nottingham.ac.uk/economics/credit/.

McKay, Andrew, Chris Milner and Oliver Morrissey (2005), 'Some Simple Analytics of the Welfare Effects of EU-ACP Economic Partnership Agreements', *Journal of African Economies*, vol. 14, no. 3: 327-358.

Panagariya, Arvind (1998), 'Rethinking the New Regionalism', in John Nash and Wendy Takacs (eds), *Trade Policy Reform. Lessons and Implications*, Washington, DC: World Bank, pp. 87-145.

Schiff, Maurice and L. Alan Winters (2003), *Regional Integration and Development*, Washington DC: The World Bank.

Appendix – Modelling Framework

As noted in the text, three particular cases were estimated.

Consumption effects only

In those sectors where the EU is globally efficient and therefore the dominant supplier to a particular EAC market, we assume that only consumption effects would follow from the EPA. For those sectors where the EU is the dominant supplier we estimate the consumption effect alone (ΔM^C) relative to the existing EU import levels as:

$$\Delta M^C = \left[\frac{t}{1+t}\right].e_M^D.M_O^{EU}.UV_O^{EU} \qquad (1)$$

where t = current tariff against imports from EU
e_M^D = price elasticity of demand for imports
M_O^{EU} = current volume of imports from EU
UV_O^{EU} = current average unit value of imports from EU

The revenue (ΔR^C) and welfare (ΔW^C) effects associated with this are correspondingly:

$$\Delta R^C = -t.UV_0^{EU}M_O^{EU} \qquad (2)$$

$$\Delta W^C = 0.5t.\Delta M^C \qquad (3)$$

Trade diversion with consumption effects

For those trade sectors in EAC imports where the ROW is the dominant supplier, we assume the EPA will divert all imports for the ROW to the EU. The upper limit of the value of trade diversion (ΔM^{TD}) is:

$$\Delta M^{TD} = M_O^{ROW}.UV^{ROW} \qquad (4)$$

where M_O^{ROW} = current quantity of imports from ROW
UV_O^{ROW} = current average unit value of imports from ROW

The tariff revenue effect (ΔR^{TD}) due to this trade diversion is given by:

$$\Delta R^{TD} = -t.UV_0^{ROW} M_O^{ROW} \qquad (5)$$

Consumption effects, assuming on average P_{EU} lies between P_{ROW} and $P^t{}_{ROW}$ are:

$$\Delta M^{TD} = 0.5\left[\frac{t}{1+t}\right].e_M^D.M_O^{ROW}.UV^{EU} \qquad (6)$$

Given the assumption about P_{EU}, we can approximate the overall welfare W^{TD} impact of the trade diversion with consumption effects as follows:

$$\Delta W^{TD} = 0.25t\Delta M^{C'} - 0.5tUV_0^{ROW} M_O^{ROW} \qquad (7)$$

Trade creation with consumption effects

For those sectors where other EAC countries provide more than 25 percent of imports we estimate the effects of trade creation (i.e., source substitution) with consumption effects in analogous fashion to the trade diversion case. The maximum value of the trade created ΔM^{TC} for the EU can be estimated by:

$$\Delta M^{TC} = M_O^{EAC} UV^{EAC} \qquad (8)$$

where M_O^{EAC} = current quantity of imports from EAC
UV^{EAC} = current average unit value of imports from EAC

The pre-EPA tariff rate against EU imports provides an (upper) estimate of the extent to which the import price can fall as a result of the EPA. Thus:

$$\Delta M^{TC} = 0.5\left[\frac{t}{1+t}\right].e_M^D.M_o^{EAC}.UV^{EU} \qquad (9)$$

In turn the combined welfare (ΔW^{TC}) effects of trade creation with consumption effects can be identified by:

$$\Delta W^{TC} = 0.5t.\Delta M^{TC} + \left(UV^{EAC} M_O^{EAC} t\right) \qquad (10)$$

9 Creating a Development-Friendly EU Trade Policy

Christopher Stevens

1. Europe's Tangled Web

The EU has a bewildering array of trade polices towards other countries – the OECD's most complex system in terms of the number of agreements. This differentiation is founded in discrimination, with some import sources treated more favourably than others. Historically, it could be claimed (contentiously, but with some justification) that the discrimination was based on some development criteria. No longer – as layer has been added on top of discriminatory layer it has become hard to provide for the EU's regime any simple rationale other than that it exists. This has made it a source of international dispute: over one-quarter of the WTO disputes between 1998 and mid-2005 that involved the EU as respondent were directly or indirectly related to the country differentiation in its trade policy.[1] It also hampers the task of assessing the economic implications of any given change to trade policy since these depend on how the complex hierarchy is shuffled.

At present the EU is busy creating even more agreements – but there is one instance where it has increased coherence, at least on paper. This is the new Generalised System of Preferences (GSP), approved by the EU Council in June 2005 (European Council, 2005). Could the GSP provide a basis for a future, developmentally coherent trade policy? The answer has a technical and a political dimension: is it feasible to construct such a policy and would the EU (and its trade partners) accept the challenges that this would create? This chapter focuses primarily on the former but identifies factors that are relevant to the latter.

2. The Patchwork

The current patchwork reflects a process that has been underway for the past three decades. This has involved increasingly wide liberalisation but excluding from this one group of states and delaying its application to two groups of products. In both cases, the groups may soon be reduced to a core that is irreducible without a fundamental policy change. The new GSP may produce this effect for countries; for products it is the combination of recent liberalisation for 'sensitive' manufactures and the failure of European agricultural reform to include substantial tariff cuts for key items that may do the same.[2]

The sources of EU imports currently fall in broad terms into three categories (figure 1):

- *the most preferred countries:* they benefit from a variety of trade agreements that differ in their details but provide broadly comparable treatment; they include the EU's older preferential trade accords (e.g., the Cotonou Agreement) and its more recent trade agreements such as those with Mediterranean countries, South Africa, and Chile, together with beneficiaries of the more liberal tranches of the GSP (see below);
- *the middle group:* countries that are party to the standard GSP but to no other regime (mainly South and East Asia, the Middle East, and parts of Latin America);
- *the least preferred (mainly industrialised countries):* they trade on the now misnamed 'most favoured nation' (MFN) terms. [3]

Over time, the size of the most preferred group has increased, mainly by countries transferring from the middle group. The size of the three groups varies from year to year, but they are of roughly comparable size. In 2003, the countries in the first group accounted for a little under, and the others for a bit over, one-third of the total.[4] In the 1970s the Lomé Convention linking the EU to a group of mainly ex-colonies in Africa, the Caribbean, and the Pacific (ACP) was at the apex of a 'pyramid of privilege'. Since then, the ACP have been joined by a host of other states.

The complexity of EU trade policy stems from three main sources. One is the growth of special trade regimes with Europe's neighbours, intended either as an alternative or as a precursor to membership. The second is the historical legacy of special trade regimes with former colonies. Both have been affected and built upon by the third source: a pragmatic attempt to respond to pressures put on the EU in a way that 'manages' market opening to maintain greater restrictions

Figure 1 Share in Total EU Import Value, 2003

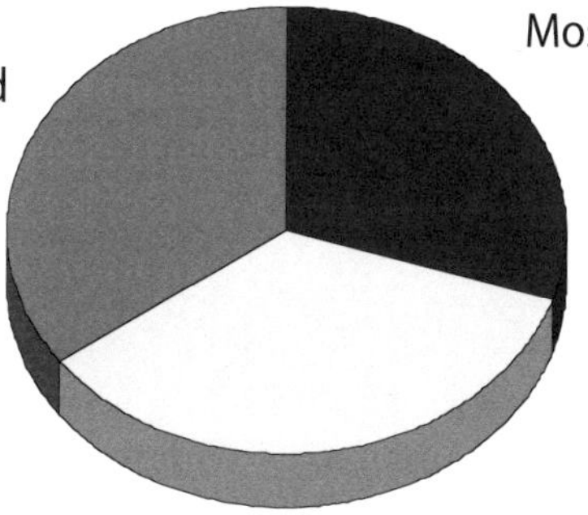

Source: derived from UNCTAD's TRAINS database

on countries deemed to be most competitive than on others (see Stevens, 1999, 2000, 2005; Stevens and Kennan, 2001). The WTO is central to this third source of pressure.

3. The WTO Link

Historically, to the extent that it attempted to justify its policies in the GATT, the EU largely followed the pattern of other industrialised countries. In the case of policies towards developing countries it either sought a waiver or argued that they were covered by the enabling clause under which GATT signatories agreed in 1979 to authorise, as a permanent feature of the agreement, the granting of trade preferences by developed to developing countries. This approach changed as it became increasingly difficult to obtain a consensus for waivers without conceding 'favours' to other members. Agreement of a waiver for the Cotonou Agreement until 2007, for example, was among the areas of brinkmanship that preceded the final agreement on a Doha Declaration in 2001.

One aspect of the EU's response strategy has been to establish new accords and to re-negotiate old ones so that they can be portrayed as falling within the ambit of article XXIV of the GATT (for goods) and article V of the GATT (for services).[5] These permit states to form free trade areas (FTAs) and customs unions

(CUs) that include industrialised countries to discriminate against non-members subject to certain constraints. Another string has been to make those tariff-reduction regimes that cannot be portrayed as FTAs or CUs more compatible with the enabling clause as its meaning has been clarified through dispute settlement. It has proved to be very difficult to marry the requirements of the enabling clause with the EU's pragmatic desire to offer more liberal market access to some developing countries but not to others. The new GSP represents the most determined attempt so far.

4. The GSP

The GSP reflects the EU's differentiation in miniature since it has provided an umbrella for no fewer than five different regimes. The broadest regime, dubbed the standard GSP in this chapter, applies to almost all developing countries. No developing country (other than the richest and most competitive or pariahs like Korea PDR and Myanmar) is offered less favourable access to the European market than that provided under the GSP. The four other tranches (which have been superceded in the new 2006 regime) were more favourable but had restricted eligibility. Because of its breadth the standard GSP is frequently not the most favourable of the EU's import regimes. Although called a 'preference' scheme, countries that benefit from it and no other accord fit into the 'the middle' section of figure 1 and are actually discriminated against when they are in competition with the 'most preferred' countries.

The creation of restricted eligibility tranches within the GSP was one of the mechanisms whereby the 'most preferred' group grew and the 'middle' group diminished. Two of the four more favourable GSP tranches were widely used; they are the ones covering the least-developed countries (LDCs) under the Everything But Arms (EBA) initiative and a select group of countries deemed to be fighting illicit narcotics. The other provisions, which were virtually unused, offered small extra preferences to countries with favourable social and environmental policies. The anti-narcotics tranche was created in the early 1990s, when it applied only to the Andean and Central American countries. It was the subject of WTO proceedings by Brazil in the late 1990s, but these never reached the panel stage. In 2001 Pakistan was added to the list – and this provoked India to take the EU to WTO dispute settlement in 2002 (CEC 2001).

5. The India Case

The essence of India's case was that the anti-narcotics regime violated GATT Article 1.1 (on non-discrimination).[6] The EU's primary defence was that the discrimination was justified by the enabling clause. The WTO Appellate Body found in India's favour in 2004, but included in its decision was a potentially important detail (WTO 2004a). India had argued that in order to claim justification under the Enabling Clause the GSP must offer 'identical' tariff preferences to all beneficiaries. The Appellate Body rejected this argument and asserted the legitimacy of providing different preferences provided that the difference responds "to a widely-recognized 'development, financial [or] trade need'..." (para. 164). The reason it upheld the main substance of the Indian complaint was that the EU's justification for its anti-narcotics regime failed to satisfy this criterion: the beneficiaries did not share a widely-recognised trade need that bound them together as different from all non-beneficiaries.

Arbitration subsequent to the Appellate Body ruling resulted in the EU being asked to amend its trade policy by 1 July, 2005 (WTO 2004b). This timetable fitted in well with a planned review of the GSP. Now over 30 years old, the GSP has been reviewed and adapted several times, most recently in 2001, and was due to expire in its current form by 31 December 2005.[7] The WTO ruling both brought forward this review and inserted into it a search for criteria that would balance the EU's two conflicting objectives: to offer higher-level preferences to a sufficiently wide and coherent group to fulfil the Appellate Body's requirement, but to keep out countries considered too competitive.

6. The New GSP

The result is that the new GSP tweaks one longstanding feature and introduces a novel one. Between them these two changes are believed by the EU to achieve the balance. They are:

- a revised graduation mechanism under which preferences are withdrawn for a particular group of products once a country accounts for a pre-set share of EU imports from developing countries; and
- a special trade regime, known as GSP+, that will be available to many developing countries (but not all of the poorest) and provide improved access to the EU (but not as good as the access available to LDCs under the EBA).[8]

In addition, around 250 items have been added to the list of products for which standard GSP preferences are available. Just under two-thirds of these are fish and fisheries products, with the remainder being mainly fresh or processed fruits and vegetables. The new products account for about one percent of EU imports from the countries for which the extension will represent a change to the status quo.[9] The main beneficiaries seem likely to be Argentina, China, Ecuador, Russia, and Thailand.

The graduation mechanism has been adjusted to limit the value of the GSP to one small group of countries. The GSP does not apply at all to some developing countries (such as Singapore and Hong Kong) on the grounds that they are too rich; others that are eligible for GSP treatment on some of their exports are 'graduated out' on certain goods for which they have to pay normal MFN tariffs. Under the old GSP graduation was determined by applying a complex formula linking market share, level of development, and specialisation. Under the new GSP a country is graduated from any section of goods in which it accounts for more than a certain share of EU imports.[10] China is graduated from the largest number of sections (15); Russia from three; Brazil, India, Indonesia, and Thailand from two each; and Algeria, Malaysia, and South Africa from one.

There is also a link between the adjusted graduation formula and the new GSP+ since the latter does not apply to countries for the goods on which they have been graduated. The GSP+ replaces the tranche struck down in dispute settlement and also the two little-used regimes linked to labour standards and the environment.[11] It covers a broader range of products and offers preferences that are a substantial improvement over the standard GSP and comparable to those available to other 'most preferred' states. In order to benefit from these additional preferences a country must have ratified and be effectively implementing 16 core human and labour rights UN/ILO conventions and at least seven (of 11) conventions related to environment and governance principles. All 27 of the conventions must be ratified by 31 December, 2008. There is to be regular monitoring by the EU and review of the beneficiary's implementation record.

But that is not all – there is another requirement; one on which the EU's hope of meeting the rules set out by the Appellate Body may founder. Countries must also satisfy two additional criteria (European Council, 2005: Article 9.3). One concerns diversification (or the lack of it): its five largest Harmonised System (HS) sections must not account for over 75 percent of its 'covered imports'.[12] The other requires the beneficiary to be relatively small (in economic, not geographic terms): the country's covered imports must represent less than 1 percent of the EU's total covered imports.[13] These criteria mean that some states are excluded a priori from the GSP+ regardless of whether they ratify all of the conventions. The GSP regulation does not list the ineligible states, but table 1 shows the countries that appear to be excluded on the basis of these criteria. They are a motley bunch, ranging in income per capita from US$ 420 to US$ 8,530. Most are not sufficiently substantial exporters to the EU to have fallen foul of the graduation formula.[14]

7. Will GSP+ Survive in the WTO?

Of particular relevance in relation to the WTO is that table 1 includes both India, the author of the last challenge, and Pakistan, which is the only country favoured under the old regime to be excluded a priori from the new. Because of this the possibility of a WTO challenge is a very real one – especially from states that

Table 1 Countries Excluded a priori from GSP+

Country [a]	*GNI per capita 2003 (US$)* [b]
Argentina	4,220
Brazil	2,860
China	960
Egypt, Arab Republic	1,470
India	470
Indonesia	710
Jordan	1,760
Lebanon	3,900
Malaysia	3,550
Mexico	5,940
Morocco	1,170
Pakistan	420
Philippines	1,030
Russian Federation	2,130
Saudi Arabia	8,530
South Africa	2,630
Thailand	2,000
Tunisia	1,990
Ukraine	780
United Arab Emirates	n/a
Vietnam	430

Sources: Data provided by the Commission; World Bank.

do not wish to follow the alternative route to improved market access for their exports, i.e., an FTA.

Whether or not the GSP+ will be subject to a WTO challenge is a question that only time will answer. Its apparent security, were there to be such a challenge, by contrast is a question on which a reasoned opinion can be given. In its ruling the Appellate Body gives an example of the 'objective standard' that could justify differential treatment for sub-groups within the GSP. The required '[b]road-based recognition of a particular need...' that would justify such differentiation is exemplified by recognition 'set out in the WTO Agreement or in multilateral instruments adopted by international organizations...' (para. 163). This statement appears to confirm the legitimacy of the special tranche for LDCs under EBA since the least developed is a recognised grouping. But does it extend to GSP+?

Whilst a plausible case can be made that the conventions that eligible countries must accept have such recognition, the same does not appear to apply to the diversification and smallness criteria. There is no obvious developmental or trade link that binds either the countries excluded from GSP+ or those included other than the diversification and smallness criteria. These are sui generis: they are not used by any other trading blocs or in any other context by the EU. Some wealthier developing countries are eligible for GSP+ (if they implement the conventions) whilst poorer ones are excluded. For example, five of the countries listed in table 1 are 'low income' according to the World Bank's definition while many potential GSP+ beneficiaries are not. Indeed, five potential beneficiary countries are wealthier than any of the states listed in the table.

A similar lack of coherence is evident in the transition regime. Whilst most countries had to apply for GSP+ by 31 October, 2005 in order to receive, if eligible, the benefits from January 2006, some received the preference immediately on a provisional basis even before they applied (European Council, 2005: Articles 10.1(1) and 10.3). Fourteen states are listed in the regulation as 'already fulfil[ing] the criteria ... at the time of entry into force' (Preamble: 8) and will receive the preference provisionally on entry into force – subject to their subsequent application. Yet three of these states appear not yet to meet the criteria in terms of convention adoption, whilst others that have done so are excluded from the list.[15]

The real justification appears to be that this provisional arrangement applies only to the beneficiaries of the superior tranches that GSP+ supersedes; the special provision is to avoid a hiatus in their terms of access to the EU market. Other than Pakistan no state that was a beneficiary of the old tranches is excluded from the list. All except two (Georgia and Mongolia) were beneficiaries of either the anti-narcotics or the labour rights tranches of the old GSP. By contrast, states that appear not only to have signed but to be implementing the conventions, such as Seychelles, are absent.

8. The GSP as an Umbrella

If the new regime were to survive a challenge at the WTO (either through a favourable verdict by the Appellate Body or by default in the absence of a complaint) it could result in a considerable change to the EU's de facto, if not its de jure, policy coherence. Seven of the 21 states listed in table 1 already have bilateral trade agreements with the EU (justified under WTO Article XXIV). If GSP+ were widely adopted the effective result could be that the polarisation resulting from the gradual increase in the most preferred and the reduction in the middle group would be complete: all developing countries other than the remaining 14 states in table 1 would have very similar and favourable access terms.

The requirements

How realistic is it to think that the new GSP could become an umbrella under which the EU's multifarious schemes could be developmentally integrated? On the one hand the case with India demonstrates the need and provides the possibility for the GSP umbrella. The ruling of the WTO Appellate Body has confirmed:

- not only that the EU's existing preferences within the GSP (apart from those for LDCs) are illegal,
- but also that differentiation within the GSP is acceptable
- provided it is related to objective and internationally accepted differences in developing country circumstance.

To become acceptable the GSP+ would need to be altered in two (not necessarily compatible) ways. It would need to be made more attractive to countries currently treated better, as well as sufficiently attractive to dissuade others from challenging it in the WTO. The ACP countries form the most substantial group for which enhancement of the GSP+ would be necessary to make it attractive; for them a suitably enhanced version would be an interesting option. This is because the ACP's current preferences under the Cotonou Agreement are vulnerable to challenge in the WTO and the ACP are in the process of negotiating a new regime based on Economic Partnership Agreements (EPAs) (see chapter 8 of the present volume).

In 1975, when the first Lomé Convention was agreed, the ACP were at the apex of Europe's trade hierarchy and accounted for over 6 percent of the EU's trade with the rest of the world; the group was second only to the Mediterranean as a regional partner from the developing world. Three decades later, the share is less than half this level. The sharpest fall in the ACP's share of EU trade was in the late 1980s and 1990s; it has since stabilised (figure 2). This fall has coloured the EPA debate. Unfortunately, it does not reflect a diversification of ACP trade towards partners other than Europe (which would be a healthy trend): ACP trade with other countries mirrors that with the EU. Africa's share of global trade, for example, has fallen from about five percent in the 1960s to less than two percent now.

Figure 2 **EU Trade with the ACP as a Percentage of Total Extra-EU Trade, 1988-2003**

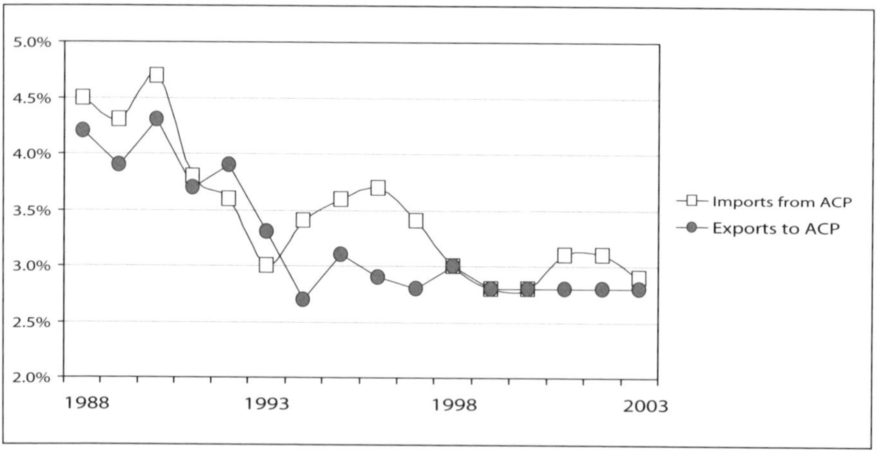

Source: derived from Eurostat data
* See file EU EU-ACP trade.xls for underlying data

As the ACP's commercial importance to the EU has declined, so has its standing in the trade policy hierarchy. In many cases the EU treats imports from the ACP the same as those from the many other highly preferred states and, in a few cases, worse. Even so, the GSP+ does not provide equivalence on all products, so it would need to be improved to make it an acceptable alternative to EPAs for some of the ACP. A basic requirement for a GSP providing treatment equal to

Cotonou is that it cover all of the products that the ACP currently export to the EU with a preference. A second, practical requirement concerns the relative treatment of the ACP and their competitors.

9. Improving the GSP for the ACP

The most obvious route for creating a regime under the GSP that is equivalent to the Cotonou provisions is to extend GSP+. Two changes would be needed to GSP+:

- to include in its ambit all products that the ACP export to the EU now or in the foreseeable future;
- to improve access terms to the Cotonou level in any cases where GSP+ is currently deficient.

Table 2 summarises the scale of the task, which is modest. It classifies the most significant ACP exports to the EU (accounting for 94 percent of the total) according to the EU's trade regime. Seventy five percent are unproblematic: they are already given duty-free treatment either under the EU's MFN tariff or under the standard GSP. A further 16 percent are already covered by the new GSP+ and, except for four items, are given duty-free access.[16]

Table 2 Non-LDC ACP exports to EU, 2003

	Value ($ bn)	Share
Total	23.3	
'Significant' items[a]	22.0	100.0%
Of which:		
MFN zero	15.4	70.2%
Standard GSP zero	1.0	4.7%
Standard GSP not zero (GSP+ zero[b])	3.4	15.7%
Not covered by GSP or GSP+	2.1	9.5%

Note:
(a) Any item accounting for 5 percent or more of any individual non-LDC ACP country's total exports to the EU in 2003 (89 items) or not meeting this criterion, but which the 36 non-LDC ACP countries in aggregate exported to the EU to a value of $10 million or more in 2003 (105 items).
(b) Other than 4 items – see footnote 16.
Source: UNCTAD, January 2005

It is these four items plus the remaining 10 percent that require further attention. Giving these products duty-free status in GSP+ would also improve the access to the EU of other scheme beneficiaries. This would spread the gains but might also lead to preference erosion for the ACP. Clearly, the EU should not agree to simply freeze current trade policy in order to maintain the ACP margin of preference. But it is not sensible to use considerable political capital to extend GSP+ if, in so doing, ACP preferences are entirely eroded.

In most cases the inclusion of these products in GSP+ would not significantly erode ACP preferences (table 3). This is because some competitors will either

Table 3 Potential for Preference Erosion

Product description (HS6/CN8 code)	*# ACP exporters to EU*[a]	*Liable to erosion?*[b]
Beef (02013000, 020230)	9	No
Bananas (08030019)	14	Yes
Oranges (ex 080520)	11	No
Fresh table grapes (ex 08061010)	3	Yes
Brown rice (10062098)	3	No
Wheat/meslin flour (110100), malt (110710)	1	No
Sugar (17011110/90, 170199), molasses 17031000, 170390)	27	No
Rum (22084051)	7	No
Rum (22084099)	9	Yes
Residues of wheat (230230), preps used in animal feed (ex 230990),	1	No
Salts (250100)	7	No
Aluminium oxide (28182000)	2	No
Skins of sheep/lambs (41051010)	4	Yes
Skins of sheep/lambs (410530), skins/hides of goats/kids (41062110/90, 41062290)	11	No
Unwrought aluminium (76011000), aluminium alloys (760120), zinc (79011100)	7	No

(a) Exporter/product combinations.
(b) 'No' denotes either that no main competitors (i.e., non-LDC, non-ACP GSP beneficiaries supplying 10 percent or more of the EU market in 2003) currently have access that is the same as or better than the ACP, or that any that do are not eligible for GSP+. 'Yes' denotes that some or all competitors whose access is currently worse than the ACP's will be eligible for GSP+.
Sources: UNCTAD, January 2005; UK Tariff 2005

be excluded from GSP+ or already enjoy duty-free access (now or within a few years) under one agreement or another. The main problems will be with sugar, bananas, and rum – all of which face serious difficulties regardless of the future EU-ACP trade regime. Until more is known about the way in which these difficulties are to be handled – and, crucially, which ACP countries decide not to join EPAs – it is not possible to determine whether or not any 'solution' may be accommodated under a GSP+ umbrella.

Extending the product coverage of GSP+ is not sufficient. Cotonou is a negotiated agreement (as will be any EPA). The GSP is an autonomous EU action: not only can it be reversed at any time, but the new regime has created great uncertainty over what will happen in 2008. Any acceptable reform would need to introduce certainty and dispute settlement into the GSP+. There are ways to achieve this. Some involve parallel action in the WTO. The GSP tariffs, for example, could be bound into the WTO given that the Hong Kong Declaration of November 2005 on duty-free and quota-free access for LDCs has broached the principle of tariff binding at levels other than MFN levels. Or a link could be made with Cotonou, to provide the ACP with a contractual guarantee that the EU's tariffs would not exceed the GSP+ level.

10. Conclusions: The Economic Effects

If it were politically feasible to extend the GSP+ in this way it would not only provide an alternative to EPAs for the ACP but also increase the chances of GSP+ having a positive, trade-creating rather than a trade-diverting effect. This is partly because the impact of the GSP+ will be determined by the number of countries that apply for, and are accepted into, the new regime. The take-up rate is vital because it will affect the balance between the new regime's trade-creating and diverting effects. The number of countries and products facing no tariff barriers in the EU will increase, resulting in more trade. However countries elevated from the 'middle' to the 'most preferred' group will find that trade is diverted to them because they pay less import tax; they have a competitive advantage over more efficient states that remain in the middle group.

Indeed, the economic effects could be superior to those likely to arise from EPAs. The EU, a large economy, would liberalise substantially and quickly. Under EPAs liberalisation by the small ACP states is likely to be partial and drawn out. This is because the ACP will have to liberalise on only 'substantially all' of their imports (which means they could entirely exclude 20 percent or so of their most sensitive imports) and can defer some liberalisation for at least 12 years (and up to 20 years if an Africa Commission recommendation is accepted).

To produce such effects, though, the EU would need to propose such a regime *and* it would need to be supported within the WTO, meaning that it has at least the tacit consent of other WTO members. And herein lies possibly the greatest challenge. In the litigious environment that has developed in the WTO no trade regime that offers some members better treatment than others is entirely safe. This applies equally to EPAs (Stevens, 2000). To reduce the danger of a challenge, therefore, the EU's strategy would need to be to move trade policy gradually along a route in which sufficient developing countries gain (or can see gains around the corner) and therefore believe that it is in their interests not to derail the process (Stevens, 2005). This will be a much greater political challenge: it means providing something, at least over time, for India, Pakistan, the Mercosur, and South East Asia. Were the EU to agree then, at last, its development policy could become developmentally coherent.

Notes

1 The absolute figures are nine out of 35 disputes, but three of these concerned sugar and involved differentiation only indirectly; the complainants did not dispute the EU's import preferences to various developing countries, but these are linked to what was in dispute: the volume of subsidised exports. Excluding these three reduces to 17 percent the proportion of disputes related directly to differentiation. The cases are: DS 134, 154, 158, 209, 242, 246, 265, 266 and 283.

2 The end of the Multi-fibre Arrangement is the most notable example of the former but there are other indicators of these trends. These include the EU's relatively liberal position in the Doha negotiations on non-agricultural goods and the evidence provided by the 2005 quota on Chinese footwear that protectionist member states are now in a minority.

3 The MFN is the highest tariff that the EU may levy on imports from WTO members, and in practice is used for non-WTO members, as well. It applies to all of the exports of countries in the least-preferred group and to any items from other countries that do not receive a concession under their trade accords with the EU.

4 The relative shares are heavily influenced by the size of the Union and, hence, of 'intra-EU' trade – which is not included in the pie. In the preceding years, when the ranks of 'the most preferred' were swelled with the EU applicants from Eastern and Central Europe, it was the largest of the three; once these states joined the EU (and therefore become even more preferred) the share fell; the 2003 figures on EU imports from TRAINS exclude the new entrants.

5 As with the replacement of the single regime with most of sub-Saharan Africa, the Caribbean, and the Pacific (the ACP) under the Cotonou Agreement with six separate Economic Partnership Agreements.

6 Initially India challenged all of the high-preference GSP regimes other than EBA, but it then concentrated on the anti-narcotics regime and reserved its position on the other two.

7 The first European Community GSP was for an initial phase of ten years (1971-81), subsequently renewed for a second decade (1981-91). The third ten-year offer was delayed pending the outcome of the Uruguay Round, and the 1991 scheme was extended with various amendments until 1994. The scheme for 1995 – 2004 was adopted on 1 January, 1995, the legislative acts being Council Regulation 3281/94 in respect of industrial products and Council Regulation 1256/96 in respect of agricultural products. The scheme was revised for the period 1 July, 1999 – 31 December, 2001 on the basis of Council Regulation 2820/98. The basic structure of the offer was not substantially modified until the end of 2001, with the adoption of Council Regulation (EC) No 2501/2001 of 10 December 2001 (OJ L 346, 21 December, 2001, p. 1), which covered the period 2002 – 2004 and fully incorporated the EBA amendment. Council Regulation (EC) No 2211/2003 of 15 December, 2003 (OJ L 332, 19 December, 2003) subsequently extended this until 31 December, 2005.

8 Under the proposed GSP+ simple ad valorem or specific duties will be suspended on all products covered by the GSP. For items subject to an ad valorem and a specific duty, the ad valorem element will be suspended. Duty suspensions will not apply to sections from which any given country has been graduated.

9 i.e., excluding imports from LDCs, countries that will be graduated, and those that may already be receiving a preference because they benefit from bilateral/regional free trade agreements with the EU.

10 The Harmonised System (HS) of trade classification used by most trading blocs divides the vast range of tradable goods into 21 broad sections (which are sub-divided into more precise sub-groups). Under the new GSP countries are graduated out from any section in which they account, on average over three consecutive years, for more than 15 percent (or 12.5 percent for Section XI – which is sub-divided for the purposes of GSP graduation into XIa (textiles) and XIb (clothing)) of the total value of 'covered imports' within that section. Covered imports are all items included in the GSP that originate in a beneficiary country, regardless of whether that country has been graduated out of the section concerned.

11 It is formally called the special incentive arrangements for sustainable development and good governance. For those countries included in the special arrangements, simple ad valorem or specific duties are suspended on all products covered by the GSP. For items subject to an ad valorem and a specific duty, the ad valorem element is suspended.

12 Additionally, the country must not have been classified by the World Bank for three consecutive years as high income. See note 15 for a definition of covered imports.

13 To be calculated using the data available on 1 September, 2004 for an average over three consecutive years.

14 By contrast, almost all of the graduated countries are to be found in the table: so they are doubly disadvantaged compared to the rest.

15 The three are El Salvador, Guatemala, and Venezuela.

16 The four exceptions to duty-free access under GSP+ are chocolate (for which the ad valorem duty is suspended but the agricultural component (AC) remains), and three shrimp items (for which the GSP+ tariff is 3.6 percent).

References

Commission of the European Communities (2001). 'Amended Proposal for a Council Regulation Applying a Scheme of Generalised Tariff Preferences for the Period 1 January 2002 to 31 December 2004', COM(2001)688 final, 2001/0131(ACC), Brussels.

European Council (2005). 'Council Regulation (EC) No 980/2005 of 27 June 2005 applying a scheme of generalised tariff preferences', *Official Journal* L 169, Vol. 48, 30 June.

Stevens, C. (1999). 'The EU and the Third World', in David A. Dyker, ed., *The European Economy*. Harlow: Longman.

Stevens, C. (2000). 'Trade with Developing Countries', in H. Wallace and W. Wallace, (eds), *Policy-Making in the European Union*. Oxford: Oxford University Press.

Stevens, C. (2005). 'An Alternative Strategy for Free Trade Areas: The Generalized System of Preferences', in O. Babarinde and G. Faber, (eds), *The European Union and the Developing Countries: The Cotonou Agreement*. Leiden and Boston: Martinus Nijhoff Publishers.

Stevens, C. and Kennan, J. (2001). 'Post-Lomé WTO-Compatible Trading Arrangements', *Economic Paper* 45. London: Commonwealth Secretariat.

UK Tariff 2005. *Integrated Tariff of the United Kingdom. 2005 Edition*. London: TSO.

UNCTAD. *Trade Analysis and Information System (TRAINS)*, powered by *World Integrated Trade Solution* (http://wits.worldbank.org/).

World Bank. *World Development Indicators Data Query* (http://www.worldbank.org/data/ dataquery.html, downloaded on 17.12.2004).

WTO (2004a). 'European Communities – Conditions for the Granting of Tariff Preferences to Developing Countries. AB-2004-1. Report of the Appellate Body', WT/DS246/AB/R, 7 April. Geneva: World Trade Organization.

WTO (2004b). 'European Communities – Conditions for the Granting of Tariff Preferences to Developing Countries. ARB-2004-1/17. Arbitration under Article 21.3(c) of the Understanding on Rules and Procedures Governing the Settlement of Disputes', WT/DS246/14, 20 September. Geneva: World Trade Organization.

10 Between a Rock and a Hard Place – Whither EU Development Policy?

Andrew Mold[1]

1. Introduction: Raising Expectations Too High?

The chapters of this book have testified to the importance of the EU both as a provider of foreign aid and in its broader influence upon the developing world. The EU and its 25 members are the largest source of Western development assistance, giving some 34.5 billion euros in 2004, accounting for approximately 55 percent of all aid flows in that year (EC, 2006: 1). Leaving aside the aid provided by individual member states, the Commission is, in its own right, an important donor, being responsible for approximately 20 percent of total aid proceeding from the EU. All in all, as Degnbol-Martinussen and Engberg-Pedersen (2003: 125) note "the EU is a potentially omnipotent aid donor in terms of the comprehensiveness of its objectives, the multitude of its instruments and the distribution of its aid." As an economic actor on the world stage, too, the EU is of crucial importance to many developing countries as a source of trade and foreign direct investment. This is particularly true of the poorest developing countries in Africa and elsewhere, which continue to have (disproportionately) important economic links with the EU. Notwithstanding the recent admission by the Commissioner for Development and Humanitarian Aid, Luis Michel, that the EU currently acts as "a financial giant and a political dwarf" (cited in SID, 2005: 1), the EU is also potentially a key actor in terms of its political sway. All this, the economic, political, and historical dimensions – provides the EU with considerable influence. But has it used that influence wisely? And could that influence be used more effectively? Those are the fundamental questions that this book has tried to answer.

In recent years, the EU's development agenda has evolved further. In chapter 1 we noted that the new security-based agenda increasingly obliges the EU to embark on a different kind of development policy. One clear manifestation of this is the way in which the EU has become increasingly involved in peacekeeping activities in recent years. It is perhaps surprising to note that until 2003 the EU as such had not mounted any foreign peacekeeping operations at all. Over the past three years, however, it has put as many as 14 peacekeeping missions into the field, turning Europe into one of the world's main purveyors of peacekeeping.[2] As *The Economist* (2006) recently noted,

> missions such as these are a visible expression of Europe's eagerness to play a bigger role in the world ... if the ability to project force is now the hallmark of an independent foreign policy, the EU could be said, at last, to be getting a bit more bloody, bold and resolute.

At the same time, the meltdown of the bloody social reengineering project in Iraq (the grounds of Fukuyama's (2006) critique of US policy) has tempered views on the ability of Western countries to intervene successfully, either politically or militarily, in the affairs of developing countries. Certainly the chaos in Iraq provides a salutatory reminder of the limits of military force.

The EU has tended to see its relations with developing countries as more enlightened than the foreign policy of the United States. In some important respects, this is undoubtedly true: whereas the EU has put poverty reduction as the overriding objective of its development policy, the politics of naked self-interest are much more evident in the US case, with far stronger links with foreign policy goals. One particularly revealing fact is that while the EU spends the equivalent of 20 percent of its combined defence budgets on development aid, the equivalent figure for the US is only 3.5 percent (Gnesotto, 2006: 142). To borrow Nye's (2004) famous analogy, in its influence on the developing world, the EU clearly prefers the approach of using 'soft' power (i.e. the power of persuasion by dint of its cultural, social and political values) rather than the 'hard' power approach of relying on military force, as the United States has tended to do.

But there is an important historical dimension to all this which should not be forgotten. Understandably, the presumption that EU policy towards the developing world is more enlightened irritates many American observers. For instance, speaking of the current situation in the Middle East Peter Suchman, a former US foreign service officer, wrote recently in the *Financial Times* (2006: 8),

> It is particularly inappropriate for European governments, whose colonial intrigues in past generations and post-first World War mendaciousness in large measure created the mosaic of failed states – Lebanon included – and undemocratic systems that nurture Islamic extremism, to consider aban-

> doning Israel ... Europe's centuries of religious bigotry, anti-Semitism and bloody persecution of its Jewish population led to the creation of Israel in this dangerous neighbourhood.

Europeans who are studious of history and are honest with themselves will recognise the large element of truth in such assertions. From Darfur to Eastern Timor, European colonialism underlies many of the contemporary conflicts involving failed states across the developing world. And despite revisionist attempts to prove the contrary,[3] Easterly (2006: 272) probably reflects the consensus view of historians and development professionals when he argues that "the old conventional wisdom was correct – the previous imperial era did not facilitate economic development. Instead, it created some of the conditions that bred occasions for today's unsuccessful interventions: failed states and bad government." Nevertheless, there is no objective reason why the EU as an institution should feel prisoner to the history of its member states (indeed, as we shall go on to argue, this is perhaps one of its prime comparative advantages vis-à-vis the bilateral engagements of its member states).

Moreover, credit needs to be given where credit is due. In terms of broad strategy, EU development policy has generally been well received. The European Commission's 'Development Policy Statement' (DPS) (approved by the Council in 2000) presented an overarching framework for EU development policy. According to the assessment of Maxwell et al. (2004: 3),

> the 2000 Development Policy correctly reflected many of the development nostrums of the time, including the emphasis on ownership, country-led development strategies, participation, and the strong linkage between aid and trade issues....on many of these issues, the EU is at the forefront of thinking, for example, on PRSPs, budget support and the mechanics of a genuinely reciprocal partnership (at least in the case of the ACP).

Of course, one could challenge the idea that these 'nostrums' are in fact the right ones (and indeed, in the final sections of this chapter, we will do just that). One could also question the DPS in terms of thematic emphasis. In reaction to concerns that the agenda had shifted since the publication of the DPS, on 20 December 2005 the Presidents of the Commission, Council and Parliament endorsed a new EU development policy statement, 'the European Consensus on Development'. This captured much of the essence of the earlier document, but now stressed a central role for the Millennium Development Goals (MDGs), as well as reflecting the new prominence given to security concerns.

Thus overtime EU development policy has tended to become even more all-encompassing. It is worth recognising the difficulty of articulating a coherent development policy when the EU has all kinds of political pressures pulling it in different directions: meeting the aspirations of candidates for membership, giving a priority to poverty reduction, maintaining financial support to EU farmers, ensuring security, promoting economic links with other regions, etc. Moreover, the agenda is not a static one – and the whole set of interests which the EU must satisfy is in a constant state of flux. In the face of growing evidence of global warming, for instance, one can perceive that environmental objectives are quickly moving up the list of priorities. Mission creep is one of the major dangers for any donor – attempting too much is a sure recipe for disaster. And, as the Director-General of the European Commission's EuropeAid office Koos Richelle (2005) has conceded, constant tensions exist as individual member states and the EuropeAid compete to cover the whole range of development priorities. In such a context, streamlining, rationalising and identifying comparative advantage for European development cooperation would seem to be an obvious priority.

Criticism can also be made on a different level. Although in many important areas of its activities the EU has established an honourable and principled set of policy stances, arguably for the more crucial strategic questions, self-interest and Bismarkean *realpolitik* still tend to dominate decision making. In this sense, as Freres notes in chapter 6 it is legitimate to ask whether the European approach is really so very different from that of the United States. In the words of Jawara and Kwa (2004: xv), "the neo-colonial attitude ... persists – a sense that the developed world knows what is best for the developing countries, and has the right to impose it." And, in the context of the aggressive promotion of policies like the EPAs, we would argue here that some current EU policies only reinforce such impressions.

The slow pace of reform of EU development aid is similarly censurable. In 2002, Clare Short, then the UK's Secretary of State for International Development memorably described the Commission as 'the worst aid agency in the world' (cited in Santiso, 2003: 4). Such judgments are perhaps overly harsh, and ignore the extent to which in recent years efforts have been made to reform the EU's aid instruments. Moreover, the EU has a lot of potential advantages in its favour vis-à-vis the programmes of member states – including economies of scale (in both procurement and delivery), a stronger field presence, and a politically more 'neutral' stance (more on which will be said shortly). But there is no denying a consistent underperformance in aid policy vis-à-vis the high aspirations set for it. As Hoebink notes (2005: 156), whatever the value of such criticisms, they suggest that the European Commission has at best a problem with its image on development cooperation.

Of course, it could be argued that perhaps it is simply a case of the goals being too ambitious. Could the EU foster a more focused, critical approach to development aid? 'Getting real' is perhaps a rather crass way of putting it, but on a number of scores, it would seem that this is exactly what the EU needs to do. It is useless, for instance, to constantly exhort policy co-ordination and coherence in aid delivery if structural constraints and bureaucratic procedures do not allow this to take place. Internally, for example, DG-Trade's objectives (and the constituency which it must keep happy) are very different from those of DG-Development.[4] Similarly, Europe's foreign policy has in the past been bedevilled by policy divisions, the most glaring recent example being the war over Iraq in 2002-2003 (with Britain, Spain, Italy, and several new EU members backing the war but France, Germany, Belgium, and others coming out vociferously against it). Thus though there is surely scope for finding more common ground on certain basic issues of mutual interest, calls for Europe to operate with one foreign policy voice are probably misplaced. As Holdar (2000: 74) notes, it may just be that the foreign policy interests of the most influential members of the EU (France, Britain, and Germany) are simply too different to be fused into any common European external policy.

How then to live with this plethora of instruments and objectives and the apparently contradictory outcomes? This final chapter makes some suggestions as to what that more streamlined agenda might be – and where the EU can more fully reap its comparative advantage vis-à-vis the more established perspectives of the World Bank and IMF. We also venture to suggest that a dramatic improvement in EU development policy may be impossible without addressing some of the fundamental problems related to policy incoherence.

2. The Thorny Issue of Democracy Promotion

Since the inception in 1994 of the European Initiative for Democracy and Human Rights, the EU has become increasingly bold in its aspirations in the sphere of democracy promotion. Yet there is no denying the continued existence of quite deep fissures in the outlooks of member states towards the developing world. One manifestation of this is the rarity of agreements between the only two European members of the UN Security Council – France and the UK. Another is the way in which the French polity often sees itself imbued in a conflict of interests with 'anglophone' countries in Africa, an attitude which sometimes seems to verge on paranoia.[5] Clearly, though, such differences go beyond a simple dichotomy between French and British interests in the African continent. Germany, Italy, the Netherlands, Spain – indeed, all European member states – promote their own particular agenda of geographic allegiances. And to some extent, these different spheres of interests have been intensified by the process of enlargement to the East. A useful typology to help understand these different sets of interests of EU member states is put forward by Emerson et al., (2005), who identify a set of 'syndromes and cleavages' which permeate EU foreign policy (table 1).

Table 1 Some Syndromes and Cleavages among the EU's Member States

Preferences from geography ▪ North prefers north ▪ South prefers south	*Sensitivities from World War II:* ▪ Germany towards Israel and Russia
Sensitivities of former colonial powers: ▪ France and Spain towards the Maghreb ▪ Austria towards the Balkans	*Alternative European visions:* ▪ A united, democratic Europe ▪ A powerful, controllable core Europe
Sensitivities of the formerly colonised or occupied: ▪ Baltic and Central European states towards Russia	*Alternative world views:* ▪ New Europe Atlanticism ▪ Old Europe Gaullism

Source: Emerson et al., 2005: 178

These cleavages often undercut the EU's declared democracy promotion objectives, and cause more than a few problems with regards to the execution of development policy too. An example is the way in which southern-tier countries in the EU have often been less willing than their northern neighbours to rock the boat and push for more ambitious reform in North Africa and the Middle East – their proximity to the southern Mediterranean heightens their concerns over illegal migration and instability and makes them adopt a more conservative approach. In contrast, northern-tier countries such as Britain and Germany have pushed for a more stringent interpretation of the human rights clause embedded in the association agreements with the North African and Eastern Mediterranean countries. As a result, the EU has found it difficult to act in concert on the issue of reform. Instead, "the European Union has often found itself captive to the lowest common denominator, and rather than launching bold initiatives to promote Middle East reform, it has acted with excessive caution" (Yacoubian, 2004).

Nevertheless, there is a positive side to cleavages of this kind, in the sense that it raises the possibility of a subtle blend of roles for both national and EU role (Emerson et al., 2005). There have been repeated examples of member states promoting deeper EU relations with their favourite neighbours, using their comparative advantages in relations with these states to the EU's advantage. Whatever its shortcomings may be (see chapters 4 and 5), the Barcelona Process (as its name suggests, very much fuelled by Spanish interests) is an example of this. Another type of situation is where the member state may be politically inhibited from championing a strong democracy promotion policy in a former colony, but sees an advantage in the EU exploiting what Emerson et al. aptly call its 'historical innocence' to pursue such policies more freely. This kind of strategy can, for example, be seen with regard to what might be considered the EU's more 'principled' stand regarding the aftermath of the Ethiopian elections in 2006, vis-à-vis the much more realpolitik reactions of European governments such as those of the UK and Germany. According to Emerson et al., this type of complementarity of EU and member states can be interpreted as a kind of 'good cop, bad cop' strategy, whereby the intimately friendly national leader may persuade the partner state's leader to understand better the case for the EU's harsher conditionality.[6]

What are the main underlying challenges for the EU in the sphere of democracy promotion? Perhaps hitherto one of the main weaknesses of EU policy has been the way in which it has tended to be linked excessively to the establishment of a formal set of institutions or processes, such as support for the celebration of elections themselves. The EU is increasingly seen as a key player in the field of election observation. And most independent assessments consider that it is a role that it is being carried out fairly effectively. In 2005, Election Observation Missions took place for presidential or parliamentary elections, or referenda, in Afghanistan, Burundi, Guinea-Bissau, Lebanon, Liberia, Ethiopia, the Democratic Republic of Congo, Venezuela and Sri Lanka. And, as the EU itself declares, "in all these missions, the EU has gained visibility while becoming an increasingly critical actor in the reinforcement of the democratic process" (EC, 2006: 8).

But a braver policy stance would be to stress the *qualitative* side of democracy instead of focusing simply on how to carry out elections. Relevant here is the important distinction made by Diamond (1996) between *liberal democracy*, where there is extensive provision for political and civic pluralism as well as individual and group freedoms, and mere *electoral democracy*. In the latter, civil freedoms are less prized and minority rights are insecure. It is indeed worrying that among many of the newer democracies, there are signs of democractic erosion or 'hollowing out', settling on the form but less so on the substance of electoral democracy (Burnell, 2005:188). In the extreme, there is the possibility that policies by the EU and other Western governments to promote democracy in developing countries might aggravate a situation whereby democratic institutions end up being nothing more than an ineffective pretence, a sham – what might be termed a 'Potemkin democracy', simply for deceiving Western visitors.[7] One is instantly reminded of Mobutu Sese Seko's response to the *volte face* of the international community in the early 1990s, who in a moment of post-Cold War fervour, suddenly insisted on 'democratisation' – he first asked how this process of democratisation should be carried out, and when it was explained to him that this should entail the formation of political parties, he hurriedly set about forming literally hundred of political parties under the epithet 'multi-Mobutism'! More recent examples are not difficult to find either. As Santiso (2003: 13) notes, many new and restored democracies have ended up in an uneasy stage of democractisation: while possessing the formal attributes of democracy, the modes of governance tend to exhibit resilient autocratic features. Moreover, in recent years, democratically elected autocrats have displayed greater sophistication and bluntness at rigging elections, as the examples of Peru in 2000, Zimbabwe in 2002, and Ethiopia in 2005 arguably show. As argued by Roderick Pace in chapter 4, such practices are widespread in North Africa too.

A further, but fundamental, consideration is that democracy only takes on a realistic character if it results in significant changes in the overall distribution of power (Rueschemeyer, Stephens, and Stephens, 1992). As Pace notes in chapter 4 of the present volume, "*gestures of political liberalisation do not necessarily mean anything unless real powers are transferred from current political elites to democratically accountable institutions*". But in the modern world, such shifts in the power balance may be becoming even more difficult: in a global economy, with many interactions with international organisations (the international financial institutions, IFIs), the donor community, multinational corporations, and other constraints on national politics, it becomes increasingly pertinent to ask whether true democracy is ever attainable, in the sense of empowering individuals to control decision-making processes? Despite, for example, the remarkable vibrancy of autochthonous NGOs in countries like Bangladesh,[8] it has still been compatible with high levels of poverty. It would seem that we are, in other words, still a long way from attaining a new 'Great Transformation' in the developing world, in the sense of a political transformation which empowers poor people (Stewart, 2006).

Perhaps key to all this is the realisation that democracy is not a set of institutions, it is a mindset. And it took many centuries to cultivate in European countries and suffered many setbacks.[9] Reaching a political compromise (rather than adopting a winner-takes-all mentality) is surely one of the most important lessons to be learned for developing countries aspiring to establish a true democracy. If the EU spent more time reflecting on ways of helping to promote this, rather than focussing simply on the putting in place of the right institutional mechanisms, a much more effective pro-democracy policy might be devised. An alternative approach for the EU then would be to increase the support given to strengthening the more qualitative side of democracy – civil society, the free press, union movements, etc. – any counterbalance to the 'constitutional power' of the state. As Nancy Birdsall (2005: 23) has argued, donors need to end their apolitical approach. This is particularly critical in the case of pro-poor reforms, since they usually undermine powerful interests and have weak domestic constituencies. Ultimately, it may be that only when developing country recipients have more voice (and votes) in the major institutions will they assume real 'ownership' of pro-poor economic and political reforms donors wish to support. Part of the strategy would also include greater support for parliamentary reform, which is currently practically non-existent (Santiso, 2003: 9).

Yet evidently the EU has been reluctant to push such an agenda very hard. The whole budget for supporting the European Initiative for Democracy and Human Rights in 2007 was only €126.7 million. External observers have noted that the Commission tends to take a technocratic approach (as have other donors), focusing on limited issues such as the capacity of government administrations to handle management of public finances, rather than a political approach, for example by supporting the democratic oversight role of parliaments (Auclair, 2006). In North Africa, for instance, so far only a small number of projects have been aimed at institutional reform, and the EU has resisted directly funding parliaments, political parties, or trade unions. Following tensions with Mediterranean governments over some MEDA programming, the MEDA II political funding became more geared towards the less controversial areas of women's and children's rights. In fact, only a small percentage of MEDA funding directly targets democracy promotion; the vast majority of its funding is more closely oriented toward a traditional development mandate (Yacoubian, 2004). In chapter 7, Crawford makes a similar point regarding EU democracy promotion in Ghana.

In all fairness to the European Commission, it needs conceding that such a path is not unproblematic. In cases of particularly fragile societies, the danger that a more overtly political policy of supporting pluralism could degenerate into chaos is of course a real one, but in the final resort it is the only long-term way to build a properly functioning democracy. In her polemical tract 'World on Fire – How

Exporting Free-market Democracy Breeds Ethnic Hatred and Global Instability', Amy Chua (2003: 198) notes that there is always an inherent instability in a combination of free markets and democracy. This is because every one of the Western democracies has alleviated the potential conflict between the rich few and the poor many through a host of devices, past and present, such as extensive social safety nets and redistribution, gradual expansion of suffrage, upward mobility, and even racism. To be sure, such systems have suffered periodic crisis (what Habermas (1973) termed the 'legitimation crisis'). But as Chua rightly observes,

> It is important to recognise that as we export free market democracy to the non-Western world, that many of these stablising devices do not exist in the developing world, that some of them are unsavoury, and that others are, practically speaking, unreproducible.[10]

An additional consideration is that, because so much is at stake for opposition parties, there is a great need for responsible behaviour on the part of donors – giving out false hopes to the opposition can be extremely dangerous. For instance, during the 2005 elections in Egypt the Muslim Brotherhood became emboldened by statements of both EU and US officials, insinuating acceptance of the results of a democratic process even if it brought Islamists to power (generally speaking, the Brotherhood's leaders and members have demonstrated a commitment to a non-violent, reformist approach to Islamism) (El-Din Shadhin, 2005: 124). But the electoral process was marred by many irregularities, including the arrest of hundreds of Brotherhood members, and the crackdown on dissidents by the Egyptian government was hardly commented upon by outside observers, giving the impression that they had been subsequently abandoned to their fate.

Ethiopia provides another case study on these dangers. Encouraged by foreigners' support, and with an economic agenda much closer to what the EU or US might like to see (a programme of economic liberalisation and privatisation of the land), during the 2005 parliamentary elections the opposition coalition Kinijit felt that it was bargaining from a position of strength. But when the crackdown came, in the wake of allegations of massive election fraud committed by the ruling party and subsequent street protests, Western governments were nothing if not subdued in their criticism of the Ethiopian government. In fact, as noted earlier, only the European Commission offered staunch criticism of the government's tactics. The recent experience of elections in Ethiopia and Uganda, two previous 'darlings' of the international aid community, leave another important lesson for donors: aid for democracy also needs to take far more seriously how to help develop 'exit strategies' for entrenched parties and leaders. Elections are useless unless the existing authorities feel comfortable about the possibility of subsequently abandoning power.

To sum up, as pointed out by Gordon Crawford in chapter 7, unfortunately on democracy promotion the large gap between rhetoric and practice is evident for all to see. And donors' professed new 'pro-democracy' focus has not been supported by actual aid flows (Brown, 2005).[11] From this point of view, it could be argued that the problem is not the policies themselves, but rather the exaggerated claims made for EU policies. The rhetoric needs to be toned down and practical political engagement stepped up if policies are to be made more coherent on this sensitive issue.

3. The Controversial Issue of Aid Conditionality

What about wider questions related to policy conditionality? Despite exhaustive studies in the past that have tended to show aid conditionality to be ineffective,[12] conditionality is still extremely popular among the donor community. Conditionality has been used extensively in order to ensure that financial aid is used to pursue the objectives that donors consider legitimate. Are constraints on actions always a bad thing? Clearly not – if a country suffers from a brutal dictator, or there is the suppression of basic liberties, a constraint on action is clearly to be welcomed. The problem should be distinguished, however, from basic freedoms to conduct economic and social policy in a way that is compatible with developmental goals. The problem is that once it is accepted that donors/finance providers may act to constrain government actions in certain fields (e.g., in defence of political rights), how can we guarantee that they won't do so in other fields? Can they be trusted to act with self-discipline in this sense? The degree to which excessive conditionality can be counterproductive has been much discussed in the literature. As Chambers (2005: 39) has noted,

> Now, to a degree that during the 1960s would have been vilified as gross neo-colonialism, in many small and low-income countries – especially in sub-Saharan Africa – lenders and donors not only fund much government expenditure (over 50 percent in Uganda, for example), but also call many of the policy shots.

Edwards (1999: 118-120) uses the 'sticks and carrots' metaphor and notes that there is some evidence that conditions can influence economic policy more than social and political change, and that 'positive' conditions can work (the carrots) better than 'negative' ones (the sticks). Nevertheless, overall the links between outside influence, internal compliance, and tangible results on the ground are weak. Moreover, where the countries are large and their dependence on aid flows relatively minor (as in the case of countries like China or Indonesia), conditionality is a fairly futile exercise. In other cases, where the implications of abandoning a country to its fate are simply too onerous for the international community to assume (as was the case with Mexico with its bailout by the IMF after the financial collapse of 1994, or perhaps as in the contemporary case of Ethiopia in the horn of Africa, where the country is considered as a bulwark of stability in an otherwise conflict-ridden, terrorist-infiltrated region), conditionality will not work under any circumstances. This effectively means that conditionality is only really applied to countries too weak to resist – hardly a fair application of development principles. In this context, in recent years there has been some recognition of the need to tone down the requirements placed on developing countries – hence a greater emphasis on the importance of broader budget support by agencies like DFID and IFIs like the World Bank, with some donors (like Canada) abandoning conditionality altogether.

In Africa at least, the rising importance of Chinese influence is rapidly changing perceptions over conditionality. Whereas Western analysts and governments tend to see the entry of China as undermining their efforts to 'discipline' certain 'errant' governments, others see it as a promising new, more workmanlike, relationship between African governments and donors. Indeed, this would explain why African countries have been so accommodating to the overtures of the Chinese in the continent – there are no political conditionalities attached, and consequently African countries know (or at least think they know) where they stand. While it is untrue to say that the Chinese have not expressed concerns over how effectively their aid is used,[13] China has been accused of turning a blind eye to human rights abuses in some African countries and of refusing to lay down governance conditionalities on its African trading partners.

What is the correct path for the European Union to tread on these matters? There is no easy answer to these questions, and to pretend otherwise would be intellectually dishonest. In terms of democratic conditionalities, it is perhaps not too bold to assert that people in many developing countries simply do not believe US or European overtures about their wishes to strengthen democracy in developing countries (particularly in the Middle East) – when strategic interests come into play (as they have arguably done in the case of Ethiopia, where concerns over human rights abuses have generally been put aside in favour of being able to count on the Ethiopian government as an important ally in the 'war on terror'), the Western countries revert to form, and conveniently forget conditionality. The current US administration has perhaps been more blatant on this score than the EU, and it could be argued that the EU needs to distance itself from the US stance and pave a more independent, principled position for itself. Detailed conditionalities clearly do not work. But in cases where a government is clearly abusing human rights and its commitment to poverty reduction is questionable, the EU needs to act boldly, and make greater efforts to ensure that its member states work in unison on these issues.

4. What is Motivating the Economic Partnership Agreements?

What can we sum up about the economic dimensions of EU relations with the developing world? According to Holdar (2000: 73),

> The historical development of EC aid programs and the geography of EC member states' aid shows that the EU lacks a consistent strategy to guide its and the EU-15's relations with aid-recipient countries. The EU still acts primarily as a customs union in its relations with Third World countries (trade and aid issues are closely linked), and it is a mix of the national interests of member states that guides the distribution of EU aid, a mix related to changes in the relative power of member states within the Community.

Is this rather harsh judgement justified? Certainly, some of the evidence that we have reviewed in this book would seem to lend support to this view. Mold notes in chapter 5 that in its dealings with developing countries, the European Commission has tended to increasingly treat trade agreements as the principal catalyst of change in forcing countries to liberalise their economies. But it might not necessarily have been the best way of inducing developing countries to accept the need for reform. And, as Freres observes in chapter 6, there is certainly a whiff of mercantilism in the form of some of these agreements (e.g., the EU-Mexican agreement).

Perhaps one of the most puzzling policies of the Commission has been its persistence in pursuing the Economic Partnership Agreements with the ACP countries (see chapter 8). The formal explanations are given by Commission officials in an emphatic manner, but arguably are not totally convincing. It is claimed that with the ending of the WTO waiver, the EU had no alternative but to propose a move towards a reciprocal agreement. Yet, as Van Reisan explains in chapter

2, the ACP-Lome-Cotonou agreements are long-standing ones, and have never suffered a challenge through the WTO. True, the EU has had to defend other elements of its trade policy from challenges via the WTO dispute mechanism. One example is its banana scheme. As Stevens points out in chapter 9, the other was the (politically-motivated) extension of the GSP+ to Pakistan.[14]

It is also argued by the EU that the previous policies of non-reciprocal access failed. This argument could be interpreted as being self-serving, and implicitly blames the developing countries themselves for their predicament. But it does not reflect on the responsibility of the EU itself for this outcome. As shown in Mold (2004a), there is a whole range of reasons as to why non-reciprocal market access may have failed to elicit the desired supply response; many of them are tied up with the actual design of the schemes, rather than on weak supply side capacities of developing countries themselves (though this undoubtedly played an important role). Stevens' argument in chapter 9 that there is a need for legally binding non-reciprocal preferential market access agreement is valid here.[15]

In any case, economic analysis generally shows a small but unambiguously negative impact from the EPAs, no matter what methodology is used. Chapter 8 in this book, by McKay, Morrissey, and Milner, provides a straightforward and clear analysis of the economic risks that the EPAs imply for the developing countries that sign them. The EU has come under a barrage of complaints from NGOs and other research centres regarding what is seen as the unequal playing field for the EPAs.[16] Cautious, if not openly critical, assessments have come from more mainstream sources, too. World Bank economists Laurence Hinkle and Richard Newfarmer claim, for example, that

> To realize their potential development benefits, the European Union must truly treat EPAs as instruments of development, subordinating its commercial interests to Africa's development needs and effectively coordinating trade and development assistance. The African countries need to use EPAs to accelerate the trade and investment climate reforms necessary to raise growth rates and integrate their economies regionally and globally. A number of important issues will need to be addressed to limit the development risks associated with EPAs. *If these issues cannot be satisfactorily resolved, the EPA process could end up being replaced by improved preferences or even abandoned.* (Hinkle and Newfarmer, 2006: 163, emphasis added)[17]

Clearly, it makes little sense for developing countries to enter into agreements knowing that such agreements will have a prejudicial impact on their economies. The offer of economic compensation, in the form of *mise au niveau* programmes or in whatever other shape or form, hardly provides much reassurance to developing country governments – as pointed out in chapter 5, although the absolute amount of funds made available could be described as moderately generous, the record of the Euro-Mediterranean Agreements in terms of disbursements is not exactly encouraging.

Perhaps one of the most revealing incidents on the EPA issue was the conflict that recently arose between the European Commission and the UK government. The UK government's *Commission for Africa* (2005: 287-288) came up with a number of sharp criticisms of the EPAs. It was argued that poor countries should not be forced to liberalise and that the EU should adopt a 'non-mercantilist approach' in their negotiations with the ACP countries (implying of course that this is what it is now doing). It was suggested that individual African countries should be allowed to sequence their own trade reforms in line with their own poverty reduction and development plans, and that a gradualist timeframe should be introduced for any reciprocal requirements ('over 20 years if necessary'). Furthermore, additional financial assistance should be provided to support developing countries in building the capacity they need to trade and adjust to more open markets. The sting in the tale was left until the end: "The EC should commit itself more explicitly to this development-orientated approach, rather than a 'trade negotiator' approach that seeks concessions from ACP countries."

The response from the European Commission was no less vehement. According to a leaked internal Commission document,[18]

> The UK statement represents a major and unwelcome shift in the UK Position as it focuses exclusively on the potential risks and how the Commission must limit these and makes no mention of the opportunities. Some recommendations move well away from agreed EU positions set out in the Cotonou agreement and negotiating directives. Others are not compatible with WTO agreements. This makes the statement counterproductive as it could well make progress with EPA negotiations more difficult by reinforcing the views of the more sceptical ACP states, and raising the prospect of alternatives that are, in reality, impractical. This happened in fact already during technical meetings with Central Africa where the UK paper had been distributed.

The advocates of the EPAs in the Commission obviously feel that they are on strong technical grounds in making these charges. But the idea that the UK has been guilty of propagating views that have been uncritically taken up by ACP states might be seen as patronising – the Africa Commission report was simply reflecting concerns raised not only by members of the Africa Commission itself, but also the many countries and bodies that were consulted during the whole process.[19]

The argument in favour of the EPAs would be more convincing if the EU had previously expended more energy trying to renegotiate the Cotonou agreement, instead of simply presupposing the impossibility of a further extension within the WTO. Moreover, one gets the distinct feeling that the EU is itself of two minds about the EPAs. DG-Development, from whose remit the EPAs were transferred, is distinctly cooler about the whole project than DG-Trade. The EC's own mid-term Report on Sustainability Impact Assessments[20] warns that EPAs 'might accelerate the collapse of the modern West African manufacturing sector' and could also 'further discourage the development of processing and manufacturing capacity in the ACP countries in export-oriented and other industries'. Such institutional misalignments do little to restore confidence in what seems to be a flawed process of negotiations.

Perhaps most controversially of all is the way in which the EPAs are seemingly being used to pursue the 'Singapore Issues' – investment, competition policy, transparency in government procurement, and trade facilitation. Despite the insistence of the European Commission on these issues in multilateral fora, in face of firm opposition from developing countries they were considered too divisive during the Doha Round of WTO negotiations and were subsequently dropped. The fact that they have reappeared in the EPA negotiations makes many suspect that the EU is guilty of imposing its own agenda over poorer developing countries simply by dint of its economic and political power. As Jawara and Kwa (2004: xxii) have argued,

> Since Cancun, many have bemoaned the possible demise of multilateralism, represented by the WTO; its replacement with bilateral negotiations has been held over the developing countries as a dire threat. This is a false choice. For the USA and EC, bilateral agreements and the WTO are not alternatives but two parts of the same strategy. What cannot be attained in one arena is pursued in the other, and 'progress' in one strengthens the other.

Of course, if such interpretations of intentionality are accurate, the more powerful developing nations – India, South Africa, Brazil, China, and perhaps Nigeria – may feel that they can resist the pressures from the EU or the United States. These large countries have been able to choose the pace and degree of liberalisation, whereas small African countries generally had to take the medicine in one go, with Latin American countries in an intermediate position (Stewart, 2006: 8). In such a scenario, what we can look forward to is not the catastrophic implosion of developing country aspirations as a whole, but rather what Churchill once called 'the agony of little nations'. This would surely constitute a step backwards for development policy.

5. A Deeper Dilemma with Development Policy?

On a deeper level, the difficulties currently being experienced by EU development policy can perhaps be seen as part of a wider problem with development policy in general and development economics (the self-appointed crown prince of the social sciences) in particular. In chapter 3 of this volume, Marjorie Lister documents the long-standing frustration with development theory and policy. The patent but uncomfortable truth for development professionals is that development policy in general has been failing, no matter where it originates from. Over the last 50 years, aid in aggregate has not had the positive impact that many of its advocates had hoped. Too often, what has been dressed up as progressive development policy is in fact motivated by self-interest. And frequently it seems that there is a mismatch, with policymaking leading to progress in one field being offset by prejudicial policies in another. We have certainly seen elements of this in European policymaking. Why is this?

One explanation is simply the level of the debate. Within the international development community there are some unspoken truths that are not supposed to be challenged – for instance, that 'trade liberalisation is the way to accelerated growth', 'democracy is a prerequisite for any kind of development', 'good governance is indispensable for poverty reduction', etc. Much of the development discourse has also become pervaded by clichés, with words like 'empowerment', 'mainstreaming', and 'participation' being bandied around so frequently that they have become emptied of their meaning.[21] Many critics associate this kind of discourse exclusively with the Bretton Woods institutions (in particular, the World Bank and the International Monetary Fund), but it is of course also very much true of the European Commission (as well as many NGOs and UN bodies). In *Kicking Away the Ladder*, the Korean economist Ha-Joon Chang (2002) dares to challenge many of these sacred cows. His book is a passionate assault on the economic orthodoxy as espoused by the IFIs and supported by the majority of our leading academic institutions. In an attempt to defy the Hegelian proposition that 'the only thing we learn from history is that we learn nothing from history', Chang revindicates the importance of history as a tool for learning about development strategies. The core of the book involves an in-depth analysis of historical records of the now-industrialised countries during their own period of economic, social, and political transformation, drawing a number of important lessons from their experience for today's developing countries. The principle message that Chang conveys is that, on most of the major issues, the policy advice given to developing countries over the last two decades has not only been fundamentally wrong, it also ignores the historical experience of the industrialised countries themselves in their own struggle towards development. Consequently, the policy advice they receive is not only mistaken – it is essentially hypocritical.

Take the issue of free trade. There is a great need to deconstruct the myth that the now-developed countries adopted free-trade policies during their own industrial revolutions. It is no small irony that the United States (the country which now extols the virtues of free-trade regimes more aggressively than any other) resorted to extensive tariff protection during crucial moments in the development of its own emergent industries. But in fact, *none* of the now-industrialised countries adopted a free-trade regime in the nineteenth century, not even Britain (whose subsequent shift in the latter half of the nineteenth century towards free trade coincided with the country's demise as the world's leading manufacturing producer). Indeed, bearing in mind the lack of other policy instruments in existence then to promote infant industry, 'tariff protection was a far more important policy tool in the nineteenth century than it is in our time' (Chang, 2003: 17). Yet through bilateral pressure and the workings of the World Trade Organization (WTO), it is a tool which the industrialised countries steadfastly deny to today's developing countries.

On governance, too, there is a clear gap between the contemporary discourse and historical reality. The historical fallacy of the good governance approach is to imagine that the advanced industrial economies developed by first introducing stable property rights, establishing democracy, and eradicating corruption. As Cramer (2006: 41) points out, this argument is wrong on every count: Democratic institutions arrived very late in the day in most Western countries, and their implementation generally preceded the economic transformation in their societies towards industrialisation. In fact, most Western states only brought in male political citizenship rights as late as the early twentieth century and, in many cases, universal suffrage was brought in only as late as the mid-twentieth century (Hobson, 2004: 290). Moreover, it could be argued that the idea of the importance of 'good governance' has always been intellectually flawed (who would want 'bad' governance?) 'Good' is a loaded word and tends to be defined in terms of hegemonic conceptions of what is deemed 'good'. This is certainly true with regard to institutional design and for a whole range of institutions (e.g., social welfare, patenting laws, central banking, bankruptcy laws, securities regulation, and, pointedly, democratic political systems) standards in the industrialised countries were found wanting during their own surge towards development: many of the respective laws were either non-existent or inoperative and the quality of bureaucratic institutions often highly questionable. In contrast, nowadays the quality of the institutions prevalent in developing countries is generally much higher than when the industrialised countries were at a comparable level of development. So why all the fuss about 'good governance' now, unless the intention is to set standards so high that developing countries will inevitably fail? In addition, the needless insistence on state-of-the-art institutions in poor countries implies a waste of scarce bureaucratic time and resources that could be used for much better ends.[22]

On one level, such arguments contain little that is new: the main message is all there to read in classic works like Eric Hobsbawm's (1975) *The Age of Capital* or Paul Bairoch's (1971) *Le Tiers Monde dans l'Impasse*. But although these authors deal with some of the same themes, the merit of the aforementioned book by Chang is the way that it brings the arguments together in a concerted fashion for the first time and stresses the relevance of these historical experiences to contemporary debates on the problems of the developing world. Chang argues that, intentionally or not, contemporary policy advice to developing countries is impeding economic progress in the poorest developing countries – 'kicking away the ladder', so to speak – so that developing countries cannot follow in the footsteps of the industrialised countries. On a whole range of issues, from trade and technology policies, the establishment of democratic institutions, to the use of child labour, the industrialised countries are now compelling developing countries to reach standards and adopt policies that they are either incapable of meeting or, if they do, will impede their own development.[23]

In fact, arguments regarding inappropriate policy advice and the excessive demands placed upon developing country institutions could be taken a step further; it could be maintained that most economists and policymakers do not even apply orthodox economic principles coherently – they focus excessively on particular issues, like international trade and the importance of liberalising capital movements, and almost completely ignore other issues that may be equally or more important from the point of view of theoretical coherence, but are consciously or subconsciously deemed politically off-limits. Take, for instance, the incoherent application of restrictions on migration. Under free market principles, in the same way that the IFIs and orthodox economists argue passionately in favour of the free movement of capital, they should also be vigorously lobbying for the removal of all restrictions on migration.[24] Yet, with one or two notable exceptions, orthodox economists are usually conspicuously silent on the issue of immigration, despite quite considerable evidence that 'mode 4' liberalisation (i.e., the free movement of workers) would provide benefits several times those estimated to be derived from trade liberalisation.[25]

What implications does all this have for the way in which policy advice is given and received? Neoliberal ideology (even when dressed up in a more progressive language) has become so pervasive that institutions and countries are increasingly constrained in their actions and, more seriously, their policy options ('policy space'). There is, in other words, a straitjacket on development thinking, and except within narrowly defined limits, experimentation with alternative policies is not permitted. Lots of elements that were intrinsic to the development of the industrialised countries, like the elaboration of an industrial policy or the protectionism of domestic firms, have become effectively out of bounds.

Yet one thing that supporters of the new set of policies cannot hide is the poor economic results that it has produced. Simply on an intuitive level, there is something fundamentally wrong when mass unemployment, like the kind that exists in many parts of the developing world today, can coexist with so many unmet basic needs. Something is clearly failing in the economic system if the right set of incentives cannot be put in place to provide meaningful work for so many people. Even in terms of economic growth (the overriding objective), neoliberal policies have failed to produce the expected results. In the two decades since the policies were first applied, growth rates have declined significantly compared to the period prior to the reforms. A few years ago, even the IMF felt obliged to concede that "progress in raising real incomes and alleviating poverty has been disappointingly slow in many developing countries, and the relative gap between the richest and poorest countries has continued to widen." (IMF, 2000: 113).[26] This is more than a little ironic, because the policies were originally sold precisely on the grounds that they would improve economic performance.

Against this backdrop, the growing frustration in developing countries with the orthodox set of policies is understandable. Moreover, the justification used to explain this poor performance is beginning to wear thin – the policies would have worked, it is often argued, if only they had been applied with more vigour and developing country governments had been prepared to stay the course. This kind of argument is common in Africa nowadays: In the post-independence period, blame for the ills of the continent were squarely (and often fairly) laid on the colonial powers by, for example, not having built up domestic capacities (lack of education and institutional development), for having built infrastructures that did not serve to develop the local economy, and for having created balkanised and unviable political structures. In the era of the post-Washington Consensus, however, the whole argument has shifted back to the other extreme: Once again, everything, it is implied, is Africa's fault – *their* poor governance, *their* poor implementation of policies, *their* corruption. No matter that the policies applied were generally designed and shaped by foreign experts and donors and the feasibility of their implementation never tested. In a generally overlooked, but deeply insightful book, Atul Kohli (2004: 12) notes that

> the nearly exclusive focus in the literature on appropriate policy choices is incomplete, even misleading. Policy choices matter, of course, but these choices must be explained. More important, the impact of the same policy applied in two different settings may vary because of the contextual differences, some of the more obvious being varying global conditions and different initial conditions of an economy.

From this point of view, there is no one 'correct' policy, nor one 'incorrect' one. Implementation is the key. If this diagnosis is right, there is a need for development policy to engage in a realistic evaluation of policy options – in other words, a return to *political economy*. Peter Nolan (2004: 97) is quite right when he argues that "far too often, economic advice has been little more than slogans. Too rarely has it consisted of careful, pragmatic political economy".

6. The Malaise of Development Economics

There may be an even simpler explanation for the poor policy-making advice and institutional obligations thrust upon developing countries. And here a heavy dose of self-criticism by the economics profession is sorely needed. The Malawian economist Thandeka Mkwandawire (2004: 2) has argued that, in order to explain the domination of one particular economic idea, we need to know more about how ideas are formed and disseminated within the economics profession and how these ideas are related to political power structures:

> In this age of deconstruction of intellectual schemas, and from rhetorical and sociological approaches to methodology, we have learned to accept that ideas that become accepted at any given time are not necessarily the 'best ones' but those that 'win out'.

In large measure, the resurgence of neoclassical economics has been associated with the immense resources at the disposal of the Bretton Woods institutions and the governments of the industrialised countries to propagate orthodox economic ideas and theories (Chang, 2003a). As Robert Wade (2004) has noted, '*in the rhetoric battle, the paradigm which provides certainties wins. But it is not necessarily right for that.*' The vast consultancy budgets at their disposal has given the IFIs a particularly powerful sway over economic thinking. Within the academic world, peer-group and professional pressure mean that the reputation of an economist is largely determined by the number of publications they achieve in a few select journals – most of these are published in the developed countries (particularly the US), and most have a very narrow view of economics. Moreover, salaries for professional economists are so low in most developing countries that a World Bank or IMF consultancy can be irresistible. In sum, the pressures within the economics profession to conform to what Albert Hirschman once eloquently termed 'monoeconomics' are enormous.[27]

The irony here is that, despite their often quite different philosophy and approach to development economics, continental European countries have done little to promote an 'alternative world view'. The EU's aid apparatus sorely lacks the research capacities of institutions such as the World Bank and thus encounters difficulties in setting its own agenda and having its voice heard in multilateral forums (Santiso, 2003: Maxwell et al., 2004). This is somewhat paradoxical. Many European research centres on development are excellent – and there is a strong tradition in development studies that is generally conspicuous by its absence in the United States. In comparison with the abstract theory that tends to emerge from the economics departments of the best US universities, the more historically-based and multidisciplinary approaches to teaching development dominant in Europe have potentially far more relevance to developing countries. But despite the efforts of European-wide associations like EADI, the EU lacks the dense network of policy think tanks that inform US foreign aid policy.

It is also worth noting that in practice European countries have been markedly pragmatic in their approach to economic policy. It was observed a long time ago that there is no obvious correlation between the success of an economy and the intellectual distinction and prestige of its economic theorists – countries like Germany or France,which thrived in the post-war period, produced few acknowledged geniuses of economic science (Hobsbawm, 1980). This observation provokes the response that contemporary economic theory may not only often be wrong – it might also be irrelevant. Certainly, as Lawson (1997: 3) notes,

> Contemporary academic economics is not in a healthy state. Over many years now problems have regularly come to light which throw considerable doubt on the capacity of many of its strands to explain or even always address, real world events or to facilitate policy evaluation.[28]

Why is the economics profession apparently failing developing countries so dismally? One reason, which we hinted at earlier, may be the way in which so much time and effort is dedicated by economists to subjects that are of marginal interest to the real problems of development. Prichett and Woolcock (2004: 192) are arguably right when they comment

> Most agree the debate about the Washington consensus is blown far out of proportion. At times 90 percent of the ink spilled addresses 10 percent of the development battle; in the end, no matter who is right about trade policy, fiscal deficits and the like, these policies do not add up to anything like a complete development agenda ... Policies such as trade openness, fiscal probity, etc. need to be seen as part of, not a substitute for, a coherent development strategy. Even the 'augmented Washington consensus' that adds the provision of some key services (such as education) to the standard policy agenda leaves wide open the standard policy question of how things will actually be accomplished. In general economists have focused their tools on the question of what governments should do, with relatively less attention given to the economics and politics of how to accomplish the 'what'.

In this context, one of the most glaring weaknesses of modern economic theory is the almost obsessive concentration on prices, exchange, and macroeconomic stability, and the lack of attention regarding how to enhance productive capacities. The ironically named'supply-side revolution' of the 1980s ('ironic' because it actually dedicates little or no attention to the actual conditions of supply), led by the governments of Margaret Thatcher and Ronald Reagan, had a deeper influence on economic thinking than is commonly thought – vanished were the ideas of Keynes regarding the importance of avoiding coordination failures and maintaining a high level of aggregate demand, despite abundant evidence that many developing countries are suffering the consequences of precisely this kind of problem. And, although the idea has been creeping back in the watered-down form of Poverty Reduction Strategy Paper (PRSPs) and Comprehensive Development Frameworks (CDFs), gone too are most attempts to provide a planned, strategic response to the challenges of development. Ideas on strengthening the supply side tend to be limited to 'getting prices right' and liberalisation. If the private sector fails to spontaneously respond to such incentives, so the argument goes, then it is their fault for demonstrating a lack of business acumen and entrepreneurship.

Fortunately, orthodoxies have a nasty habit of turning on their promoters. There are clear signs of chinks in the intellectual armoury of neoliberal thinking. The fact that such a respected orthodox economist as Stiglitz defected several years ago to the *other side* was clearly a sign that things were changing.[29] The subtle but marked shift in the position of institutions like the World Bank and the International Monetary Fund (which now, for example, accepts that there may be a case in favour of capital account controls) is also illustrative as to how far the debate has moved on in recent years. Heterodox development economists may have lost many intellectual battles in the past, but might well end up winning the war. With the possibly definitive abandonment of the Doha Round, the globalisation project is perhaps at risk of unraveling itself.

7. Towards a Conclusion: How Can the EU Genuinely Help Restore 'Policy Space'?

This intellectual detour has had, as its purpose, to put the apparent failings of EU development policy in a broader perspective. The problems identified in this volume are not simply a function of the failure of European policy towards the developing world, but a much wider malaise with development policy. If the arguments put forward here are correct, there is an urgent need to restore a balance to contemporary debates on development – to re-establish a sense of proportion regarding what is important in achieving development.

So, where do we go from here? Clearly, the policy advice stemming from analysis like that contained in Chang (2002) and Kohli (2004) is that there is a need for developing countries to retain more independence in the elaboration and execution of their own policies ('policy space'). How could the EU contribute to this objective? Such a viewpoint might be construed as naïve, but the EU is sufficiently powerful, as an institution and as individual member states, to help developing countries win greater autonomy within the international fora like the WTO. Rather than simply err on the side of caution and reinforce traditional alliances (especially the transatlantic partnership), more concerted efforts could be made to establish deeper partnerships with developing countries, along the lines discussed by Lister in chapter 3 and Freres in chapter 7. The EU could also be instrumental in providing greater freedom from the overbearing external pressure placed upon developing countries by donors and the IFIs. For these aspirations to become a credible reality, those institutions would have to undergo a process of democratisation themselves – something again in which the EU could be instrumental and play a constructive role, if it so wished.

Nor is the EU immune from criticism on this score: With its complex and delicate balance between the Council of Ministers, the Commission and Parliament, the decision-making process within the EU is not wholly legitimate. Although the system is generally considered to have worked well in the initial stages of European integration, successive enlargements of the EU have led to questions regarding their respective roles. As spelt out in chapter 2 of this volume, many of the problems with EU development policy identified in this volume ultimately stem from archaic and inefficient institutional arrangements. Reform of EU institutions themselves may therefore be a prerequisite for articulating a more coherent development policy. It is difficult to justify lecturing developing countries on the merits of democratic institutions when the EU's own system of decision making is so far from perfect.

All this should put European aspirations to promote democracy and good governance in the developing world into perspective. In his controversial but thought-provoking recent book, William Easterly (2006: 156) argues that "the official aid agencies simply don't know how to change bad governments into good governments with the apparatus of foreign aid. Bad government has far deeper roots than anything the West can affect." Analyses contained in chapters 4 and 7 of this book and elsewhere would certainly seem to back up this assessment. In the final resort, as Adrian Leftwich (2000) notes in his comprehensive review of the empirical evidence on the relationship between democratisation and development, the best way to guarantee democratic consolidation in the developing world is through enhancing economic performance. Getting development policy 'right' is thus key and, as the world's major donor, the EU has a responsibility to contribute to this outcome.

Several of the chapters in this book identify a need for the EU to lay out its own strategy more explicitly. As Santiso (2003: 23) has argued,

> The need for more coherent aid policies and strategies should not lead the EU to adopt the IFIs agenda, but rather to influence and challenge it. In particular, and unlike the IFIs, the identity of EU aid is founded on its distinctively political character and approach. Challenging the intellectual monopoly of the IFIs on aid policies and the predominance of economic approaches to development will require the EU to enhance its credibility as an innovator and leader in development thinking.

In this context, recent plans for the EU to introduce its own annual 'Development Report' (Maxwell et al., 2006) are to be welcomed, as a first step on the way of articulating a more coherent 'European view' of development policy. Despite the existence of many excellent research centres in Europe, such as the Institute of Social Studies (ISS) in The Hague, or the Institute of Development Studies (IDS) in Brighton, research efforts are at present too fragmented and there are insufficient cross-border collaborations. Strengthening existing European-wide networks on development research, particularly Bonn-based EADI, would also be a prime way of providing the catalyst for a new 'European approach' to development.

Finally, it is quite evident from the chapters in this book that not much progress can be expected unless the EU tackles major policy incongruencies like the Common Agricultural Policy. Beyond the problems invoked earlier in aid strategy and delivery, the damage done through policy incoherence in other areas (such as requesting excessively onerous concessions in trade deals or condoning abusive fishing policies of member states) can potentially far outweigh the benefits accruing from development aid. The first development rule should be 'do no harm' and, regrettably, on a number of scores, the EU does not currently pass this test.

We would not however like to end this final chapter on a negative note. As the title of this chapter ('Between a Rock and a Hard Place') alludes, it needs acknowledging that the choices for European development policy makers are not easy ones. In this context, Hoebink's (2005:163) evaluation of European development aid is probably one of the most adroit:

> The answer to the question 'Is the EU a "good" aid donor?' has to be mixed: the EU is a slow, bureaucratic donor, demanding a lot of paperwork, effective in some sectors and clearly inefficient in others. But the EU is also generous, imposes low levels of conditionality, with fewer strings attached to aid than most other donors.

As suggested in the introduction to this book, the EU enjoys considerable influence in its relations with the developing world. It can use this influence either to pursue its own agenda, or genuinely allow developing countries more 'policy space'. That would require a major rethink of policies such as the EPAs, the Euro-Mediterranean agreement, or indeed on areas related to democracy promotion. Articulating more fully a 'European view' on development policy (without subsequently imposing that view) would go some way to helping achieve this objective. Hopefully, this current volume will help provide some useful reflections in this process.

Notes

1 The views expressed herein are those of the author and do not necessarily reflect the views of the United Nations, nor should they be attributed collectively to the authors of this book. The author would like to thank Gordon Crawford for some very insightful comments on an earlier draft of this chapter. Any errors of course remain the responsibility of the author.

2 One recent example is the involvement of the EU in trying to establish a UN mission to keep peace between Lebanon and Israel. Another is the border between Ukraine and the breakaway Moldovan region of Trandsniestria which is patrolled by EU forces. The EU's influence goes further afield too. For instance, in Indonesia EU troops are monitoring the peace in Aceh. EU soldiers have also been sent to supervise Congo's recent election.

3 For instance, on his first ever visit to Africa the UK's Chancellor of the Exchequer Gordon Brown declared boldly that "I've talked to many people on my visit to Africa and the days of Britain having to apologise for its colonial history are over. We should move forward. We should celebrate much of our past rather than apologise for it." See "It's Time to Celebrate Empire, says Brown", by Benedict Brogan, The Daily Mail online, 15 January 2005, http://www.dailymail.co.uk/pages/live/articles/news/news.html?in_article_id=334208&in_page_id=1770. It might be added that similar declarations by politicians from other European countries with long and not always noble colonial histories, such as Belgium, France and Spain, are not difficult to find.

4 Several such institutional inconsistencies, which are difficult to resolve without undertaking a thorough internal reorganisation, are discussed by van Riesen in chapter 2 of this volume.

5 The perceived 'loss' of Rwanda to the Anglophone government of the Rwandan Patriotic Front (RPF), in the aftermath of the genocide of 1994, is one such instance. Djibouti, too, is increasingly 'passing to the other side'.

6 Ana Gomes, the EU official in charge of the Election Observation Mission, was far more outspoken in her criticisms of government repression during the post-election crisis than her counterparts in the British and German Embassies, and was subsequently barred by the Ethiopian authorities from entering Ethiopia. Whether such an outcome can really be called a 'strategy' (the different positions taken do not appear to have been planned or intentional, but rather the fruit of genuinely different perspectives on the crisis) might be debateable of course.

7 The term 'Potemkin village' derives from the apocryphal tale of Catherine the Great's Field Marshall Grigory Potemkin's attempt to hide the failure of a gigantic scheme for the colonisation of the Ukrainian steppe by erecting artificial villages to be seen by the empress as she inspected progress.

8 Stewart (2006: 13) notes, for instance, that total micro-credit provision in Bangladesh is estimated to extend to over 13 million people, and that the health and nutrition programmes of the NGO BRAC are estimated to cover over 30 million people (http://www.brac.net/about.htm).

9 None of this is to subscribe to the Eurocentric idea that development of democracy is inimitable to European civilisation. As Amartrya Sen (2003) eloquently argues, democracy as a concept has universal roots. Moreover, although it may be argued that our contemporary understanding of democracy has Greek origins, this may well have been forgotten had it not been for the Arab-Islamic heritage that conserved the idea of democracy during the European Dark Ages (Tibi, 2005).

10 Although Chua does not acknowledge this, her ideas on this subject constitute a revisiting (2001) of Polanyi's ideas, as embodied in his classic text 'The Great Transformation'. For an excellent discussion of the relevance of 'The Great Transformation' to the contemporary situation in developing countries, see the aforementioned paper by Stewart (2006).

11 Particularly scathing criticism of this has recently been made by William Easterly (2006: 132-33), who notes that "foreign aid is used as political reward to allied governments, no matter how unsavoury they are ... so we had the world's twenty-five most undemocratic government rulers (out of 199 countries the World Bank rated on democracy) get a sum of $9 billion in foreign aid in 2002."

12 For example, Mosley, Harrigan, and Toye (1995), or Crawford (2000).

13 For instance, see Anver Versi, (2006), 'A Meeting of Minds and Needs', *African Business*, who discusses Chinese intervention in Angola to stop its aid money diverted to other uses.

14 This occurred at the time of the war in Afghanistan when the US administration was negotiating to enlist the support of the Pakistani government for its 'war on terrorism'. The EU was pressured to do something in support of this objective and so extended its GSP-drugs (GSP+) scheme to Pakistan, despite the fact that this scheme had really only been intended for Latin American countries suffering from serious problems related to drug-trafficking and production.

15 The question of making such preferential access legally binding has also been raised in other fora (e.g., Mold, 2005). Perez (forthcoming) makes the interesting, but controversial, proposal that rather than switching to EPAs, a simple expansion of the GSP might make an attractive alternative.

16 See, for instance, the websites of ActionAid http://www.actionaid.org.uk/1412/epas.html or Christian Aid http://www.christian-aid.org.uk/indepth/505epas/index.htm.

17 In private, this author has in fact heard an evidently well-meaning EU official acknowledge that the African ACP countries are in no condition to compete with the EU, and that the result of the EPAs would probably be the decimation of many domestic industries and a concomitant huge increase in imports (the capital account permitting, of course). But the same official suggested that this would be a good thing – it would break down 'rent-seeking' activities and oblige the state to renounce its control on economic activity. This turns the conventional wisdom on the merits of export-orientation and liberalisation on its head and suggests that through 'export failure' and a massive surge in imports an economy can be turned around. It does also reflect what is arguably a rather naïve and one-dimensional view of the political economy of African countries.

18 See EPA Watch, www.epawatch.net/documents/doc287_1.doc

19 Even the UN General Secretary Kofi Annan argued in his address to the ACP heads of state that the EPA's 'threaten to further hinder [their] ability to achieve the Millennium Development Goals' (Oxfam, 2006: 15).

20 Available at http://trade-info.cec.eu.int/doclib/

21 It is perhaps revealing that many of these words were not even used in development circles a few decades ago – they might, in some sense, be considered completely artificial artefacts. As Chambers (2005: 98) notes, "Language has changed. In the 1970s we did not use many of the words that are current today. 'Equity' and 'poverty' were there. But of the six power-and-relationship words now in common use, the only one I have found in what I wrote is 'participation': there was no trace of 'empowerment', 'ownership', 'partnership', 'accountability' or 'transparency'. These concepts and priorities had no yet been articulated."

22 Moreover, for critics, institutions like the World Bank and the IMF can hardly be regarded as the most qualified institutions to lecture developing countries on governance, given their own tainted record on transparency and democratic decision making. See, for instance, Raghavan (2004).

23 This viewpoint might be labelled excessively pessimistic. But on another level, it could be argued that the current situation, although regrettable, is entirely understandable. History shows us that hegemonic powers have always attempted to bend the rules in their favour. In this sense, rule-bending by the US is no more blatant than that carried out by, say, the British in India, with the suppression of the Indian textile industry, or in China, with the opium wars (Bairoch, 1993).

24 Appealing to factor-price equalisation through the workings of the Stolpher-Samuelson theorem (i.e., claiming that trade substitutes for the free movement of labour) does not totally let them off the proverbial hook. On two grounds, the argument is particularly shaky: first, convergence between countries would be very much accelerated through the free movement of labour; secondly, the Stolpher–Samuelson theorem significantly weakens the case for the free movement of capital, which is considered by orthodox economists as the cornerstone of the international system, because it inevitably leads to the question 'why have one but not the other?'

25 The degree of selectivity in the orthodox discourse is often startling. For example, whereas there are continual exaltations for developing countries to harmonise labour and environmental legislation to industrialised country standards, there has never to date been any serious attempt to propose global standards with respect to taxation. Why are international standards in one area considered beneficial and another not? Tax competition clearly distorts the decisions of market agents, affecting the allocation of resources, and has potentially serious effects on a state's ability to finance its expenditures on social and infrastructural development (Mold, 2004c). Yet the granting of selective tax holidays or other exemptions to encourage investment abroad has been positively encouraged by the IMF and World Bank (Shutt, 2001: 80).

26 Chambers (2005: 97-98) recalls that "the conditions, approaches and outlook in Eastern Africa in the late 1960s and early 1970s were strikingly different from those in the early 21st century. In the earlier period, in sub-Saharan Africa, many conditions were better. The outlook was optimistic. Neither I, nor any but the most dire pessimists, could have dreamt of the downturns that were to come. In Eastern Africa, 30 years later, it is appalling to see how much has changed for the worse."

27 It is also highly significant that the liberal pro-market philosophy almost all comes from outside the developing world, being led by names such as Milton Friedman (US), Tibor

Scitovsky (US), Ian Little, (UK), Bela Balssa (US), Anne Kruger (US), with Deepak Lal and Jagdish Bhagwati (from India, but educated in the UK) almost the sole developing country representatives (Stewart, 2006: 8).

28 Elsewhere, Chang (2003b) has questioned the usefulness of economists for tackling the problems of underdevelopment and suggested that developing countries intent on establishing a good economic bureaucracy and management should put more emphasis on recruiting people of generally high calibre, rather than looking for specialists in economics. The experience of countries like Taiwan and South Korea, where the representation of career bureaucrats with technical backgrounds in field such as engineering is far more predominant than in Western governments, would seem to bear out this evaluation.

29 Other economists from within the World Bank are also showing increasing signs of rebellion against the official line. Milanovic (2002: 1), for instance, argues that "It is only by a serious misreading of the recent evidence that the partisans of globalisation are able to argue for its unmitigated munificence".

References

Auclair, Denise (2006), 'The EU's Good Governance Agenda in Development : Europe Should Prioritise National Accountability', *World Economy and Development in Brief*, 25 September, available at www.wdev.eu).

Bairoch, Paul (1971), *Le tiers-Monde dans l'Impasse*, Paris: Gallimard.

Bairoch, Paul (1993), *Economics and World History – Myths and Paradoxes*, Chicago: University of Chicago Press.

Brown, Stephen (2005), '*Foreign Aid and Democracy Promotion: Lessons from Africa*', *European Journal of Development Research*, vol. 17, no. 2, June.

Burnell, Peter (2005), 'Democratization' in Peter Burnell and Vicky Randall (eds.), *Politics in the Developing World*, Oxford: Oxford University Press, Chapter 12, pp. 185-202.

Chambers, Robert (2005), *Ideas for Development*, London: Earthscan.

Chang, Ha-Joon (ed.) (2003a), *Rethinking Development Economics*, Anthem Press: London.

Chang, Ha-Joon (2003b), *Globalisation, Economic Development and the Role of the State*, London: Zed Books.

Chang, Ha-Joon and Ilene Grabel (2004), *Reclaiming Development – An Alternative Economic Policy Manual*, London: Zed Books.

Chua, Amy (2003), *World on Fire – How Exporting Free-Market Democracy Breeds Ethnic Hatred and Global Instability*, London: William Heineman.

Commission for Africa (2005), 'Our Common Interest – Report of the Commission for Africa', London: DFID.

Cramer, Chris (2006), *Civil War is Not a Stupid Thing – Accounting for Violence in Developing Countries*, London: Hurst and Company.

Crawford, Gordon (2000), *Foreign Aid and Political Reform: a comparative analysis of democracy assistance and political conditionality*. Basingstoke, Palgrave.
Degnbol-Martinussen, John and Poul Engbert-Pedersen (2003), *Aid – Understanding International Development Cooperation*, London: Zed Books.
Diamond, Larry (1996), *Developing Democracy: Towards Consolidation*, Baltimore: The John Hopkins University Press.
Easterly, William (2002), 'Growth in Ethiopia: Retrospect and Prospect', Center for Global Development Institute for International Economics, April.
Easterly, William (2006), *The White Man's Burden – Why the West's Efforts to Aid the Rest Have Done So Much Ill and So Little Good*', London: Penguin Press.
The Economist (2006), 'Abroad Be dangers – Doubts over Sending Troops to Lebanon Say Much about the European Union's Aspirations to Play a Bigger Role in the World', August 24.
Edwards, Michael (1999), *Future Positive – International Co-operation in the 21st Century*, London: Earthscan Publications.
El-Din Shahin, Emad (2005), 'Egypt's Moment of Reform: A Reality or an Illusion?', in Michael Emerson (ed),. *Democratisation in the European Neighbourhood*, Brussels, Centre for European Policy Studies,
Emerson, Michael (ed.) (2005), *Democratisation in the European Neighbourhood*, Brussels: Centre for European Policy Studies.
Emerson, Michael, Senem Aydin, Gergana Noutcheva, Nathalie Tocci, Marius Vahl and Richard Youngs (2005), '*The Reluctant Debutante: The EU as Promoter of Democracy in its Neighbourhood*', in Michael Emerson (ed.), *Democratisation in the European Neighbourhood*, Brussels, Centre for European Policy Studies.
Fukuyama, Francis (2006), *America at the Crossroads: Democracy, Power, and the Neoconservative Legacy*, New Haven: Yale University Press.
Gnesotto, Nicole (2005), 'Europe and America's different visions of how to help the Third World', *Europe's World*, Autumn, available at http:///europesworld.link.be/europesworld/Body.htm
Habermas, Jurgen (1973), *The Legitimation Crisis*, London: Beacon Press.
Hinkle, Laurence and Richard Newfarmer (2006), 'Risks and Rewards of Regional Trading Arrangements in Africa: Economic Partnership Agreements between the European Union and Sub-Saharan Africa', in Richard Newfarmer (ed.), *Trade and Development*, Washington: World Bank.
Hobsbawm, Eric (1975), *The Age of Capital*, London: Weidenfeld and Nicolson.
Hobsbawm, Eric (1980), *Historians and Economists*, Lecture given at Faculty of Economics, Cambridge, reprinted in 'On History' (1997), London, Abacus.
Hobson, John M. (2004), *The Eastern Origins of Western Civilisation*, Cambridge: Cambridge University Press.

Hoebink, Paul (2005), 'Assessing Europe's aid effort', Europe's World, Autumn, pp.156-163, available at http:///europesworld.link.be/europesworld/Body.htm

Holdar, Sven (2000), 'European Foreign Aid – South, East, Both, or Neither?', in Richard Grant and Jan Nijman (eds), *The Global Crisis in Foreign Aid*, Syracuse: Syracuse University Press.

International Monetary Fund (2000), 'World Economic Outlook – Asset Prices and the Business Cycle', May, available at http://www.imf.org/external/pubs/ft/weo/2000/01/index.htm

Jawara, Fatoumata and Aileen Kwa (2004), (updated edition), *Behind the Scenes at the WTO – The Real World of International Trade Negotiations: The Lessons of Cancun*', London: Zed Books.

Kohli, Atul (2004), *State-Directed Development – Political Power and Industrialisation in the Global Periphery*', Cambridge: Cambridge University Press.

Lawson, Tony (1997), *Economics and Reality*, London: Routledge..

Leftwich, Adrian (2000), *States of Development – On the Primacy of Politics in Development*, Cambridge: Polity Press.

Maxwell, Simon, Dirk Messner, Francoise Moreau, and Laurence Tubiana (2006), 'European Development Report – A Prospectus', mimeo produced for DG-Development.

Milanovic, Branko (2002), 'The Two Faces of Globalization: Against Globalization as We Know It', Washington, World Bank Research Department, May (draft).

Mkandawire, Thandeka (2004), 'The Spread of Economic Doctrines in Post-colonial Africa', UNRISD, Geneva, mimeo.

Mold, Andrew (2004a), 'Trade Preferences and Africa: The State of Play and the Issues at Stake', Work in Progress Policy Paper no. 12, African Trade Policy Centre (ATPC), UNECA, Addis Ababa.

Mold, Andrew (2004b), introduction to *Retirar la Escalera – La Estrategia del Desarrollo en Perspectiva Histórica* by Ha-Joon Chang, Madrid: La Catarata.

Mold, Andrew (2004c), 'Paying a Fair Share? A Proposal for Unitary Taxes on the Profits of Multinational Enterprises', *The CEPAL Review*, no. 43, April.

Mold, Andrew (2005), 'Taking Politics Out of Preferences: The Need for a New Deal for Africa', *Bridges*, Year 9, No. 1, January, ICTSD.

Mosley, Paul, John Harrigan and John Toye (1995) *Aid and Power: The World Bank and Policy-based Lending*, 2 vols., second edition, Abingdon: Routledge.

Nolan, Peter (2004), *Transforming China – Globalisation, Transition and Development*, London: Anthem Press.

Nye, Joseph S. Jr. (2004), 'The Decline of America's Soft Power', *Foreign Affairs*, May/June

Oxfam (2006), 'Unequal Partners: How EU – ACP Economic Partnership Agreements (EPAs) Could Harm the Development Prospects of Many of the World's Poorest Countries', Oxfam Briefing Note, available at http://www.oxfam.org.uk/what_we_do/issues/trade/bn_epa.htm.

Perez, Romain (forthcoming), 'Are the Economic Partnership Agreements a First-Best Optimum for the ACP Countries?', *Journal of World Trade*, vol. 40, no. 6.

Pritchett, Lant and Michael Woocock (2004), 'Solutions when the Solution is the Problem: Arraying the Disarray in Development', *World Development*, vol 32, no. 2, pp. 191-212.

Raghavan, Charavarthi (2004), 'Choose IMF Head Through Transparent and Participatory Process, says G24', *Third World Economics – Trends and Analysis*, Issue 324, 1-15 March.

Richelle, Koos (2005), 'How Brussels has overhauled its "dire" aid apparatus', *Europe's World*, Autumn, pp. 146-151, available at http://europesworld.link.be/europesworld/Body.htm

Rueschemeyer, Dietrich, Evelyne Huber Stephens and John D. Stephens (1992), *Capitalist Development and Democracy*, Cambridge: Polity Press.

Santiso, Carlos (2003), 'Sisyphus in the Castle: Improving European Union Strategies for Democracy Promotion and Governance Conditionality', *European Journal of Development Research*, vol. 15, no. 1, June, pp. 1-28.

Sen, Amartya (2003), *La Démocratie des autres – Pourquoi la liberté n'est pas une invention de l'Occident*, Paris: Editions Payot & Rivages.

Society for International Development (SID) (2005), 'Will Europe make a difference? Future of the European Development Policy', Briefing Session Report, Brussels, 1 September, available at http://www.euforic.org/docs

Stewart, Frances (2006), 'Do we need a new 'Great Transformation'? Is one likely?', Queen Elizabeth Working Paper Series QEHWPS136, February.

Tibi, Bassam (2005), 'Islam, Freedom and Democracy in the Arab World', in Michael Emerson (ed.) (2005), *Democratisation in the European Neighbourhood*, Brussels: Centre for European Policy Studies

Wade, Robert (2004), '*Democracy, Development and the Case for the Developmental State*' presentation at Symposium, held at the Sheraton Hotel, Addis Ababa, 30th August.

About the Authors

Dr. **Gordon Crawford** is Senior Lecturer in development studies in the School of Politics and International Studies at the University of Leeds, UK. He specialises in the politics of development, including issues of human rights, democracy, and development. He has published widely in the area of aid policy and democracy promotion, including *Foreign Aid and Political Reform: A Comparative Analysis of Democracy Assistance and Political Conditionality* (Palgrave Macmillan 2001).

Dr. **Christian Freres**, Research Associate at the Instituto Complutense de Estudios Internacionales (ICEI) and advisor at the Spanish Agency for International Coperation (AEIC), is a specialist on European-Latin American relations. He has published widely, lectured at various universities and carried out numerous consultancies on this topic. Among recent publications, he co-edited the book *América Latina y la Unión Europea. Estrategia para una asociación necesaria* (Icaria, 2006).

Dr. **Marjorie Lister** is Senior Lecturer in European Studies, University of Bradford, UK. She has written extensively on European development policy and, among other publications, is the editor of the book *European Union Development Policy* (1998).

Professor **Andrew McKay** is Professor of Economics and International Development at the University of Bath, UK. He is also a part time research fellow at the Overseas Development Institute (ODI), London. In addition to academic research Professor McKay has many years experience of undertaking advisory work for Department for International Development (DFID) and different African governments, among others.

Professor **Chris Milner** is Professor of International Economics and Head of School at the University of Nottingham, UK. He is a Research Fellow of both the Leverhulme Centre for Research on Globalisation and Economic Policy (GEP) and the Centre for Research on Economic Development and International Trade (CREDIT). His research interests lie in the area of applied trade and trade policy analysis in both a developed and developing country context. He has published widely in academic journals and authored or edited a number of books in these areas.

Dr. **Andrew Mold** works as an economist at the United Nations Economic Commission for Latin America (ECLAC), Santiago, Chile. He previously worked at the United Nations Economic Commission for Africa (UNECA), based in Addis Ababa, Ethiopia, and the Instituto Complutense de Estudios Internationales (ICEI), Madrid. Since 2003 he has been the Editor of the *European Journal of Development Research*.

Professor **Oliver Morrissey** is Professor of Development Economics and Director of the Centre for Research in Economic Development and International Trade (CREDIT) at the University of Nottingham, UK. His primary areas of research interests include macroeconomic effects of aid and in trade policy reform in Africa. He has published many articles in international journals, mostly on aid policy and effectiveness, trade policy reform, conditionality and adjustment.

Dr. **Roderick Pace** is currently Director of the European Documentation and Research Centre at the University of Malta and lecturer in international relations and European Studies. His research interests are in the theories of European integration, small states in world affairs and Euro-Mediterranean relations.

Sheila Page is a Senior Research Associate of the Overseas Development Institute, London. From 1982 to 2005 she was a Research Fellow there. Previously she was at Queen Elizabeth House, Oxford, 1972, and the National Institute of Economic and Social Research, 1972-82. She was President of the European Association of Development Research and Training Institutes (EADI), 1999-2002. Recent publications include *Trade and Aid: Partners or Rivals in Development Policy* (Cameron May, 2006) and *Special and Differential Treatment for Developing Countries in the WTO*, with Peter Kleen (2005).

Mirjam van Reisen is Director of Europe External Policy Advisors – EEPA (www.eepa.be) based in Brussels, Belgium. She is the author of the book *EU Global Player, The NorthSouth Policy of the European Union* (International Books, 2000).

Dr. **Christopher Stevens** is Director of Programmes (International Economic Development) at the Overseas Development Institute, London. He was previously at the Institute of Development Studies (IDS), Brighton. He has written extensively on EU trade with developing countries, most recently on Economic Partnership Agreements, rules of origin, and the effects of reform to the Common Agricultural Policy.